Making the Poor Free?

Making the Poor Free?

India's Unique Identification Number

S.K. Das

OXFORD
UNIVERSITY PRESS

OXFORD
UNIVERSITY PRESS

Oxford University Press is a department of the University of Oxford.
It furthers the University's objective of excellence in research, scholarship,
and education by publishing worldwide. Oxford is a registered trademark of
Oxford University Press in the UK and in certain other countries

Published in India by
Oxford University Press
YMCA Library Building, 1 Jai Singh Road, New Delhi 110 001, India

© Oxford University Press 2015

The moral rights of the author have been asserted

First Edition published in 2015

ISBN-13: 978-0-19-945329-0
ISBN-10: 0-19-945329-2

Typeset in Adobe Garamond Pro 11/13
by The Graphics Solution, New Delhi 110 092
Printed in India by Rakmo Press, New Delhi 110 020

Contents

✌✍

Tables and Figures

Tables

Figures

Abbreviations

∞୧ୡ∞

AAY	Antyodaya Anna Yojana
ABIS	Automated Biometrics Identification System
ACH	Automatic Clearance House
ADG	Assistant Director General
AGM	annual general meeting
AIDS	acquired immune deficiency syndrome
AmI	Ambient Intelligence
API	application programming interface
ASHA	Accredited Social Health Activist
APL	above the poverty line
ATM	automated teller machine
BATF	Bangalore Action Task Force
BC	business correspondent
BJP	Bharatiya Janata Party
BoP	bottom of the pyramid
BPL	below the poverty line
BSNL	Bharat Sanchar Nigam Limited
C&AG	Comptroller and Auditor General
CBS	Core Banking Solution
CCEA	Cabinet Committee on Economic Affairs
CCTV	closed-circuit television
CDB	core database
CEDAC	Community Economic Development Assistance Corporation
CEO	Chief Executive Officer
CESP	Centre for Economic Studies and Planning
CIDR	Central Identities Data Repository
CPI(M)	Communist Party of India (Marxist)

CPU	central processing unit
CRANTI	Citizens Resource and Action Network Initiative
CRM	customer relationship management
CSC	common service centre
CSMS	core subsidy management system
DDG	Deputy Director General
DG	Director General
DoE	Department of Expenditure
EBT	electronic benefit transfer
EGoM	Empowered Group of Ministers
EPIC	Electoral Photo Identity Card
ERP	enterprise resource planning
FCI	Food Corporation of India
FIP	fair information principle
KFO	Key Field Officer
FMCG	fast-moving consumer good
FMR	false match rate
FNMR	false non-match rate
FPS	fair price shop
GDP	gross domestic product
GFR	General Financial Rule
GoM	Group of Ministers
GP	Gram Panchayat
GPRS	general packet radio service
GPS	Global Positioning System
HIV	human immunodeficiency virus
IAS	Indian Administrative Service
IB	Intelligence Bureau
ICD	International Classification of Disease
ICDS	Integrated Child Development Scheme
ICRIER	Indian Council of Research on International Economic Relations
ICT	information and communication technology
ID	identification
IIM	Indian Institute of Management
IIT	Indian Institute of Technology
IRDA	Insurance Regulatory and Development Authority

IT	Information Technology
IVRS	interactive voice response system
JNNURM	Jawaharlal Nehru National Urban Renewal Mission
JNU	Jawaharlal Nehru University
KDD	knowledge discovery in database
KYC	Know Your Customer
KYR	Know Your Resident
LPG	liquefied petroleum gas
MFI	microfinance institution
MGNREGS	Mahatma Gandhi National Rural Employment Guarantee Scheme
MIC	modest-income consumers
MIS	management information system
MLA	Member of Legislative Assembly
MNIC	Multi-purpose National Identity Card
MoHA	Ministry of Home Affairs
MoU	memorandum of understanding
MPs	Members of Parliament
MSP	Minimum Support Price
NASSCOM	National Association of Software and Services Companies
NBFC	non-banking financial company
NCAER	National Council of Applied Economic Research
NCERT	National Council of Educational Research and Training
NCPEDP	National Centre for Promotion of Employment for Disabled People
NDA	National Democratic Alliance
NGO	non-governmental organization
NIC	National Informatics Centre
NIN or NINO	national insurance number
NIST	National Institute of Standards and Technology
NPCI	National Payments Corporation of India
NPR	National Population Register
NREGA	National Rural Employment Guarantee Act
NSS	National Sample Survey
NSSO	National Sample Survey Organization

OPD	outpatient department
PAN	permanent account number
PDS	public distribution scheme
PER	purchase–entitlement ratio
PIN	Personal Identification Number
PMU	Project Management Unit
PoC	Proof of Concept
PoS	point of sale
RBI	Reserve Bank of India
RSBY	Rashtriya Swasthya Bima Yojana
RTE	Right to Education
RTI	Right to Information
SBI	State Bank of India
SC	Scheduled Caste
SEBI	Securities and Exchange Board of India
SLBC	State Level Bankers Committee
SSA	Sarva Shiksha Abhiyan
SSN	social security number
SSS	School of Social Science
ST	Scheduled Tribe
TPDS	Targeted Public Distribution Scheme
UID	unique identification
UIDAI	Unique Identification Authority of India
UPA	United Progressive Alliance
URL	uniform resource locator
UTL	United Telecom Limited

Introduction

Tembhli is a dusty village tucked away in a far corner of Maharashtra state. It is inhabited by Bhils, a tribal community that traces its descent to Eklavya, the fabled archer of the Mahabharata. The Bhils of Tembhli are desperately poor. They live in small huts made of mud and *khaprail*, and thatched with straw. The miserable patch of land that they own does not give them food for more than a few months. So, for nine months a year, they migrate to Gujarat for work as farm labour, or to Saurashtra, for doing seasonal jobs like cutting sugarcane.

In 2010, it was already September but the villagers had not left for Saurashtra yet. They should have been there at least three weeks ago. They had been asked by the government officers to stay back because Dr Manmohan Singh, the then Prime Minister of India, and Sonia Gandhi, the President of United Progressive Alliance (UPA), were coming to their village to give them something very special.

Tembhli wore a festive look to welcome its distinguished visitors. The buildings in the village gleamed with a fresh coat of paint. New roads had been laid. The government fair price shop had issued food rations to the villagers after a very long time. New electric meters had been installed in all the houses. Everyone was ready for the big day. Maibai, who had been born and brought up in Tembhli and had never set foot outside the village, told everyone that their village had finally been blessed. On the day before the big day, she proclaimed in a voice nearly choking with gratitude: 'Nobody else gives us anything. We got food grains for the first time in three years. Whoever is coming tomorrow is like God for us. All the work was done quickly and we got a month's worth of ration' (Byatnal 2010: 17).

Excitement was in the air. Nothing could mar that excitement. Not even the nasty power failure barely two hours after the prime minister had handed over the first set of 12-digit identification numbers to 10 tribal families of Tembhli, marking the launch of India's proud initiative to provide unique identification (UID) numbers to its billion-plus citizens. Speaking on the occasion, the prime minister said:

> UID will help hundreds of people in India, whose pride was hurt for so many years because of the lack of an identity. This will be their source of recognition from now on. Nandurbar was chosen because this is a symbol that this scheme will first benefit the tribals and the needy people in this country. Before this, no other country has made use of such technology on such a large scale. (*The Hindu* 2010c: 1–2)

Sonia Gandhi, the President of the UPA, declared:

> With this, Tembhli has got a special importance in the map of India. People of Tembhli will lead the rest of the country. It is a historic step towards strengthening the people of our nation. Starting from this tiny hamlet, the scheme will reach more than a billion people of this country. UID will give the poor the right to all government schemes, especially in places like Nandurbar where the tribal people still don't benefit from welfare schemes…Our idea is not just to focus on development, but to bring about inclusive growth amongst our people. This scheme will make sure people get what they deserve. (*The Hindu* 2010c: 1–2)

Villagers of Tembhli were told that the UID number would bring them all kinds of benefits from the government and help them in their day-to-day activities. The villagers were euphoric that they were going to get so much. 'Now I can get a license, a mobile number, or show my ID card and get rations in Bhavnagar, which I can't get currently,' said an elated Sanjay Pawar, who works at a caustic powder company in Bhavnagar (*The Hindu* 2010c: 1–2).

The freshly painted slogans on the walls in the village proclaimed in bold letters that the UID number would make it easy for them to get jobs. The number would enable them to get a ration card anywhere in the country and to get job cards, among many other facilities. The villagers were told that the Aadhaar number would help them to open bank accounts without any hassle. S.K. Jain, the

General Manager of Bank of Baroda for the Maharashtra region, was there in person to tell the villagers, 'We will roll out bank accounts for all Tembhli villagers in the next few days' (Jore 2010: 2). Anil Thakre, a young lad of 12 years studying in the local school, declared in a voice choked with excitement that he was looking forward to opening a bank account now that he has the coveted UID number (Jore 2010: 2).

Yuvraj Rajput, the then Tehsildar of Sahada, had already prepared a list for giving the villagers concrete houses, and self-employment schemes that would get them grants for buying cycle rickshaws, setting up flour mills, and opening eating houses (Swamy 2011: 2). He told them that this was possible only because they now had their own unique identification numbers. The villagers of Tembhli were delighted to hear all this emancipatory talk. This was music to their ears. This was a language of freedom that the hapless Bhils had never heard before. They were now confident that the card they were holding in their hands, containing the UID number, was finally going to make them free.

This book is an attempt to understand how the government programme of UID number will make India's poor free. The book has 15 chapters. Chapter 1 is about the governmentality approach that the book adopts as a conceptual framework for its analysis. Governmentality is a concept first developed by the French philosopher Michel Foucault in the 1970s. Foucault argued that a certain mentality, that he termed governmentality, had become the common ground of all modern forms of political thought and action. The concept, as it has been refined over the years, focuses on the rationalities, practices, and technologies of government. Central to contemporary strategies of governing is the creation of freedom. Subjects are obliged to be free and are required to conduct themselves responsibly and to account for their own lives in terms of their freedom.

Chapter 2 looks at the genesis of the idea of the UID number programme (which is now called Aadhaar). The idea of having a comprehensive identity registration system was mooted by Simon Szreter, an English historian. Szreter argues that one of the fundamental determinants of an individual's well-being is whether or not the individual has an acknowledged existence. Nandan Nilekani, the chief programmer of India's UID number programme, was inspired by Szreter's idea of giving every individual an acknowledged existence. The Aadhaar programme seeks to give every Indian an acknowledged existence by providing him/her with an identity. But Nandan Nilekani's formulation is novel in that it puts identification in the human rights framework and invests it with a transformational capacity by linking it with the quality of, and access to, public services.

Chapter 3 traces the evolution of different schemes of the Indian government that have, over the years, sought to provide identification. Originally, the scheme of providing identification was conceived, primarily, as a security measure for issuing separate identity cards to citizens and non-citizens. Eventually, the scheme was modified to create a comprehensive National Population Register. In a parallel process, a separate scheme was envisaged to issue identification numbers to families below the poverty line. Finally, the Aadhaar programme, which seeks to identify every resident through the biometric route, was thought of. It has taken the Indian government almost two decades to conceive and create a comprehensive identity infrastructure for all Indians.

Chapter 4 is a study of the brochures, documents, blueprints, and background papers of the Aadhaar programme. According to this literature, the inability to prove identity has prevented India's poor from claiming their basic political and economic rights. In particular, the lack of identity has worked to the detriment of the poor who live in India's social, political, and economic periphery. The literature claims that there are immense benefits from a mechanism that can uniquely identify a person and thus, ensure instant identity verification. A clear identity number, apart from bringing down transaction costs for the poor, will have the capacity to transform the delivery of public services by making them more inclusive of communities now cut off from such benefits. It will also enable the government to shift from indirect to direct benefits, and help verify whether the intended beneficiaries do actually receive these benefits. The literature claims that a single, universal identity number will be transformational in eliminating fraud and duplicate identities, since individuals will no longer be able to represent themselves differently to different agencies.

Chapter 5 is about the process of enrolment in the Aadhaar programme. Enrolment in the programme is not legally mandated but is demand driven. The basic advantage, which drives this demand, is that the Aadhaar will be one universal number that can be used to prove identity and will be accepted as proof of identity across service providers. Actual enrolment will be done through a multitude of partners, drawn from both public and private sectors, and with the active involvement of civil society groups and community networks. This partnership model is the basis on which the Aadhaar programme will create an ecosystem. The fact that Aadhaar programme will have multiple partners, each of which has a constituency of its own, and the sum of the partners covers the whole of India's population, will give Aadhaar the leveraged model to reach almost everyone in the country.

Chapter 6 looks at the process of authenticating identity. Confirming 'you say who you are' is the primary goal of all identity systems. The Aadhaar process, which consists of online authentication with biometric check, is a strong authentication system and gives the Aadhaar programme significant ability to confirm an individual's unique identity. That being the case, the literature claims that the Aadhaar programme's ability to provide identity authentication can help in bringing about transparency and efficiency in delivery of public services.

Chapter 7 is about the Unique Identification Authority of India (UIDAI), the organization that will implement the Aadhaar programme. The programme has many challenges, involving as it does, the enrolment of 1.2 billion Indians by building an ecosystem of partnerships with state and non-state actors, harnessing frontier technologies to achieve what essentially is a developmental objective, and laying the foundation for the re-engineering of public services. To meet these challenges, the UIDAI has assembled a team of experts, which includes some of the finest minds in the world, drawn from academic institutions, private sector, and the government. The UIDAI, though an attached office of the Planning Commission, functions with total autonomy and independently of the government. Consequently, people believe that the UIDAI, an autonomous body that embodies knowledge, skill, and expertise, will be in a position to deliver socially relevant outcomes.

Chapter 8 analyses the legal framework. A bill—the National Identification Authority of India Bill—has been introduced in Parliament in 2010. It provides for the creation of National Identification Authority of India for issuing identification numbers to individuals and authenticating them in order to facilitate access to government benefits and services. Although the UIDAI now functions as an attached office of the Planning Commission and has already issued identification numbers to a large number of people, it was realized that the act of issuing unique identification numbers involved certain key issues that could be addressed only by the authority of a statute, and hence, the Bill. The Bill is currently under scrutiny in the legislature.

Chapter 9 deals with dataveillance. Dataveillance refers to the use of personal information of citizens for purposes other than the one for which the information is collected. The Aadhaar programme, for example, collects a lot of personal information that can be used for purposes other than providing identification to individuals. The chapter examines various safeguards (protocols, data protection law, regulations, industry self-regulation) that are proposed to be put in place to protect the personal information of citizens in order to safeguard privacy. The chapter, however, finds that there is considerable scope for dataveillance, which will make it possible for the Aadhaar programme to bring the market into the lives of the poor.

Chapter 10 is about the role that the Aadhaar programme envisions for itself in the implementation of the public distribution scheme (PDS). The PDS provides subsidized food and fuel to India's poor. According to the UIDAI literature, the poor, who are the intended beneficiaries of the PDS, cannot get their entitlements because commodities meant for them are pilfered and diverted, and because of inclusion and exclusion errors and the existence of duplicates and ghost beneficiaries. The literature claims that using Aadhaar for identification and authentication will enable clear targeting of PDS beneficiaries, inclusion of excluded groups, and provision of expanded coverage of the poor through elimination of fakes and duplicates. It is also claimed that implementing Aadhaar-based authentication across the PDS would enable the government to guarantee food delivery to the poor. The UIDAI also claims that, in addition to streamlining PDS processes, an Aadhaar-enabled management information system (MIS) would make possible a more transparent, flexible system. The chapter analyses the validity of these claims.

Chapter 11 looks at the role that the Aadhaar programme can play in the implementation of the Mahatma Gandhi National Rural Employment Guarantee Scheme (MGNREGS). The UIDAI literature claims that the Aadhaar programme will help MGNREGS in meeting implementation challenges, such as payment of wages, theft from beneficiaries, theft from taxpayers, ghost beneficiaries, beneficiary misuse, beneficiary management, social audit, and transparency. The chapter analyses the extent to which the Aadhaar programme can help with these implementation challenges of the MGNREGS.

Chapter 12 is an analysis of what the Aadhaar programme can do for public health. The UIDAI literature claims that the Aadhaar programme can create a demand for public health in the country, help in the implementation of Rashtriya Swasthya Bima Yojana (RSBY) by providing an additional and authenticated source of registration of the poor, and, in conjunction with linkages to a routine health information system, can improve the implementation of public health programmes in terms of efficiency and outcomes. The chapter analyses the validity of these claims.

Chapter 13 is about the role that the Aadhaar programme can play in elementary education. The UIDAI literature claims that giving Aadhaar numbers to all the children in the age group of 6–14 years will provide details about children who are out of the educational system and help in monitoring dropouts. It is also claimed that the Aadhaar programme will help in tackling the problem of inflated enrolment, and in ensuring a uniform teacher–student ratio. It will also ensure that students from migrant families face no problems in getting admitted to schools in the new places. It is also claimed that the provision of Aadhaar number at birth will help planners of elementary education system in terms of planning for schools, teachers, and other logistics. The book analyses the validity of these claims in the context of the Right to Education (RTE) Act, 2009 and the Rules.

Chapter 14 deals with financial inclusion of India's poor. The UIDAI claims that the Aadhaar programme can play a critical role in enabling access to formal financial mechanisms by helping the poor to easily authenticate their identity. This, in turn, can significantly improve the effectiveness of existing financial strategies and address the challenges that the poor now face in accessing financial services. The solutions that the Aadhaar programme offers for financial inclusion of the poor include: creation of a micropayment platform; addressing the last-mile problem; streamlining the delivery of government benefits; and providing access to finance to those who have so far been excluded. The chapter analyses the validity of these claims.

Chapter 15 is about what the Aadhaar programme can really do for India's poor. The book finds that, while the Aadhaar programme's contribution in the implementation of PDS, MGNREGS, education, and public health can only be modest, it will be in a position to create a platform for financial inclusion of the poor. Using this platform, the government can pay its subsidies and benefits in cash directly to the beneficiaries. The scope that the Aadhaar programme offers for dataveillance will make the market interested in India's poor as potential consumers for its products and services. The Aadhaar programme, by making financial inclusion possible for the poor, will bring them subsidies and benefits directly in cash, and give them the wherewithal for being consumers for the market. The market, by offering a choice of products, services experiences, and lifestyles, will enable the poor to define who they are or want to be. That is how India's poor will become free and enterprising individuals who will govern themselves and will, therefore, need only limited direct governance by the state.

CHAPTER ONE

Governmentality

'We need to cut off the king's head,' Michel Foucault, the French philosopher, wrote in 1976, 'in political theory that has still to be done' (Rabinow 1984: 63). What Foucault meant was that the thought about politics was trapped by analysis of the government as an authority needing to be legitimized or a power needing to be tamed (Rabinow 1984: 63). For Foucault, it was important that government should be seen as an activity and an art, which concerns all and which touches each (Rabinow 1984: 63). Foucault was interested in government as an activity or practice, and in arts of government as ways of knowing what that activity consisted in and how it might be carried on (Gordon 1991: 3).

Between 1970 and 1984, Foucault delivered a series of lectures at the College de France in Paris on 'governmentality' (Foucault 2008, 2010, 2011). In these lectures, Foucault argued that a certain mentality, that he termed as governmentality, had become the common ground of all modern forms of political thought. Governmentality, Foucault said, can be 'understood in the broad sense of techniques and procedures for directing human behaviour. Government of children, government of souls and consciences, government of a household, of a state, or of oneself' (Rabinow 1984: 82). That is why Foucault defines government as 'conduct', or more precisely as 'the conduct of conduct', and thus, as a term which ranges from 'governing of the self' to 'governing others' (Lemke 2000: 2).

Foucault understood the term 'government' in a comprehensive sense: as it was understood in the sixteenth century. He refers to a series of treatises on the 'art of government' that began to appear from the middle of the sixteenth century (Rabinow 1984: 15). These treatises did not dwell upon the nature of the state and neither did they talk about how best the prince could guard his power. They spoke of the 'governing of a household, souls, children, a province, a convent, a religious order, a family' (Rabinow 1984: 90). Political reflection was thus broadened to include almost all forms of human activity, from the smallest stirrings of the soul to the largest military manoeuvres of the army (Rabinow 1984: 90). As Foucault says:

> This word [government] must be allowed the very broad meaning which it had in the sixteenth century. 'Government' did not refer to only the political structures or the management of states; rather it designates the way in which the conduct of individuals or states might be directed; the government of children, of souls, of communities, of families, of the sick. It did not cover only the legitimately constituted forms of political or economic subjection, but also modes of action, more or less considered, which were designed to act upon the possibilities of action of other people. To govern, in this sense, is to structure the possible field of action of others. (Foucault 1982: 221)

So, for Foucault, 'government', in addition to management by the state or administration, includes problems of self-control, guidance for the family and for children, management of the household, directing the soul, etc., and structuring the possible field of action of others. That is why Foucault defines government as 'the conduct of conduct': a form of activity aiming to shape, guide, or affect the conduct of some person or persons. As Foucault said, government is 'an activity that undertakes to conduct individuals throughout their lives by placing them under the authority of a guide responsible for what they do and for what happens to them' (Foucault 1997: 68).

While delivering his lectures at the College de France, Foucault used the concept of governmentality as a guideline for the analysis he offered of a historical period starting from ancient Greece through to modern neo-liberalism (Lemke 2000: 2). In his analysis, Foucault traced a movement to a form of reason that took, as its particular object, the political problem of population (Rose et al. 2006: 84). Foucault found that in mid-eighteenth century, authorities had come to realize that the population had a reality of its own, which was not the same as that of the individuals who composed it (Foucault 1991:

99). For Foucault, this was a major finding because it had implications for the art of government. As he says:

> Population comes to appear above all else as the ultimate end of the government. In contrast to sovereignty, government has at its purpose not the act of government itself, but the welfare of the population, the improvement of its condition, the increase of its wealth, longevity, health, etc., and the means that the government uses to attain these ends are themselves all in some sense immanent to the population. Interest at the level of the consciousness of each individual who goes to make up the population, and interest considered as the interest of the population regardless of what the particular interests and aspirations may be of the individuals who compose it, this is the new target and fundamental instrument of the government of population; the birth of a new art, or at any rate of a range of absolutely new tactics and techniques. (T)he population is the object that government must take into account in all its observation and savoir [knowledge], in order to be able to govern effectively in a rational and conscious manner. (Foucault 1991: 100)

What are the implications of this 'new' art of governing or the range of new tactics and techniques? Now, the individuals were no longer seen only as those who must obey the laws passed by a sovereign authority, nor as isolated individuals whose conduct was to be shaped, but as existing within a field of relations between people and people, people and things, and people as events (Rose *et al.* 2006: 87). The authorities had to know and understand these relations, and govern using a whole range of strategies and tactics based on this knowledge (Rose *et al.* 2006: 87). To govern, therefore, whether a household, a ship, or a population, it was necessary to know that which was to be governed, and to govern in the light of that knowledge (Rose *et al.* 2006: 87).

In his 1979 lectures, Foucault focused on the study of liberal and neo-liberal forms of government (Lemke 2001: 2). At the beginning and end of the lecture series, Foucault talked about the liberal art of government by discussing the works of Adam Smith, David Hume, and Adam Ferguson (Lemke 2001: 2). In the lectures in between, he analysed neo-liberalism in its two forms: German post-War neo-liberalism; and the neo-liberalism of the Chicago School (Lemke 2001: 2). The theoretical foundations of German neo-liberalism were laid by a group of jurists and economists who were known as Ordo-liberals because of their association with the journal *Ordo* (Lemke 2001: 3). According to the Ordo-liberals, the market does not amount to a natural economic reality and therefore, it can only be constituted and kept alive by political interventions. Like the market, pure competition did not exist naturally and can be sustained only with the support of politics (Lemke 2001: 3).

That is why the Ordo-liberals demanded that the government should formulate a policy for the society to make it possible for the market to exist and function (Lemke 2001: 3). The social policy of the government should create the social conditions of the market, and also promote competition. According to the Ordo-liberals, the social policy should have two aspects: one is to universalize the enterprise form; and the second, to redefine law in order to universalize the enterprise form (Lemke 2001: 5). The social policy should create a social framework, which promotes enterprise as a style of conduct, diffusing the enterprise form throughout the society as its generalized principle of functioning. According to Ordo-liberals, this generalization function should do two things. First, it should generate a model for social relations from economic mechanisms of supply and demand, competition, etc. Second, this model should act as 'vital policy' and foster 'creation of ethical and cultural values' within the society (Gordon 1991: 42). An individual's life should be structured in such a way that he can pursue a range of different enterprises, and his relation to his self, his professional activity, personal property, or environment should be given the ethos and structure of the enterprise form (Gordon 1991: 42). The other aspect of the social policy should be to redefine the form of law and of the institutions of law so that the enterprise form is anchored at the very heart of the society.

Like the Ordo-liberals, the neo-liberals of the Chicago School opposed state intervention, and in the name of economic liberty, criticized the uncontrolled growth of bureaucratic apparatuses and threat to individual rights (Lemke 2001: 7). Yet, there was a significant difference between the two. For the Ordo-liberals, the conception of social policy was based on a difference between the economic and social domains, with the concept of enterprise functioning as an intermediary between the two. The coding of social existence as an enterprise was, at the same time, a politics of rendering the social domain economic and realizing the 'vital policy', which was intended to offset the negative impact of economic exchange by taking political measures (Lemke 2001: 7). This, according to the United States (US) neo-liberals, was an ambiguity and should be removed.

According to Foucault, the key element in the Chicago School's approach was the expansion of the economic form to apply to the social sphere, thus removing any difference between the economy and the social (Lemke 2001: 7). While the Ordo-liberals in West Germany advocated the idea of governing the society in the name of the economy, American neo-liberals sought to redefine the social as a form of the economic (Gordon 1991: 43). According to the Chicago School, the model of economic action should serve as a principle for justifying and limiting governmental action, and more importantly, the government itself should become a sort of enterprise that universalizes competition and invents market-shaped systems of action for individuals, groups, and institutions (Lemke 2001: 7). Economics, thus, becomes an approach capable of addressing the totality of human behaviour and therefore, of envisaging a purely economic method of programming the totality of governmental action (Gordon 1991: 43).

Neo-liberalism generalizes the scope of the economic in order to accomplish two things (Lemke 2001: 8). First, it works as an analytical principle in the sense that it investigates non-economic areas and forms of actions in terms of economic categories. Social relations and individual behaviour are deciphered by using economic criteria, and their eligibility or ineligibility is determined within economic terms. Second, it is programmatic in the sense that it enables an evaluation of governmental practices by means of market concepts. It allows these practices to be evaluated in order to determine whether they are excessive, and to filter them in terms of the interplay of supply and demand. In the neo-liberal approach, the government is judged against the principle of the market and the market becomes, in Foucault's words, 'a kind of permanent economic tribunal' (Lemke 2001: 8).

Foucault uses the example of the theory of human capital to illustrate neo-liberalism's linking of the analytical and the programmatic (Lemke 2001: 8). Neo-liberalism posits an economic understanding of human work. For a worker, the wage is not the price of selling his/her labour power, but it represents an income from a special type of capital. Work for the workers means the use of resources of skill, aptitude, and competence that comprise the worker's human capital (Gordon 1991: 44). This 'human capital' is not capital like other forms, because ability, skill, and knowledge cannot be separated from the person who possesses them. This is composed of two components: (i) an innate component of bodily and generic equipment; and (ii) an acquired component of aptitudes and skills that has been acquired as a result of investments in the corresponding stimuli: nutrition, education, training, and also, love and affection. An aptitude is defined as a quasi-machine for production of a value; this applies not only to the production of commodities but also to the production of satisfactions (Gordon 1991: 44). Education, which confers on its possessor the capacity for such satisfaction, can be considered economically akin to a consumer durable, which is inseparable from its owner. In the neo-liberal model, the workers are no longer the employees dependent on a company, but are autonomous entrepreneurs with full responsibility for their own investment decisions, and in seeking to produce surplus value, they are entrepreneurs of themselves. So, the individual producer–consumer becomes not just an enterprise but also an entrepreneur of himself or herself (Gordon 1991: 44).

How is Foucault's concept of governmentality useful in analysing neo-liberalism? It is useful in correcting the diagnosis of neo-liberalism as an expansion of economy in politics that takes for granted the separation of state and market. The perspective of governmentality makes possible a form of analysis that does not limit itself to stating the 'retreat of politics', or 'retreat of the state', or the 'domination of the market' but deciphers the so-called 'end of politics' itself as a political project. It helps us to see that the so-called 'retreat of the state' is, in reality, a prolongation of government. It is only by using the perspective of governmentality that we begin to understand that the neo-liberal agenda for the 'withdrawal of the state' is, in essence, a restructuring of government techniques, shifting the regulatory competence of the state on to 'responsible' and 'rational' individuals (Lemke 2001: 12).

NEO-LIBERAL GOVERNMENTALITY

Foucault's governmentality approach gives us sufficient insights to attempt an analysis of neo-liberal governmentality. A caveat is in order here. Any analysis of neo-liberal governmentality has to look at both the technologies of power and the political rationality underpinning them. This is needed because of semantic linking of 'governing' and 'mentality' (rationality) in the term 'governmentality' (Lemke 2000: 2). 'Governing' refers to modes of power (a technology), following a specific form of reasoning (a rationality) (Lemke 2000: 5). 'Rationality' of government means a way or system of thinking about the nature of the practice of government (who can govern; what governing is; what or who is governed), capable of making some form of that activity thinkable and practicable both to its practitioners and to those upon whom it is practised (Gordon 1991: 2).

Rationality

Neo-liberalism is a political rationality that links reduction in state welfare services to an increasing call for subjects to become free, enterprising, and autonomous individuals (Rose 1999: 87). The government can then begin to govern its subjects, not through intrusive state bureaucracies armed with legal powers, but through structuring the possible field of action in which they govern themselves, to govern them through their freedom (Rose 1999: 87). Through the transformation of subjects with duties and obligations into individuals with rights and freedoms, modern individuals are not merely free to choose but obliged to be free, 'to understand and enact their lives in terms of choice' (Rose 1999: 87). It is a freedom for the individual to realize his potential and his dreams through reshaping the way in which he conducts his life.

Technologies of Power

There are two main groups of technologies of power: the technologies of the self; and technologies of the market.

Technologies of the Self

Technologies of the self are the ways in which human beings come to understand and act upon themselves within certain regimes of authority and knowledge, and by means of certain techniques directed to self-improvement (Rose *et al.* 2006: 90). In other words, particular self-governing capabilities are to be installed so that individuals can conduct themselves in alignment with political objectives (Rose 1996: 155). These capabilities are enterprise and autonomy. Enterprise means an array of rules for the conduct of our everyday existence: energy, initiative, ambition, calculation, and personal responsibility (Rose 1996: 155). Autonomy is about taking control of our undertakings, defining our goals, and planning to achieve our needs through our own powers (Rose 1996: 159). The enterprising self makes an enterprise of its life, seeks to maximize its own human capital, projects itself a future, and seeks to shape life in order to become what it wishes to be. The idea is to promote an enterprising self that acts upon itself in order to better itself (Rose 1996: 154).

Technologies of the Market

Technologies of the market are those based around buying and selling of products and services that enable us to define who we are, or want to be. The technologies of the market and the technologies of the self are not always distinct, as both borrow bits of each other. Technologies of the market are mechanisms that induce desire in individuals that they work to satisfy. Marketers create wants and needs through advertising goods, experiences, and lifestyles that seek to convey the sense of individual satisfaction which will be brought about by the purchase or use of the advertised product or service (Rose 1999: 86). Individuals come to desire these things and act in a manner that allows them to achieve these things. Thus, individuals are governed into purchasing commodities through their desire. The technologies of the market also utilize the power of commodities to shape identities (Rose 1999: 76). It is like what the brand names usually do in their advertisements: individuals come to perceive that consumption of these commodities would place them within a certain form of life, thereby proclaiming the kind of person they are, or want to be. Thus, marketing governs individuals into choosing those products or services that correspond to the identity that they would like to have.

The technologies of the self and the market are the particular mechanisms whereby individuals are induced to becoming free, enterprising individuals who govern themselves and thus, need only limited direct governance by the state. These technologies are underpinned by a rationality that seeks to transform citizens into free, enterprising, and autonomous individuals.

Expertise

Expertise has a very important role in neo-liberal governmentality. Expertise operates through a relationship with the self-regulating capabilities of individuals. By means of expertise, self-regulatory techniques are established in citizens that align their personal choices with the ends of the government (Rose and Miller 1992: 188–9). It works through the logic of choice: through inculcating desires for self-development that expertise itself can guide (Rose 1999: 88). Expertise grounds its authority in a claim to knowledge and objectivity. The personage of the expert, embodying objectivity, authority and skill in a wise figure, and operating according to an ethical code beyond good and evil, sets up the necessary background (Rose and Miller 1992: 187).

Expertise produces a new relationship between knowledge and government and therefore, is given a key role in the formulation of government programmes and in the technologies that seek to give effect to these programmes (Rose 1996: 156). Expertise helps in establishing vital links between the sociopolitical objectives of the government and the minutiae of daily existence of citizens (Rose 1996: 156). For example, experts enter into a kind of double alliance. On the one hand, they ally themselves with political authorities, focusing upon their problems and problematizing new issues, translating political concerns of economic productivity, innovation, industrial unrest, social stability, law and order, normality, pathology, and so forth, into the vocabulary of management, accounting, medicine, social science and psychology. On the other hand, they form alliances with individuals themselves, translating their daily worries into a language claiming the power of truth, and offering to teach them the techniques by which they might manage better and earn more (Rose 1996: 156). That is how expertise plays a crucial role in establishing the possibility and legitimacy of government (Rose and Miller 1992: 188).

Governing from a Distance

Another element of neo-liberal governmentality is how to make an extension of the government possible by replacing the direct government of society by the state with a form of government at a distance (Donzelot and Gordon 2008: 54). It invents or utilizes a range of techniques that enables the state to divest itself of many of its obligations for its citizens, devolving them to autonomous entities such as enterprises, communities, and professional organizations, or to the citizens themselves. In such cases, there appears to be a destatification of government, which goes hand in hand with the appearance of social technologies that delegate the responsibilities for citizens to autonomous organizations or to the citizens themselves (Donzelot and Gordon 2008: 54).

How Does the Governmentality Approach Help in Analysis?

In his essay on governmentality, Foucault quotes Guillaume de la Perriere: 'government is the right disposition of things, arranged so as to lead to a convenient end' (Foucault 1991: 93). This quotation seems innocuous, but Foucault reads it as indicating a major shift in political thinking (Rabinow 1984: 15). He points out that for traditional theories of sovereignty, there was a fundamental link between the sovereign and a territory: the source of sovereign's legitimacy was his connection to a realm. In Guillaume de la Perriere's definition, there is no mention of territory. Rather, a complex relationship of men and things is given priority. This leads Foucault to argue that:

> Now, with the new definition given by La Perriere, with his attempt at a definition of government, I believe we can see emerging a new kind of finality. Government is defined as a right manner of disposing things so as to lead not to the form of the common good, as the jurists' texts would have said, but to an end which is 'convenient' for each of the things that are to be governed. (Foucault 1991: 95)

Guillaume de la Perriere was a minor administrator and the book he wrote was by no means a grand text on political thought, but Foucault shows us how seemingly mundane statements by minor administrators can indicate major shifts in political thinking and take on a new significance.

So, the governmentality approach focuses not on the grand texts of political philosophy but on the more minor texts of programmers, administrators, and polemicists. It pays attention to the mundane little techniques and tools, such as interviews, case records and diaries, brochures, manuals, and blueprints generated by programmers and administrators (Rose *et al.* 2006: 89). This is useful because such blueprints are, empirically, the real plans and diagrams generated by programmers of various kinds. This makes governmentality approach a creative analytical framework because of its ability to generate an empirical mapping of government rationalities and techniques through studying the mind and texts of the programmer (Rose *et al.* 2006: 99).

In essence, the governmentality approach provides us with a new perspective on political power. It views such power as operating in terms of specific rationalizations and directed towards certain ends that arise within them (Rose *et al.* 2006: 84). Such a perspective makes it possible to ask the following questions. Who is to be governed? Why should they be governed? How should they be governed? To what ends should they be governed (Rose *et al.* 2006: 84)? Thus, as an analytical perspective, the governmentality approach is useful because the questions it asks of the phenomena it seeks to understand are questions which can be answered through empirical enquiry.

These are the questions that the book seeks to ask of the Aadhaar programme in the next few chapters by studying the mind and texts of the programmers, and by analysing interviews, brochures, manuals, background papers, and blueprints generated by the programme and its programmers.

The Idea

❦

Nandan Nilekani, the chief programmer of the Aadhaar programme, has been India's most visible new-age entrepreneur. As the co-founder of Infosys Technologies, one of the country's largest information technology (IT) services companies, he has been a key player in India's growth story. In 2006, he became one of the youngest entrepreneurs to join the World Economic Forum Foundation Board, and *Time* magazine listed him as one of the 100 most influential people in the world. In 2007, he was named *Forbes* Businessman of the Year for Asia.

Nilekani has been remarkably active in helping governments in formulating public policy in important areas. He was the Chairman of the Government of India's IT Task Force for Power. He is a member of the National Knowledge Commission and the review committee of the Jawaharlal Nehru National Urban Renewal Mission (JNNURM). He is part of the National Advisory Group on e-Governance. He is the Chairman of the Technology Advisory Group on Unique Projects as well as the Chairman of the Task Force for Direct Transfer of Subsidies on Kerosene, LPG (liquefied petroleum gas), and Fertilizer.

His book, *Imagining India: Ideas for the New Century* (2008), has been hugely influential. In the book, Nilekani asks important questions of India's future: how will India, as a global power, avoid the mistakes of earlier development models? Will further access to the open market continue to stimulate such extraordinary growth? While providing answers to these questions, Nilekani points out that India is in the middle of a huge transformational change, and only a safety net of ideas can transcend political agendas and safeguard the country's future. One of these ideas is the single citizen identification (ID). Nilekani says in his book:

Today Indians can have a multitude of numbers with which to identify ourselves, depending on when and where we interact with the state. When we get a passport we get a passport ID, a ration card gets us another number, when we pay taxes we need a permanent account number (PAN), when we register our vote we get a voter ID card, and on to barcode infinitum. 'Our barcodes are in these disconnected silos,' the chief election commissioner N. Gopalaswami says. This makes zeroing on a definite identity for each citizen particularly difficult, since government departments work in a different turf and with different groups of people... India's ministries and departments are also quite isolated, with separate fund flows and intricate, over-hyphenated authority levels. As a result these systems require paperwork-choked processes each time citizens approach the state. A common technology and process platform for government schemes and departments—especially now that they have such large budgets—would be a huge improvement in coordinating information between departments, and getting rid of redundancy and triplicate forms.

Identity systems linked up with an IT-enabled process that interlinks our various departments would, besides making citizen information and identity more verifiable, make the relationship between the state and the citizen infinitely less traumatizing in both time and energy wasted.

Such a 'national grid' would require, as a first and critical step, a unique and universal ID for each citizen. Creating a national register for citizens, assigning them a unique ID and linking them across national databases, like the PAN and passport, can have far-reaching effects in delivering public services better and targeting services more accurately. Unique identification for each citizen also ensures a basic right—the right to 'an acknowledged existence' in the country, without which much of the nation's poor can be nameless and ignored, and governments can draw a veil over large-scale poverty and destitution...

A national smart ID could be transformational. Acknowledging the existence of every single citizen, for instance, automatically compels the state to improve the quality of services, and immediately gives the citizen better access. No one else can then claim a benefit that is rightfully yours, and no one can deny their economic status, whether abjectly poor or extremely wealthy. More than anything else, this recognition creates among all parties concerned a deeper awareness of their rights, entitlements and their duties. It becomes far more difficult for both the citizen and the government to dodge any of these. (Nilekani 2008: 367–70)

The most important thing about Nilekani's blueprint is that it moots the idea of a single citizen ID as a means of realizing a basic human right: the right to an acknowledged existence. Without this right, Nilekani asserts, the country's poor will be nameless and ignored, and this will enable the government to hide the fact of large-scale poverty and destitution. If the citizen ID can give this right to the poor, their existence would have been acknowledged, compelling the state to improve the quality of public services and giving the citizens better access to services. This, as Nilekani suggests, could be transformational.

Nilekani got this idea from Simon Szreter, a Cambridge historian. Szreter (2011: 1) argues that one of the fundamental determinants of an individual's well-being is whether or not the individual has an acknowledged existence. According to Szreter (2011: 1), the right to identity registration at birth is a human right, which almost every state in the world has endorsed through ratification of the United Nations (UN) Convention on the Rights of the Child. But, many of the world's poorest countries have no identity or vital registration system. As a result, the poor of the world are anonymous. This is an impediment to their capacity to exercise and enjoy their human rights, their entitlements, functioning, or capabilities. Szreter suggests that policies to promote individuals' identity registration are not economic luxuries but necessities for encouraging broad-based, liberal market development. Szreter (2011: 2), however, has an important caveat to make. Identity registration should be seen as creating a category of public information that is private property, and it should not be accessible for use by commercial or state agencies (Szreter 2011: 2).

According to Szreter (2011: 3), British history indicates that an identity registration system in conjunction with collective provision of social security can both be institutions of fundamental importance for stimulating economic growth, even in relatively poor agrarian economies. Britain's history of economic development shows how the identity registration system and the social security system played a key part in facilitating mobility of both labour and capital in economic development. The English Poor Law worked in tandem with two other institutions: the national identity registration system; and the system of magistrates to administer cheap and accessible justice in the localities. Before the nineteenth century, no other country in the world had the advantage of all three of these institutions working together: magistrates, Poor Law, and an accessible identity registration system (Szreter 2011: 4). A national system of registers of baptisms, marriages, and burials was put in place by the state in the mid-sixteenth century. This system was maintained for legal and economic purposes, directly related to the needs of individuals operating in England's nascent property markets. This vital registration system operating in England's parishes was an important institution which made possible the world's first case of self-sustaining market growth (Szreter 2011: 5).

Szreter (2011: 5) points out that the identity registration system did several things in Britain. First, it facilitated the workings of a legal system that gave ordinary individuals their identities and enabled them and their families to exercise their property and other rights. Second, it was an example of the effective working of the British state and its ability to protect property rights of the individual (the maintenance of parish registers shows that the writ of the British state ran right down to the level of the parish and the individual subjects). Third, the parish register system was the key to the sustaining of the political and legal credibility of the social security system of the English Poor Law. This, in turn, was important in providing legitimacy to an expanding market economy by giving it the means to address the serious social problems of disruption caused by market growth and the mobile markets in land, capital, and labour.

Szreter (2011: 7) says that the English Poor Law and its enforce-ment by magistrates created, in England, a public system that ack-nowledged the collective responsibility for the subsistence of all. The Poor Law, funded entirely from local taxation, created a set of responsibilities on those with the means to support those without. The Settlement Acts were crucial for the functioning of the Poor Law as a locally devolved system. Thus, the combination of Poor Laws and Settlement Laws was able to work effectively as a system of relief, providing social security to the entire population because both the magistrates' courts and the parish registration system facilitated it. This meant that, while some disputes between parishes about relief liabilities for particular individuals under settlement rules could be resolved locally by the magistrates, in some of these cases, reference to the identity records held in the parish registers was sufficient. Thus, identity registration was an important institution, which contributed to the consolidation of the English social security system over two centuries. The security system, in turn, played a big role in giving the British agrarian economy its high level of labour mobility during the century of rising economic productivity and commercial expansion, which ultimately produced the industrial revolution (Szreter 2011: 9).

According to Szreter, the lack of universal civil identity registration systems in many poor countries is a fundamental obstacle to their development. He makes out a case for installing identity registration systems in these countries urgently. However, he points out that, since such identity registration systems create categories of public information about persons, they should be considered to be the private property of the individual to whom it relates and therefore, serious thought must be given to the kinds of identity information systems that are created, the precise technology of construction, and modes of access which should be essentially by private individuals and opaque to state or commercial uses (Szreter 2011: 12). Szreter counsels that attention must be given to the laws authorizing the use of the system and the possibility of invoking international sanctions on any state or private company abusing this aspect of an individual's human rights. According to Szreter (2011: 12), such invoking of international sanctions would be perfectly legitimate because this also applies to the violation of any of the other human rights of citizens of those states who are participants to the UN covenants and charters. These systems of identity registration should best be constituted as autonomous institutions, independent of elected national governments and their changing political agendas, and ultimately, answerable only to the UN and international law (Szreter 2011: 12).

On the whole, according to Szreter (2011: 13), the lack of identity registration systems in many poor countries is both a human rights scandal and a fundamental development obstacle, which international organizations should treat as their highest priorities to address, while taking note of the point that these systems, though necessarily supported with the authority and resources of national governments, need to be protected against possible abuses. Identity registration systems should be created for the liberty and the use of private individuals, and not to serve the purposes of commercial organizations or states (Szreter 2011: 13).

There are two things about Szreter's formulation of an identity registration system that stand out. First, an individual's identity registration is as much about the individual's right to an acknowledged existence as a necessary condition for encouraging broad-based, liberal market development. Second, identity registration should be viewed as creating a category of public information that is private property, and should be maintained in such a way that it is not accessible for commercial or state agencies. These are two points that will be discussed later in the book.

The idea of a single citizen ID that Nandan Nilekani suggested in his book, based on Szreter's formulation, became very influential in government policy circles. It encouraged the Planning Commission to make a policy statement in its official document for the Eleventh Five Year Plan. The statement listed under the chapter 'Governance' said:

Unique Identifiers

In a citizen-centric system of governance, the citizen's satisfaction becomes the measure of success of both service delivery as well as programme delivery. A citizen's identity, therefore, becomes important both in developmental as well as regulatory administration. The absence of a reliable system for such purposes has been an impediment to improving targeting of developmental schemes and reducing leakages in the delivery system. Many major individual-oriented government programmes incorporate a provision for collection of information at the individual/family level. In most cases, this is undertaken as a de novo exercise without reference to similar exercises undertaken in the past by other government departments and sometimes even by the same department. The absence of a system of updation of such purpose-specific databases and the lack of a system for corroboration among such departments are also factors leading inevitably to expensive, time consuming and error-prone de novo surveys for data collection for each scheme. To create a common platform for service/ programme delivery, it is proposed to create a unique ID (UID) in the G2C domain as unique identifiers of citizens.

UID for Indian Residents

The long-term objective of the UID project is to create a Core Database (CDB) for all residents, each having a unique identification number, which is regularly updated and easily available to, and used by, all departments for identification of residents in the country. This CDB would be used as the basis for identifying a person and enabling a cross-linkage of major databases in the country. It is envisaged that the UID could significantly reduce identity related fraud, reduce leakages and allow for better targeting of government schemes. The implementation strategy involves creation of a Central and State UID authorities who would be responsible for implementation and maintaining the UID.

Smart Cards

The UID Project will eventually become the underpinning of the Citizens Smart Card Project of the Ministry of Home Affairs... Any subsidy received by any individual would be entered in his/her smart card when the goods or service is delivered/charged for by the authorized supplier (for example, the fair price shop, kerosene/LPG dealer, fertilizer outlet). The rules and regulations for delivery of subsidy and its reimbursement to the goods/service supplier would be defined by the concerned department. The data entered on the smart card should, however, be accessible by all monitoring/evaluating agencies so that they can put together a picture of what subsidies are being received by whom, as well as those who are not receiving a subsidy for which they are eligible. (Planning Commission 2008a: 231–2)

Interestingly, it was not for the first time that the idea of an ID was being mooted in India. Different agencies of the government had proposed issuing of identity cards to achieve a variety of objectives. What is novel about Nilekani's formulation is that it puts identification for each citizen firmly and unequivocally in the human rights framework (the right to an acknowledged existence) like Simon Szreter does, but, in addition, invests it with a transformational capacity by linking it with the quality of, and access to, public services, particularly to benefit India's poor. Nilekani's UID number is expected to eliminate duplicate and fake identities by uniquely verifying and authenticating genuine beneficiaries and legitimate claimants of public services. More importantly, it plans to make India's poor free from the multiple and vexed bureaucratic layers that they have to negotiate, the multiplicity of documents that they do not have but have to produce in order to avail of public services, and the poverty premiums or bribes that they have to pay to access everything from food, fuel, and employment to health care.

CHAPTER THREE

Evolution

As early as 1994, the Election Commission of India took up a project to issue identity cards to voters (Election Commission of India 2008: 1). These cards are called Electoral Photo Identity Cards (EPICs) and are issued for identifying voters under Rule 28 of the Registration of Elector Rules, 1960 (Election Commission of India 2008: 1). The Commission stipulates the details to be captured on the card: name of the voter; relation's name; date of birth; gender; address; and the photograph of the voter. Every EPIC has a unique number of alphanumeric strings with three alphabetical codes followed by seven numerical digits, the last seventh digit being the checksum (Election Commission of India 2008: 1).

The idea of issuing an EPIC with a unique number is to prevent chances of impersonation and bogus voting so that the voting rights of genuine voters can be protected. In order to preclude and prevent any forgery of the EPIC, the Commission mandates affixing of a security-featured hologram pasted half on the photograph and half on the vacant space on the left of the photograph in the card. The hologram is serially numbered and carries the national emblem, *Satyamev Jayate*, inscribed in Devanagari script, in the centre (Election Commission of India 2008: 1–2).

MULTI-PURPOSE NATIONAL IDENTITY CARD

In 2002, the Government of India started the Multi-purpose National Identity Card (MNIC) project. The plan was to issue an MNIC to citizens and an identity card to non-citizens of a different colour and design. The MNIC project was a child of the Kargil War (Ramakumar 2011a: 4). The Kargil Review Committee, which was appointed in the wake of the Kargil War, mooted this idea. The Committee was chaired by K. Subrahmanyam and had, as its members, B.G. Verghese, Satish Chandra, and K.K. Hazari (Ramakumar 2009: 2). In its report submitted in January 2000, the Committee suggested that immediate steps should be taken to issue ID cards to villagers in border districts, pending its extension to other parts of the country (Ramakumar 2009: 2).

In 2001, a Group of Ministers (GoM) of the National Democratic Alliance (NDA) government submitted a report to the government, titled *Reforming the National Security System*. This report was based largely on the findings of the Subrahmanyam Committee. The report noted: 'Illegal migration has assumed serious proportions. There should be compulsory registration of citizens and non-citizens living in India. This will facilitate preparation of a national register of citizens. All citizens should be given an MNIC and non-citizens should be issued identity cards of a different colour and design' (Ramakumar 2009: 2).

In 2003, the NDA government initiated a series of steps for the preparation of the national register of citizens, as suggested by the GoM. At that time, it was suggested that the best way of preparing the national register would be to link it with the Census of India (Ramakumar 2009: 2). But such linking was essentially problematic because the Census Act of 1948 contained certain stringent provisions for protecting the privacy of the respondents. For example, the Census Act has an express provision regarding confidentiality of information: Section 15 categorically makes the information that people give to the census agency 'not open to inspection nor admissible in evidence' (Ramakumar 2009: 2). The Census Act authorizes information to be collected so that the state has a profile of the population as a collectivity, but it is specifically designed not to profile the individual. Obviously, the census data collected under the provisions of the Census Act could not have been used for preparing the national register of citizens.

That being the case, it was decided to amend the Citizenship Act of 1955. The Citizenship Act was amended in 2003. The amended Act provided for the creation of the National Population Register

(NPR), to be taken up as an initiative of the Registrar General of India (Ramakumar 2009: 2). The amended Act provided for the creation of the post of Director of Citizen Registration, who was also to function as the Director of Census Operations in each state (Ramakumar 2009: 2). It is important to note that the NPR exercise is one that is taken up under provisions of the Citizenship Act of 1955 and the Citizenship (Registration of Citizens and Issue of National Identity Cards) Rules. In terms of the Citizenship Rules, which were notified in December 2003, the onus for registration is on the citizen. Rule 7(3) states: 'It shall be the responsibility of every citizen to register once with the Local Register of Citizen Registration and to provide correct individual particulars' (Ramakumar 2011a: 5). Rule 3(3) provides that information on every citizen in the NPR should compulsorily have his/her national identity number. Rule 17 specifies punishments for citizens violating certain important provisions of the Rules. It says: 'any violation of provisions of rules 5, 7, 8, 10, 11 and 14 shall be punishable with fine, which may extend to one thousand rupees' (Ramakumar 2011a: 5).

THE UID PROJECT

Initially, the Planning Commission conceived the UID project as an initiative that would provide a clear and unique ID number for each resident across the country and could be used as the basis for efficient delivery of welfare services (UIDAI 2010a: 6). The Planning Commission suggested that the number could also be used as a tool for effective monitoring of various programmes and schemes of the government. Official discussion on the concept of UID was first initiated when the Department of Information Technology sought administrative approval for its project, 'Unique ID for BPL Families', in March 2006 (UIDAI 2010a: 6). The idea was that the National Informatics Centre (NIC) would uniquely identify all the poor families in the country over a period of 12 months.

In July 2006, a Processes Committee was set up to suggest processes for updation, modification, addition, and deletion of data fields from the CDB to be created under the 'Unique ID for BPL Families' project (UIDAI 2010a: 6).The Committee was set up under the chairmanship of Dr Arvind Virmani, Principal Adviser to the Planning Commission (UIDAI 2012a: 1). The Committee got M/S Wipro Ltd to prepare a vision document on the subject. Wipro prepared a paper, 'Strategic Vision on the UID Project', and submitted it to the Committee. The vision document envisaged the close linkage that the UID project would have to the electoral database. Acting on this vision document, the Processes Committee, in its seventh meeting held in August 2007, decided to furnish a detailed proposal to the Planning Commission for seeking its in-principle approval (UIDAI 2012a: 1). The Committee also suggested that a UID Authority could be established as the institutional mechanism for the purpose. This, according to the Committee, could be done through an executive order and the Authority could be set up under the aegis of the Planning Commission. The idea was to ensure a pan-departmental and neutral identity for the Authority and, at the same time, to enable a focused approach for the realization of the goals of the Eleventh Five Year Plan.

In a parallel process, the Registrar General of India was taking steps to create the NPR and issue MNICs to citizens of India.

EMPOWERED GROUP OF MINISTERS (EGoM)

The prime minister, however, took note of the parallel and independent efforts of these two schemes to create an identity infrastructure for the country and decided to constitute an EGoM to collate the two schemes: the NPR under the Citizenship Act, 1955; and the UID number project of the Department of Information Technology (UIDAI 2012a: 7). The EGoM was also asked to look at the methodology and setting up of specific milestones for early and effective completion of the project and take a final view. The EGoM was constituted on 4 December 2006.

The first meeting of the EGoM was held on 27 November 2007. It recognized the need for an identity-related resident database, regardless of whether the database was created based on a de novo collection of individual data or based on the existing data such as the voter's list. It also recognized that there was a need to identify and establish an institutional mechanism that will own the database and be responsible for its maintenance and updating on an ongoing basis (UIDAI 2010a: 7). The second meeting of the EGoM was held on 28 January 2008. It finalized the strategy for the collation of NPR and UID. It also approved the proposal to establish a UID Authority under the aegis of the Planning Commission (UIDAI 2010a: 7).

The third meeting of the EGoM was held on 7 August 2008. The Planning Commission submitted a detailed proposal to the EGoM for setting up the UID Authority. The meeting decided that certain issues, which had been raised by the members in respect of the proposed UID Authority, would require detailed scrutiny by an official-level committee. The EGoM referred the matter to the Committee of Secretaries to examine and give its recommendations to the EGoM for taking a final decision (UIDAI 2012a: 7).

The Committee of Secretaries submitted its recommendations, and the EGoM considered them in its fourth meeting held on 4 November 2008. The EGoM took the following decisions on the recommendations of the Committee of Secretaries:

1. Initially, the UIDAI should be notified as an executive authority. Investing the Authority with statutory authority could be taken up for consideration later at an appropriate time.
2. The UIDAI should limit its activities to the creation of an initial database from the electoral rolls/EPIC data. The UIDAI may, however, additionally issue instructions to agencies that undertake creation of databases to ensure standardization of data elements.
3. The UIDAI will take its own decision as to how to build the database.
4. The UIDAI would be anchored in the Planning Commission for five years, after which a view could be taken as to where the UIDAI would be located in the government.
5. The EGoM approved the constitution of the UIDAI with a core team of 10 personnel at the central level. It directed the Planning Commission to separately place a detailed proposal with a complete structure, details of the rest of staff, and organizational structure of the UIDAI before the cabinet secretary for his consideration before seeking approval under normal procedure through the Department of Expenditure/Cabinet Committee on Economic Affairs (DoE/CCEA).
6. The EGoM approved the constitution of the state UID authorities to be established simultaneously with the central UIDAI, with a core team of three personnel each.

7. The UID was given the target date of December 2009 for data to be made available for usage by an initial set of authorized users.
8. The EGoM directed that, prior to seeking approval for the complete organizational structure and full complement of staff through DoE/CCEA as per the existing procedure, the cabinet secretary should convene a meeting to finalize the detailed organizational structure, staff, and other requirements (UIDAI 2012a: 1–2).

On 22 January 2009, the cabinet secretary, in pursuance of the decision of the EGoM, considered the proposal submitted by the Department of Information Technology regarding the governance structure and recommended:

1. The notification for constitution of the UIDAI should be issued immediately.
2. A High-level Advisory, Monitoring and Review Committee headed by deputy chairman, Planning Commission, should be constituted to oversee the work of the authority.
3. A member, Planning Commission, or the secretary, Planning Commission, should be assigned the task of looking after the work proposed by the chief UID commissioner.
4. Core team should be put in place (UIDAI 2012a: 2).

The UIDAI was constituted and notified by the Planning Commission on 28 January 2009, as an attached office of the Planning Commission with an initial core team of 115 officials. The role and responsibilities of the UIDAI were laid down in the notification. In terms of the notification, the UIDAI was given the responsibility of formulating the plan and policies to implement the UID scheme. The notification also indicated that the UIDAI should own and operate the UID database and would be responsible for its updation and maintenance on an ongoing basis. On 2 July 2009, Nandan Nilekani was appointed as the Chairman of the UIDAI. He assumed charge on 23 July 2009 (UIDAI 2010a: 8).

CABINET COMMITTEE

The government constituted a Cabinet Committee on UIDAI on 22 October 2009 (UIDAI 2012a: 2). It is headed by the prime minister and has as its members: the minister of finance; minister of agriculture; minister of consumer affairs, food, and public distribution; minister of home affairs; minister of external affairs; minister of law and justice; minister of communication and IT; minister of labour and employment; minister of human resource development; minister of rural development and panchayat raj; minister of housing and urban poverty alleviation; and minister of tourism (UIDAI 2012a: 2). The deputy chairman, Planning Commission, and chairman UIDAI are special invitees. The functions of this Cabinet Committee are specified as all issues relating to the UIDAI, including its organization, plans, policies, programmes, schemes, funding, and methodology to be adopted for achieving the objectives of the authority (UIDAI 2012a: 2).

Prime Minister's Council

The Prime Minister's Council on the UIDAI was constituted on 30 July 2009 (UIDAI 2012a: 2). The Council advises the UIDAI on programme, methodology, and implementation in order to ensure coordination between ministries/departments, stakeholders, and partners. The first meeting of the Council took place on 12 August 2009. The Council took a number of decisions with respect to the following:

1. legislative framework;
2. broad endorsement of the strategy;
3. budgetary support to partners;
4. setting biometric and demographic standards;
5. UIDAI structure contours;
6. flexibility in personnel and other issues;
7. deployment and repatriation of officers;
8. government accommodation eligibility;
9. broadbanding of posts;
10. hiring of professionals from the market;
11. setting up of Global Advisory Council;
12. interns and sabbatical; and
13. global procurement (UIDAI 2012a: 2).

The Council also declared the UIDAI as the apex body to set standards in the area of demographic and biometric data (UIDAI 2012a: 2). Accordingly, the UIDAI set up two committees: (i) biometric standards committee; and (ii) demographic data standards and verification procedure committee (UIDAI 2012a: 2).

BIOMETRIC STANDARDS COMMITTEE

The Biometric Standards Committee was constituted under the chairmanship of Dr B.K. Gairola, the Director General (DG) of NIC. As biometric attributes of residents were to be used as the basic signature for de-duplication and to ensure uniqueness, the mandate of the Committee was to go into the question as to what should be the type and specifications of biometrics to be collected at the time of enrolment. The Committee gave its report on 7 January 2010. The UIDAI examined the report and accepted the standards for various biometric attributes as recommended by the Committee, as also other recommendations regarding collection of biometrics and their quality. The UIDAI also decided that biometric attributes such as face, all 10 fingerprints, and both iris scans should be collected at the time of capturing the demographic and biometric details of a resident. This would enable ensuring the uniqueness of the IDs at a scale of 1.2 billion residents (UIDAI 2010a: 13).

DEMOGRAPHIC DATA STANDARDS AND VERIFICATION PROCEDURE COMMITTEE

The Committee was headed by N. Vittal and had 15 members. The charter of the Committee was:

1. To recommend the demographic data standards (the data fields and their formats/structures) that will ensure interoperability and standardization of basic demographic data, systems, and processes used by various agencies that use the UID system. This would involve the review of the existing standards of demographic data and, if required, modify/extend/enhance them so as to serve the specific requirements of the UIDAI and its partners.

2. To recommend the process of verification of the demographic data in order to ensure that the data, captured at the time of enrolment of the residents into the UID system, are correct (UIDAI 2010a: 12).

With respect to data fields, the Committee recommended the following:

1. name;
2. date of birth;
3. gender;
4. father's/husband's/guardian's name and UID (optional for adult residents);
5. mother's/wife's/guardian's name and UID (optional for adult residents); and
6. introducer's name and UID (in case of lack of documents) and address (UIDAI 2010a: 12).

With respect to the verification process, the Committee recommended three categories:

1. document-based;
2. introducer-based (in case of lack of documents); and
3. community-based verifications, a process which will be followed during the creation of the NPR (UIDAI 2010a: 12).

The UIDAI accepted the recommendations of Vittal Committee (UIDAI 2010a: 12). These recommendations met a key requirement of the UID system to capture demographic data in a standardized manner so that identity information could work across various systems. In order to achieve interoperability across various government and private agencies that would be using the UID system, it was important that the capture and verification of basic demographic information for each resident was standardized across all partners of the UID system. There was yet another important aspect of demographic data collection: it was to ensure the correctness of data at the time of enrolment of residents into the UID system. While an elaborate verification system based on local enquiries and existing documents issued by various agencies could be used to verify the correctness of data to a large degree, it was likely to result in exclusion of the poor who normally did not have any documents to prove their existence and addresses. As the main purpose of the UID was inclusion of the poor, the verification process had to be formulated in such a manner that, while it did not compromise the integrity of inputs, it should not lead to the exclusion of the poor.

With the finalization of biometric and demographic data standards, the registrars were in a position to use these standards/specifications, processes, and systems for enrolment of people. The stage had finally been set for the implementation of the Aadhaar programme by creating a platform to establish identity and perform authentication that could be used by several public and private service providers.

UID: Experiences of Other Countries

As we can see, it has taken the Indian government the best part of two decades to initiate definitive steps to create an identity infrastructure to provide identity to all Indians. We need to recognize that it is not an easy task because issues relating to the creation of an identity infrastructure, such as the categories of public information to be gathered about persons, the precise technology of construction and modes of access, and to what use this infrastructure should be put, depend on the political rationality of the government of the day. This comes across clearly from the experience of other countries that have sought to issue national identity cards to their citizens. While for some countries, it has been an easy exercise, for others, it has been rather controversial.

In Pakistan, it was an easy exercise. Since the 1960s, Pakistan has been issuing national identity card numbers to its citizens. These numbers are assigned at birth, and then a national identity card with the same number is issued at the age of 18 years (*The Economic Times* 2012f: 10). In 2001–2, Pakistan started issuing 13-digit national identity card numbers, along with their new biometric ID cards (*The Economic Times* 2012f: 10). The number is a requirement for many activities such as paying taxes, opening a bank account, and getting utility (phone, cell phone, gas electricity) connection (*The Economic Times* 2012f: 10).

While China declared its intention to introduce ID cards, it later withdrew the clause to have biometric data stored in such cards (*The Economic Times* 2012f: 10). In China, an ID card (resident identity card) is mandatory for all citizens who are over 16 years (*The Economic Times* 2012f: 10). The 18-digit ID number is used for residential registration, army enrolment registration, marriage/divorce, going abroad, taking part in various national examinations, and other social or civil matters (*The Economic Times* 2012f: 10).

In Australia, the idea of issuing ID cards to its citizens was mooted but was dropped subsequently (Ramakumar 2009: 4). The primary reason why the idea of ID cards has not found favour in some countries is because of the unsettled debate on how to protect privacy. It has been repeatedly pointed out that there is a risk that the data collected and the information stored may be used for other purposes, and this will be an invasion of privacy (Ramakumar 2009: 3).

The two countries where the issue of invasion of privacy was debated comprehensively are the US and the United Kingdom (UK). In the US, following the Great Depression, the government came up with the Social Security Act, which led to the issuing of the social security number (SSN). When the SSN scheme was started in 1936, it was done to facilitate provision of social security benefits. A nine-digit SSN is issued to citizens, permanent residents, and temporary (working) residents. Interestingly, the SSN in the US was never conceived as an identity document. The original purpose was to identify individuals for the purposes of social security, but it soon became a de facto national ID number (*The Economic Times* 2012f: 10). This led to a situation where service providers (both government organizations and private firms) were allowed to mandate the SSN in order to deliver services (*The Hindu* 2011a: 8). But the disclosure of the SSN to private agencies was stopped in 1989 following a public outcry (Ramakumar 2009: 4). A system of security card was proposed when Bill Clinton was the President, but the proposal did not find favour even after the government assured 'full protection for privacy and confidentiality' (Ramakumar 2009: 4).

In 2005, the George Bush government opted for an indirect way of providing ID cards to the US citizens. In what came to be known as the 'de facto ID system', the REAL ID Act made it mandatory for all US citizens to get their drivers' licences reissued, replacing old licences (Ramakumar 2009: 4). In the application form for reissue, the Department of Homeland Security added new questions that became part of the database of driving licence holders. As almost all citizens in the US have a driving licence, this became an informal electronic database of citizens (Ramakumar 2009: 4). However, these cards cannot be used in the US for any other requirement, such as in banks or airlines (Ramakumar 2009: 4).

The same thing happened in the UK. After World War II, the government in the UK came up with the national insurance and national health service numbers. This was to implement the Beveridge Report, which had recommended that the state should accept responsibility for tackling the 'five giants of Want, Disease, Idleness, Ignorance and Squalor' through a nationalized health service, a commitment to full employment, and a social insurance system (Rose 1992: 192). A national insurance number, generally called an NIN or NINO, is used to administer state benefits and for getting jobs, but it has not gained the ubiquity of its US equivalent, and is not considered a proof of identity (*The Economic Times* 2012f: 10).

Tony Blair's government proposed the issue of identity cards, ostensibly to reduce leakages from the national health system (Rose 1992: 192) and other entitlement programmes, and also to protect citizens from terrorism and identity fraud (*The Hindu* 2011a: 8). This was proposed to be done by creating a National Identity Register through the Identity Cards Act, 2006. Under the provisions of the Identity Cards Act, while identity cards were intended to 'secure the efficient and effective provision of public services' in ways which potentially involve a large array of departments and agencies that relate to specific service fields, they were also supposed to serve the traditional Home Office functions regarding law enforcement, immigration and asylum, national security, and counterterrorism (Surveillance Studies Network 2006: para 11.2.6). A key element was the provision of a unique reference number for each person, facilitating the integration of a vast number of data sources (Surveillance Studies Network 2006: para 11.2.6).

However, Tony Blair's push for identity cards ended in disaster. A House of Commons Select Committee report complained about the disturbingly unclear range of proposed functions of identity cards (Surveillance Studies Network 2006: para 11.2.6). The most controversial issue was regarding potential threats to privacy through the surveillance involved in the establishment and use of the National Identity Register to be created under the proposed Identity Cards Act (Surveillance Studies Network 2006: para 11.2.6). In particular, indications that the government did foresee interaction between the public and private sectors in the use of the identity card, including access to the National Identity Register, added further concerns about limitations and privacy safeguards for this potential extension of surveillance (Surveillance Studies Network 2006: para 11.2.6). Finally, the Cameron government scrapped the Identity Cards Act in 2010, thus ending the identity cards project and plans for the creation of the National Identity Register.

The experience of these countries with proposals for national ID cards shows how the objectives of establishing identity infrastructures can change, corresponding to the political rationalities of the government in power at the time. In India, various attempts for creating identity infrastructures through the last two decades have been underpinned by different objectives. In the first instance, it was for electoral purposes. Later, under the MNIC project, identity cards were proposed in order to distinguish citizens from non-citizens for security reasons by issuing multi-purpose identity cards to citizens and identity cards to non-citizens of a different colour and design. This eventually led to the project for the creation of the NPR, which is an ongoing initiative of the Registrar General of India. There was also the project to issue unique IDs to families below the poverty line (BPL) so that targeted programmes for poverty alleviation have an objective and transparent method for identifying the poor. The Aadhaar programme is for creating a comprehensive identity infrastructure, driven by the latest biometric technology, to give unique identities to India's poor and lay the foundation for re-engineering of public services delivery so that the poor can have easy and hassle-free access to these services.

Political rationalities change constantly in the face of some newly identified problem or solution. So do technologies. The photo identity cards issued to voters by the Election Commission use only a simple camera, carrying an optical image, so that the officials in the polling station can distinguish the real from the impersonator by looking at the photograph pinned on the identity card. Then, there are the personal identification numbers (PINs) and passwords. Now it is biometrics used by the Aadhaar programme. The beauty of biometrics is that it finds an anchor for identity in the human body to which data and information can be fixed so that the biometric identifier becomes the access gateway to the data field. In that sense, biometrics is a more potent marker than an optical image, or PINs, or passwords as an identifier. Photographs may turn yellow with age; PINs and passwords may be forgotten or lost; but the body will always provide a constant, direct link between the record and the person, and give the person the right to an acknowledged existence.

CHAPTER FOUR

The Programme

Ram Sewak Sharma, the DG and Mission Director of Unique Identification Authority of India (UIDAI), cites an instance from the history of his own family to emphasize how vitally important an ID can be (*The Economic Times* 2011c: 13). Sharma's family is from a village near Ferozabad in Uttar Pradesh. The Government of Uttar Pradesh gives Rs 40,000 to a family in case its breadwinner dies. When his cousin passed away, Sharma's sister-in-law received a cheque from the government. But she did not have a bank account and so, she could not encash the cheque. She could not open an account in the bank either, because she did not have an ID of any kind. So, Sharma says, 'People feel the need for some identity document that is also valid across the country' (*The Economic Times* 2011c: 13).

The stated objective of the Aadhaar programme is a simple one: it is to issue a unique identity number (Aadhaar) to every resident in the country that is (i) robust enough to eliminate duplicate and fake identities; and (ii) can be verified and authenticated in an easy and cost-effective way (UIDAI 2010a: 1). The idea of issuing an Aadhaar number to all Indians, according to the UIDAI literature, is to fill a significant gap that has so far characterized the country's regulatory infrastructure. India has long lacked the identification infrastructure that is in place in most countries around the world. The absence of such infrastructure in India, the UIDAI literature argues, has been one of the biggest barriers that the poor face in accessing welfare and social services effectively, as it increases costs and effort of identification as well as the risk of duplicates.

THE MANDATE

The Aadhaar programme's mandate is to provide a unique number to residents of India, collect basic demographic and biometric information, guarantee non-duplication through biometrics, and offer online authentication services that can be used across India. The idea is to improve benefits of service delivery, especially to the poor and marginalized sections of the society. The UIDAI's task is to create a platform to establish identity and perform authentication that can be used by several government and private service providers. That is why a key requirement of the Aadhaar system is to capture necessary demographic and biometric data in a standardized manner so that this identity information can work across various systems.

RESPONSIBILITIES OF THE UIDAI AND STAKEHOLDERS

The responsibilities of the UIDAI and the stakeholders are very clearly spelt out in the UIDAI literature (UIDAI 2010a: 10). The UIDAI will be responsible for creating, administering, and enforcing policy. It will prescribe guidelines on the biometric technology, and on the various processes around enrolment and verification procedures, which are to be followed to enrol residents into the Aadhaar system. It will also design and create the institutional microstructure to implement the policy. This will include a Central Identities Data Repository (CIDR), which will manage the central system, and a network of registrars that will establish resident touchpoints through enrolling agencies.

The UIDAI will set standards for enrolment and authentication, which have to be universally followed. It is responsible for designing, developing, and deploying Aadhaar applications with the help of service providers. Subsequently, the entire operation is to be expanded and run by an external service provider. In addition to providing product and services, the UIDAI has the responsibility for recruiting registrars, approving enrolment agencies, and providing a list of introducers. Moreover, the UIDAI is expected to help in the creation of services that will depend on Aadhaar authentication.

Registrars

Registrars are public and private organizations that will provide services to residents (UIDAI 2010a: 10). They will operate on behalf of the

UIDAI in order to provide Aadhaar services (such as enrolment) to their constituents. In the category of public organizations, registrars are either the state governments or ministries and departments of the central government, or the Life Insurance Corporation. Registrars may also be from the private sector, such as banks and other financial institutions, and insurance or telephone companies. The UIDAI will enter into memorandum of understanding (MoU) with individual registrars, and enable their incorporation into the Aadhaar system (UIDAI 2010a: 10).

The registrars, on their part, will be responsible for making changes to their processes to be Aadhaar compatible. The UIDAI will support them in this, and also in linking them to the CIDR, connecting them to the Aadhaar system, and adding Aadhaar fields to their databases. The registrars are expected to take steps to ensure that clean and correct data flow into the CIDR. Their key role in the system is in aggregating enrolments from sub-registrars and enrolling agencies, and forwarding them to the CIDR. Each registrar will adopt UIDAI standards in the technology used for biometrics, as well as in collecting and verifying resident information, and submitting to audits. In case of those registrars who intend using the CIDR solely for authentication purposes, the UIDAI will enter into separate agreements with them. Service providers adopting the Aadhaar system for identity authentication during service delivery are required to follow certain specified processes and standards, and to re-engineer their internal processes (UIDAI 2010a: 10).

Registrars may collect documentation—such as proof of residence and proof of identity—from residents. Registrars are required to store such documents and make them available for later investigations/audits. Registrars may also receive and have access to some of the data specifically collected by the UIDAI (for example, demographic data and photograph of the resident). Registrars may store the Aadhaar number in their systems, as well as print it on artifacts to be provided to the resident (such as card or a letter). Certain registrars may store biometric data such as fingerprint and iris image in a secure manner on smart cards for offline authentication purposes. The data may not be stored on their servers or used for online authentication. To ease the process of registration for the poor, registrars may provide a list of introducers who may introduce residents, thus waiving certain proofs, as required by the Know Your Resident (KYR) document. The list of introducers is registrar specific. Registrars are also authenticators, and can use the authentication interfaces to confirm the details for residents who may have already enrolled in the UIDAI system (UIDAI 2010g: 2).

Sub-registrars

These are departments or entities that report to a specific registrar. For instance, the line departments of the state government, such as the Department of Rural Development and Panchayati Raj, would be sub-registrar to the state government, which will be the registrar (UIDAI 2010a: 11).

Enrolment Agency

Enrolment agencies directly interact with and enrol residents into the CIDR (UIDAI 2010a: 11). For example, the hospital where a baby is born will be the enrolment agency for the baby's Aadhaar, and will report to the municipality, which will be the sub-registrar. For performing their duties, enrolment agencies will enter into a contract with the registrar, subject to certification by the UIDAI. Enrolment agencies will provide assistance to operators and supervisors for setting up enrolment stations in the field, and also create necessary conditions for optimal enrolment of residents. Enrolment agencies must collect demographic data prior to the actual enrolment. They must notify residents and the UIDAI for the assistance of registrars. However, registrars will be free to engage any other enrolment agencies.

Introducer

An introducer is a well-known person authorized by the UIDAI or by a registrar to introduce individuals for enrolment (UIDAI 2010g: 3). This mechanism is specifically created to allow the UIDAI system to reach out to poor people who may not have sufficient documentation to meet proof of identity or address published in the KYR norms. The introducer provides an assurance that the individual applying for an Aadhaar number is indeed a resident, and to the best of his/

her personal knowledge, they are who they say they are. Registrars may provide a list of introducers with their name and Aadhaar card numbers. For various registrars, it is expected that the list would include officials (elected, gazetted, and others), schoolteachers, headmasters, *anganwadi* workers, etc(UIDAI 2010g: 3).

Outreach Groups

The UIDAI, along with the registrars, will also partner with civil society groups and community networks which will promote the Aadhaar number and provide information on enrolment of hard-to-reach segments of poor people (UIDAI 2010a: 12). In fact, the UIDAI plans to seek the help of non-governmental organizations (NGOs) and other civil society organizations to provide additional registrars to improve the coverage of marginalized groups. A carefully crafted enrolment strategy, based on the support of a strong, reliable introducer network will be put in place by the UIDAI to reach out to the poor and marginalized sections of the society (UIDAI 2010g: 3).

Resident

A resident is defined as a natural person, usually residing in India. Residents who wish to obtain an Aadhaar number need to provide documentation to meet the KYR norms or to be introduced by an introducer (UIDAI 2010g: 3). Further, they are expected to provide biometric information to the UIDAI. Residents will have access to their data, and the ability to identify when they were authenticated (for a period of time). Access to data of other residents is to be restricted by the UIDAI.

Authenticator

An authenticator is an agency that uses the UIDAI system to authenticate a resident. Authenticators may use demographic data and/or biometric data in addition to the resident's Aadhaar number. The authenticator is expected to use the appropriate form of authentication that provides the necessary assurance for the transaction. Authenticators are required to register with the UIDAI and provide an estimated usage (primarily for the provisioning).

Authenticators may have presence at multiple locations, at each of which they need to deploy authentication devices. Authenticators are billed by the UIDAI for certain service levels. The billing relationship will require additional data. The UIDAI is expected to enable creation of service platforms and standards that will allow authenticators to be associated with the Aadhaar programme easily (UIDAI 2010g: 3).

The CIDR

The CIDR is the central data repository and functions as a managed service provider (UIDAI 2010a: 10). It implements the core services around the Aadhaar programme: it stores resident records; it issues UID numbers; and it verifies, authenticates, and amends resident data. The CIDR holds only that much of information as is required to identify the resident and ensure that there are no duplicates. As the UIDAI literature indicates, the applications hosted by the CIDR can be very broadly categorized into core applications and supporting applications (UIDAI 2010g: 3). In the core category, there are the enrolment and authentication application services. The category of supporting applications consists of applications required for administration, analytics, reporting, and fraud detection interfaces to logistics provider, contact centre, and the portal (UIDAI 2010g: 3).

Enrolment application is expected to serve the client enrolment request for providing an Aadhaar number. The application orchestrates the enrolment workflow by integrating various sub-systems such as address normalization, third-party de-duplication, and Aadhaar generation. As an exception, manual workflow is required to respond to enrolment requests which cannot be resolved automatically. Basic letter printing and delivery functionality is made available for servicing exceptions to normal workflow (UIDAI 2010g: 3).

Authentication application provides the identity authentication services. Various types of authentication requests such as demographic, biometric, and simple or advanced authentications are supported by this application. The Aadhaar number submitted is used for one-to-one match for the resident's record. The inputs are then matched against the resident information found in the biometric database (UIDAI 2010g: 3).

Fraud detection application is deployed to detect and reduce identity fraud. For example, identifying fraud scenarios, which the application needs to handle, are: misrepresentation of information; multiple registrations by the same resident; registration for non-existent residents; or personification as somebody else (UIDAI 2010g: 3).

Administrative application takes care of user management, roles and access control, business process automation, and status reporting. It ensures a trust network across both internal and external entities. The external entities could be registrars, sub-registrars, enrolment agencies, field agencies, introducers, and authentication clients. For example, the administrative application is required to manage user accounts for registrars or introducers who vouch for identity of individuals who lack proper documentation. The internal entities could be system administrators, customer service agents, or biometric and fraud detection agents. The administrative application allows administrators to track status of other applications, and provide mechanisms to deal with failures or delays (UIDAI 2010g: 3–4).

Analytics and reporting application provides enrolment and authentication statistics for both members of the public and partners. It supports visual representation of statistics and allows drill down at regional levels. All the information available for this application is only at the aggregate level, thereby ensuring that individual identity is completely protected. The information portal provides administrative and information access for internal users, partners, and members of the public. Besides the above-mentioned application, interface application for logistics and contact centre is also available in the CIDR. While the contact centre interface application provides query and status update functionality, the logistics interface application interfaces with the logistics provider for letter printing and delivery. It is used for sending and receiving raw data, sending Aadhaar data for letter printing, and delivering and receiving periodic status updates on the inbound and outbound communication (UIDAI 2010g: 4).

FEATURES OF THE AADHAAR PROGRAMME

UID Number

The UID number is a numeric that will be unique across all 1.2 billion residents in the country (UIDAI 2010a: 10). It provides a 12-digit ID number to every person residing in India, after getting and verifying their biometric and demographic information. The following data fields and biometrics are collected for issuing the Aadhaar number (UIDAI 2010a: 10):

- name;
- date of birth;
- gender;
- father's/husband's/guardian's name and Aadhaar number (optional for adult residents);
- mother's/wife's/guardian's name and Aadhaar number (optional for adult residents);
- introducer's name and Aadhaar number (in case of lack of documents);
- address; and
- all 10 fingerprints, photographs, and both iris scans.

What is unique about the ID number? A UID is a string assigned to an entity that identifies the entity uniquely (UIDAI 2010b: 1). The Aadhaar programme uses biometric ID system and checks to ensure that each individual is assigned one and only one ID number, and the process of generating a new ID number ensures that duplicates are not issued as valid ID numbers. In fact, one of the key features of the Aadhaar programme is ensuring uniqueness in issuing the ID number. This means that each resident can get one and only one number, and conversely, the number can be used by one resident alone.

The way to ensure uniqueness with a high degree of accuracy covering a large population of 1.2 billion is by the use of biometrics. Biometric characteristics are physical markers of an individual that are unique to the individual, such as fingerprints, iris patterns, and face structure (UIDAI 2010b: 4). By capturing and storing some of these biometric markers, the Aadhaar programme is in a position to uniquely identify residents, assign unique numbers to them, and authenticate them accurately during service delivery (UIDAI 2010b: 4). Since biometric information contains no ordering and hence cannot be indexed like text-based information, when a resident applies for a number with his/her fingerprints, iris, and photo of the face, these biometric markers are compared against the entire

Aadhaar database to make sure that this applicant is indeed unique and has not already been allotted a number (even under a different name, address, etc. (UIDAI 2010b: 4).

It Will Only Prove Identity, not Citizenship

The UIDAI's activities are limited to issuing of UID numbers linked to a person's demographic and biometric information. The Aadhaar number only guarantees identity, and not rights, benefits, or entitlements (UIDAI 2010a: 2). Section 6 of the proposed National Identification Authority of India Bill (PRS Legislative Research 2010c: 3) makes it clear that 'The Aadhaar number or the authentication thereof shall not, by itself, confer any right of or be proof of citizenship or domicile in respect of an Aadhaar number holder.' However, the Aadhaar number itself is an entitlement. Section 3(1) of the Bill says, 'Every resident shall be entitled to obtain an Aadhaar number on providing his demographic information and biometric information to the Authority in such manner as may be prescribed' (PRS Legislative Research 2010c: 3). The Aadhaar number, however, provides proof of identity. Section 4(3) of the Bill says, 'An Aadhaar number shall, subject to authentication, be accepted as proof of identity of the Aadhaar number holder' (PRS Legislative Research 2010c: 3).

A Pro-poor Approach

The UIDAI literature envisions full enrolment of residents, but with a special focus on enrolment of the poor (UIDAI 2010a: 2). According to the UIDAI, the registrars that it plans to partner with—MGNREGS, RSBY, PDS—will help bring a large number of poor into the Aadhaar system (UIDAI 2010a: 2). While the UIDAI intends to target registrars that have large networks among the poor and rural communities, it also plans to adopt multiple approaches to reach specific, frequently marginalized groups. The UIDAI literature also claims that the Aadhaar method of authentication will improve service delivery for the poor (UIDAI 2010a: 2).

Enrolment of Residents with Proper Verification

The UIDAI literature points out that the existing identity databases in India are fraught with problems of fraud and duplicate/ghost beneficiaries (UIDAI 2010a: 2). In order to prevent this from seeping into the UIDAI database, it plans to enrol residents into its database only after proper verification of their demographic and biometric information (UIDAI 2010a: 2). This would ensure that the data collected by the UIDAI are clean from the inception of the implementation of the programme. According to the UIDAI literature, most poor people lack identity documents and the Aadhaar number is the best form of identification they will have access to (UIDAI 2010a: 2). The UIDAI plans to make sure that KYR standards do not become a barrier for enrolling the poor, and for the purpose, it has devised suitable procedures to facilitate their inclusion without compromising the integrity of the data (UIDAI 2010a: 2).

A Partnership Model

According to the UIDAI, its approach leverages the existing infrastructure of government and private agencies across India (UIDAI 2010a: 2). In this ecosystem of partnership, the role of the UIDAI will be that of a regulatory authority managing the CIDR, which will issue Aadhaar numbers, update resident information, and authenticate the identity of residents as and when required. The UIDAI plans to partner with agencies such as central and state government departments and private sector agencies, which will be registrars for the purpose of processing Aadhaar applications, and providing connections to the CIDR in order to de-duplicate resident information and receive Aadhaar numbers (UIDAI 2010a: 2). The registrars will be either enrollers themselves or they will appoint agencies as enrollers, who interface with people seeking Aadhaar numbers. The UIDAI also plans to partner with service providers for authentication purposes.

A Flexible Model for Registrars

The UIDAI literature claims that the Aadhaar system will allow registrars to have sufficient flexibility while operating their processes, including issuing of cards, pricing, expanding KYR verification, collecting demographic data on residents for their specific requirements, and in authenticating identity (UIDAI 2010a: 2).

However, the UIDAI will prescribe standards to enable registrars to maintain uniformity in collecting certain demographic and biometric information, and in basic KYR verification.

Process to Ensure No Duplicates

In terms of the Aadhaar programme, registrars will send the applicant's data to the CIDR for de-duplication. The CIDR, which will store resident records, will perform a search on key demographic fields and on biometrics for each new enrolment in order to ensure that there are no duplicates. In essence, the incentives in the Aadhaar system are aligned towards a self-cleaning mechanism. The existing patchwork of multiple databases in India for different schemes and programmes encourages individuals to provide different personal information to different agencies. Since the de-duplication in the Aadhaar system will ensure that residents have only one chance to be in the database, individuals will be incentivized to provide accurate data. According to the UIDAI, this incentive will be suitably strengthened as and when benefits and entitlements under different schemes and programmes of the government get linked to the Aadhaar programme (UIDAI 2010a: 3).

Online Authentication

According to the UIDAI literature, the Aadhaar system plans to offer a strong form of online authentication, through which agencies will be in a position to compare demographic and biometric information of the resident with the record stored in the central database (UIDAI 2010a: 3). The UIDAI proposes to support registrars and agencies in adopting the Aadhaar authentication process, and in defining the infrastructure and processes they need to install for the purpose.

Enrolment is Voluntary

The UIDAI claims that enrolment into the Aadhaar programme is fully voluntary. In other words, the UIDAI's approach is a demand-driven one, in which benefits and services that are linked to the Aadhaar system would ensure demand for the number (UIDAI 2010a: 3). This will not, however, preclude governments or registrars from mandating Aadhaar enrolment for getting the benefits of their schemes and programmes.

BENEFITS

For Residents

According to the UIDAI literature, Aadhaar will be the single proof of identity verification (UIDAI 2010a: 4). Once the residents enrol, they can use the Aadhaar number any number of times, and consequently, they would be spared the hassle of providing identity documents every time they wish to access services such as obtaining a bank account, passport, driving licence, and so on. By providing a clear proof of identity, the Aadhaar number would also facilitate entry for the poor into the formal banking system, and give them an opportunity to avail of services provided by the government and the private sector. The Aadhaar number would also give migrants mobility of identity (UIDAI 2010a: 4).

For Registrars and Enrollers

The UIDAI literature claims that the Aadhaar programme will enrol residents only after de-duplicating their records (UIDAI 2010a: 4). According to the UIDAI, this will help registrars to clean out duplicates from their databases and in the process, enable them to achieve significant efficiencies and cost savings in their operation (UIDAI 2010a: 4). For registrars focused on cost, the UIDAI's verification processes would ensure lower KYR costs. For registrars focused on social goals, a reliable ID number would enable them to broaden their outreach into groups whose identities have been difficult to authenticate so far. The strong authentication that the Aadhaar number offers would improve delivery of services, leading to better resident satisfaction.

For Governments

As far as governments are concerned, eliminating duplication under various schemes would save substantial money for the government exchequer (UIDAI 2010a: 4). It will also provide governments with accurate data on residents, making it possible for them to deliver benefits directly to the beneficiaries, and allow government departments to coordinate investments and share information.

ANALYSIS OF THE UIDAI TEXT

As the UIDAI literature tells us, the Aadhaar programme is premised on the idea that the inability to prove identity has been an obstacle for the poor in India for claiming their basic political and economic rights. It is true that lack of identity has worked to the detriment of the poor, particularly those who live in India's social, political, and economic periphery. Across the country, public as well as private sector agencies like banks typically require proof of identity before providing individuals with products or services. The unhappy result is that, every time an individual tries to access a benefit or service, he has to undergo a full, and often tortuous, cycle of identity verification. Different service providers stipulate different requirements in the documents that they demand, the forms they want to be filled out, and the information that they seek to collect on the individual. Such duplication of effort, combined with the fact there are identity silos in government departments, increase the overall costs of identification and cause untold hardship to the poor who typically lack identity documentation. In any case, the poor in India have neither the means nor the resources to meet the costs and demands of multiple verification processes.

It is true that a number of benefits can flow from a mechanism that will uniquely identify a person and ensure instant identity verification. One significant benefit is that a unique identity and its instant verification will bring down transaction costs for the poor. Another benefit is that it can provide the means for shifting from indirect to direct benefits, and also help in verifying whether the intended beneficiaries actually receive the benefits. Yet another benefit is that a single, universal identity number would help in eliminating duplicate identities, since individuals will no longer be able to represent themselves differently to different agencies.

The UIDAI literature points out that the key role of the Aadhaar is that of an enabler: a number that will help government in designing better welfare programmes, enable residents to access resources more easily wherever they live, and allow agencies and programmes—such as MGNREGS, PDS, and Sarva Shiksha Abhiyan (SSA)—to deliver benefits and services effectively and transparently (UIDAI 2010a: 4). According to the UIDAI literature, the unique identity numbers will constitute an identity infrastructure that will provide the foundation over which multiple services and applications can be built for the resident (UIDAI 2010a: 4). That is why the programme has been named Aadhaar: the word *aadhaar* in most Indian languages means foundation.

The validity of these claims will be discussed in subsequent chapters, but what is striking about the Aadhaar programme is its leveraging of two important elements: (i) harnessing frontier technology for the programme's operations; and (ii) objective of social inclusion. Aadhaar's technology is based on a convergence of information integration and data mining with biometric identifiers. Information integration is made possible by storage capability that is undoubtedly the biggest change brought about by the IT revolution: the ubiquity of the computer database. This enables collection and use of large stores of data. Data sets are matched against each other to uniquely identify an individual. The data are also 'mined'—analysed in great depth by sophisticated technologies. The important thing about the use of these sophisticated technologies is that multiple data are now gathered, tabulated, and cross-referenced much faster and more accurately than the paper files that were once the characteristic feature of how governments worked.

While it is true that biometrics in the West has advanced very rapidly in the last decade, it has been primarily driven by applications in surveillance and security areas. What distinguishes the Aadhaar programme is that it is driven by applications in the area of social inclusion. The Aadhaar programme harnesses the biometric technology in combination with data mining and information integration to build an identity superstructure, and uses the method of de-duplication to make sure that everybody is given a unique identity. Although Aadhaar was conceived as a means for residents to clearly and uniquely verify their identity anywhere in the country, the mandate for Aadhaar now includes defining the usage of the UID number across critical applications and public services delivery. The Aadhaar programme is expected to ensure that residents across

India, including the poorest among them, are enabled to have access to benefits and services that are meant for them. The Aadhaar programme would be of critical importance to the government in achieving its goals of social justice and inclusion, and thus providing legitimacy to the government.

We need to note that the Aadhaar programme proposes to harness today's sophisticated technology to give unique identities to India's poor and uses the online authentication of identities to provide the foundation for the re-engineering of public service delivery systems so that the process of delivery becomes efficient, equitable, and effective. What is really remarkable about the Aadhaar programme is its innovative use of frontier technologies for a developmental purpose. As Nandan Nilekani says in an interview:

> What is distinguishing about what we are doing in India is the first use of biometrics on a large scale for a developmental purpose...That, to our mind, is what is so special about this project—the use of today's technology and computing horsepower and biometrics, but finally for a developmental purpose, to give an ID to a large number of Indians who do not have any papers or an ID, and then lay the foundation for the re-engineering of public services. (India Knowledge @Wharton 2010: 3)

What comes across very clearly is the Aadhaar programme's concern for India's poor. The programme envisions full enrolment of all Indian residents, but its special focus is on enrolling the poor. The pro-poor concern of the Aadhaar programme is also reflected in the fact that its principal partners are poverty alleviation programmes such as the MGNREGS, RSBY, and PDS. The process of authentication of the Aadhaar programme is also designed in a manner that improves service delivery for the poor.

In sum, what the UIDAI proposes to do is to build an identity infrastructure, which is a sort of soft infrastructure: a foundation. The whole idea of building an identity infrastructure is to use it to ensure that the welfare schemes of the government are implemented properly. As R.S. Sharma, the DG and Mission Director of the UIDAI, says:

> The Government of India spends a sizable proportion of the taxpayers' money on hundreds of welfare schemes for the benefit of millions of

people. To that effect, it recognises the importance of establishing an effective identification infrastructure for its residents and is committed to creating the same in a cost effective and secure manner. In fact, deliberations with regards to creating such an infrastructure have been taking place within policy circles since 2006. (*The Hindu* 2011b: 15)

The idea is that this identity infrastructure will provide the foundation on which new systems can be built, which can deliver socially relevant outcomes. As Nandan Nilekani says in an interview:

You can build new systems on that [Aadhaar]. The way it'll work is that when a beneficiary goes to a ration shop, the shop will only be able to deliver ration through an authentication process, which will involve the UID and biometrics. The shop will get more rations based on the evidence that the ration actually went to the correct people. That's how you stop diversion...Let's say someone moves from village A to village B, it takes him years to get a new ration card. We need to build a PDS system that allows him to do that more easily. We need a system that will move from being supply-based to being demand or replenishment based. This will allow a beneficiary the power of choice. You have to understand that all these systems today are static. Overhauling the PDS will require huge political will. But at least the UID gives you the ability and technological base to do that. Without this, there's no way you can pull it off. (*Tehelka* 2010: 27)

Another important aspect of the Aadhaar programme is the sheer scale involved in building this identity infrastructure for all Indians. As far as the scale is concerned, it is certainly the biggest in the world. By 2014, the Aadhaar programme proposes to issue UID numbers to 600 million (60 crore) Indians. For the purpose, it is necessary to photograph a staggering 600 million people, scan 1.2 billion irises, collect 6 billion fingerprints, and record 600 million addresses, in addition to gathering a whole array of other personal information. As Nandan Nilekani says, 'Certainly the scale of this project is humungous' (*Tehelka* 2010: 28).

In fact, the scale is so overwhelmingly huge that the Japanese and French governments have sent teams to study the technology that enables the scale of Aadhaar programme to be achieved. The teams sent by these two governments visited the Unique Identification Technology Centre at Bangalore to gather comprehensive inputs on how the UID number is being rolled out technologically to reach 1.2 billion Indians (*The Times of India* 2011a: 3). Speaking about the visit of these two teams, Ashok Dalwai, the Deputy Director General (DDG) of UIDAI, says in an interview:

> Experts from Japan and France interacted with us on how we are leveraging IT to give an identity. They appreciated the scale of the project, acknowledging that nowhere in the world has an identity project planned to touch more than 100 crore people. They were primarily interested in two things—the technology and method of its deployment to reach such a large population. We explained to them that the IT infrastructure put in place and the role of multiple Registrars across the country who deploy this infrastructure. We also outlined the operation of two softwares that play a crucial role in the UID process—back-end software for de-duplication and front-end one for ID generation. We discussed storage issues, pointing out that Bangalore would store all the IDs generated countrywide, while a disaster recovery centre at Delhi would be the back-up... We have planned one million IDs per day from October first week. Infrastructure has been upgraded to meet this objective. In terms of the number of IDs generated per day, India would have no parallel in the world. (*The Times of India* 2011a: 3)

On the whole, there are three things about the Aadhaar programme that stand out. One is that it is a programme based on technical expertise, knowledge, and skill. Technology undergirds the entire UIDAI system. Technology systems have a major role across the UIDAI infrastructure. The Aadhaar database is stored on a central server. Enrolment of the residents is computerized, and the exchange of information between the registrars and CIDR is over a network. Authentication of the resident's identity is online. The UIDAI plans to build technology systems for the security and safety of the information. The UIDAI is thus an organization of expertise, which will create and put in place the entire technology platform for all these diverse, complex tasks.

Second, the Aadhaar programme is special in the sense that it puts identity in the human rights framework, and proposes to invest it with a transformational capacity by linking it with the quality of, and access to, public services. It proposes to provide an identity infrastructure throughout the country, and thus lay the foundation for the re-engineering of the public services delivery system so that service delivery is made efficient, equitable, and effective. It seeks to provide the ecosystem and the interfaces so that government departments and agencies delivering public services can plug Aadhaar into their operations easily and build their applications on it.

Third, while the Aadhaar is programmatically meant for all the residents in the country, it is primarily addressed to India's poor. This comes across very clearly when we read the mind of the chief programmer. In the course of an interview, Nandan Nilekani has said:

The genesis of this project lay in the fact that a large number of Indians don't have any recognized identity by the State. It's allright for you and me. We have passports, credit cards, etc. But there are hundreds of millions of people who have no identity. They don't have birth certificates or school certificates. They are basically bereft of any form of acknowledged existence. That becomes a form of exclusion. Increasingly, more and more benefits—either public services or private benefits—depends on proving who we are. When you don't have a basic identity, you're completely shut out from these things. Identity becomes a form of divide. People get trapped in a cycle of documentation. To get a driver's license, you need a ration card, to get a ration card you need a birth certificate.

The problem is compounded by patterns of migration. Today, India has about 100–120 million migrants. Papers that might have value in your village have less value outside your village and certainly outside your state. So at the very basic level, we are giving a unique identity embodied in a number to every Indian resident—man, woman and child. This will now be a national identity, a portable identity, because the number will be verifiable anywhere in the country. That's one big intention. (*Tehelka* 2010: 26)

The Aadhaar programme is meant for hundreds of millions of India's poor who do not have authenticated identities acceptable to providers of all manner of services. In essence, it is to India's poor that the Aadhaar programme is addressed.

CHAPTER FIVE

Enrolment

According to the UIDAI literature, enrolment into the Aadhaar programme is not through a mandate; it is demand driven (UIDAI 2010a: 3). The momentum for the Aadhaar programme is expected to come from people enrolling in order to access products and services associated with it. It is assumed that the basic advantage which can drive this demand is that the Aadhaar number will be one number, which can be used to prove identity for life. Once an individual gets the unique Aadhaar number, it will be accepted as identity proof across service providers in the country.

ENROLMENT PROCESS

The process of enrolment for the Aadhaar number begins with an individual submitting his/her personal information to the enrolling agency with supporting documents. The information is verified in terms of a verification procedure, which is laid down by the Committee on Demographic Data Standard and Verification Procedures (Vittal Committee). To ensure that the poor are not excluded, the UIDAI has prescribed guideline for applicants without documents. Once the enroller verifies the information provided by an applicant, it submits the application request through the registrar to the CIDR. The CIDR, then, runs a de-duplication check, comparing the applicant's biometric and demographic information to the records in the central database in order to ensure that the applicant is not already enrolled. Since the process of de-duplication also involves comparison of biometric records, it will identify individuals enrolling with a different set of demographic details. The assumption is that since the Aadhaar system is both de-duplicated and universal, it will discourage people from giving incorrect data at the time of enrolment (UIDAI 2010a: 14).

Issuing the Aadhaar Number

Once the Aadhaar number is assigned, the UIDAI sends a letter to the applicant that contains his/her registered demographic and biometric details. The letter also has a tearaway portion, which contains the Aadhaar number, name and photograph, and a 2D barcode of the fingerprint minutiae digest. If there are mistakes in the demographic details, the applicant can contact the relevant registrar/enrolling agency in accordance with a procedure that is prescribed by the UIDAI.

When the registrar issues a card, it is stipulated that the card should contain the Aadhaar number, name, and photograph. However, the registrars are free to add any more information related to their services (such as customer ID in case it is a bank). They are also free to print/store the biometric collected from the applicant on the issued card. If more registrars store such biometric information in a single-card format, the card becomes interoperable for offline verification.

All data entry that the enrolling agencies take up on behalf of the registrars is done in English. It is, then, converted into the local language using standard transliteration software, and verified for accuracy by the registrar. The letter that the UIDAI sends to the applicant will consequently contain all demographic details in English as well as the local language of the state in which the applicant resides. In this respect, the UIDAI follows the procedure evolved by the Election Commission of India.

ENROLMENT STRATEGY

Pro-rural and Pro-poor Orientation

The UIDAI literature emphasizes that the approach of the Aadhaar programme to enrolment is pro-rural and pro-poor (UIDAI 2010a: 16). The registrars targeted for rural India, such as the MGNREGS, PDS, and social security pension schemes, are governmental agencies with large rural networks and significant bases among the poor. That is why the UIDAI expects that initial enrolment would be fairly rapid in both large and small rural areas. In addition to these enrollers, the UIDAI is partnering with the Registrar General of India, who is in charge of preparing the NPR, in order to reach as many people as possible and enrol them in the Aadhaar database. This has called for incorporating some additional procedures into the Registrar General's data collection mechanism so as to make it Aadhaar friendly.

A Focused Effort to Enrol the Poor and Hard-to-reach Groups

The UIDAI claims that it has also emphasized the following approaches to reach specific, frequently marginalized groups (UIDAI 2010a: 17).

Urban Poor

One of the objectives of the Aadhaar programme is to reach out to the urban poor. According to the UIDAI literature, the urban poor are the most ignored and disadvantaged people in India (UIDAI 2010a: 18). The main constraint in enrolling the urban poor is that this group consists largely of migrant workers with temporary or seasonal jobs. The following are the ways in which the Aadhaar programme seeks to enrol the urban poor (UIDAI 2010a: 18).

Co-resident Enrolment   The bulk of India's urban poor work as drivers, maids, or workers associated with a family or business. The UIDAI's approach to reach them consists of efforts to get in touch with the head of the family or business to enable these members (who are co-residents/co-workers) to get enrolled into the Aadhaar programme with the same address proof that the business or the family uses. The UIDAI offers a host of financial incentives to enrol such co-residents.

Financial Institutions   The urban poor often borrow from micro-finance institutions and other sources, and these could serve as enrolment points for them. There are established chit funds, which the Aadhaar programme will use as enrolment points to reach out to the urban poor and improve its coverage.

Non-governmental Organizations (NGOs) and Non-profits   Several established non-profits work in urban slums and marginal neighbour-hoods in areas of education, health care, and social empowerment. The UIDAI has strategized to utilize their services as access points to educate the poor on the benefits of the Aadhaar programme, with the aim of enrolling them into the Aadhaar programme and also, to help endorse identity for those of the poor who lack documentation.

Children

India is a young country with over 400 million residents below the age of 18 years. While the UIDAI has incorporated agencies implementing family-based government schemes into the ecosystem of partnership to operate as registrars and help in enrolling children, it has also adopted the following measures to specifically target the children population (UIDAI 2010a: 18).

Integrated Child Development Scheme (ICDS)   ICDS is one of the world's largest integrated early childhood programmes, with over 40,000 centres nationwide. The programme covers over 5 million expectant and nursing mothers and 25 million children under the age of 6 years. The UIDAI plans to use these centres as information and enrolment points for children who are outside the school system.

School Admission   The UIDAI has planned that children should have the Aadhaar identification number or enrol for one at the time they join school (Class 1) for the first time. The UIDAI believes that this is the way that children can be tracked for progress during their educational career and targeted for direct benefits. The UIDAI also plans to enlist the services of agencies implementing the SSA to enrol children in the 6–14 years age group into the Aadhaar programme. This would enable better child tracking, in addition to bringing about abiding improvements in the implementation of the mid-day meal scheme.

The UIDAI believes that as far as children are concerned, the advantages flowing to them from the Aadhaar programme would be substantial (UIDAI 2010a: 18). One of the gray areas in the implementation of child-related programmes in India is that the authorities administering these programmes often rely on inaccurate, aggregate data at school/cluster/block levels, making these programmes ineffective. Now that the concept of universal child tracking (the ability to track every child and ensure his/her all-round development) is gaining ground, an accurate database of children with Aadhaar numbers would be immensely beneficial to agencies implementing women and children welfare programmes, as well as educational programmes, so that they can track developments in *anganwadis* and progress of children in government schools on the basis of the Aadhaar numbers. The UIDAI believes that the Aadhaar number will also be useful in eliminating child labour.

Women

The UIDAI has already enlisted the services of agencies delivering family-based government services in both urban and rural India, such as the PDS and RSBY, as enrollers. In addition, the UIDAI has evolved a strategy to cover women outside this net as in the following (UIDAI 2010a: 19).

Financial Institutions Robust collective organizations of women exist within the framework of microfinance institutions and self-help groups across the country. According to the UIDAI, these women collectives are important and effective enrolment points for women. In addition, there is the institutional infrastructure of Mahila Samakhya in the nine states of Karnataka, Kerala, Andhra Pradesh, Gujarat, Uttar Pradesh, Uttarakhand, Assam, Jharkhand, and Bihar. These institutions operate in several thousands of villages of the country, empowering women through a shelf of educational programmes. These can act as touchpoints for education and enrolment of women.

The National Commission for Women This is the apex national-level body in the country for the protection and promotion of the interests of women. The National Commission of Women has a massive programme that can reach out to disadvantaged women and get them to enrol for Aadhaar. The UIDAI believes that the Aadhaar programme has the potential of being costructively used as a unique handle for a variety of services to be rendered to these women.

Differently Abled People

According to the UIDAI, India has over 60 million differently abled people, and providing identity for this population is a big challenge (UIDAI 2010a: 19). The Disability Act of 1995 mandates a certain percentage of employment for the differently abled. But without identifying such individuals clearly and unequivocally, it is difficult to enforce the provisions of the Disability Act. The UIDAI believes that there is an obvious incentive for organizations like National Centre for Promotion of Employment for Disabled People (NCPEDP) to promote the Aadhaar programme and enable residents with disability to register for a range of benefits (UIDAI 2010a: 19). The UIDAI considers that the NGOs and rights group associated with NCPEDP would be an effective way to reach out to this section of the population and enrol them into the Aadhaar programme.

Tribals

India's tribal population of 90 million is concentrated in a few states (UIDAI 2010a: 19). The UIDAI believes that government programmes for the 697 notified tribes in the country can be used for enrolment and information dissemination. According to the UIDAI, governments and NGOs, which are active in these states with high tribal concentration, would be ideal candidates for being appointed as registrars for the tribal population (UIDAI 2010a: 19).

The approaches just outlined are indicative of the strategy that the UIDAI plans to follow to reach the marginalized groups. In addition, the UIDAI plans to reach out to other marginalized groups such as homeless people and individuals in shelter homes, remand homes, and asylums.

Civil Society Outreach Strategy

According to the UIDAI literature, the organization plans to partner with civil society groups and community networks to promote the Aadhaar number and provide information on enrolment to be disseminated to hard-to-reach, marginalized, and deprived populations such as tribal and homeless people (UIDAI 2010a: 10).

SETTING UP ENROLMENT CENTRES

The UIDAI literature describes several steps needed to set up an enrolment centre. They are:

1. Enrolment agency submits the plan and detailed schedule for the roll-out of Aadhaar enrolment to the registrar for approval.
2. Enrolment agency identifies the building or space for setting up the enrolment centre, and procures hardware and other infrastructure based upon the number of enrolment centres, duration of the drive, and population size to be covered.
3. UIDAI shares the content for awareness and publicity with the registrar.
4. Registrar creates awareness among residents.
5. Enrolment agency helps the registrar in creating awareness among residents.
6. Enrolment agency ensures availability of certified operators and supervisors.
7. Registrar provides pre-enrolment data.
8. Enrolment agency sets up the enrolment stations.
9. Enrolment agency ensures site readiness using the checklist.
10. Registrar's supervisor audits site readiness (UIDAI 2010e: 7).

According to the UIDAI literature, the idea is that the enrolment centres should be located in places which are easily accessible for all the people of the target area (UIDAI 2010e: 8). Usually, such locations are schools, anganwadi centres, gram panchayat offices, etc. While the enrolment agencies set up the enrolment centres, the registrar supervises the operations. The registrar checks that the house/hut/building where the enrolment centre is set up does not leak or have defects in construction. Care is taken to ensure the comfort of people who come in for enrolment and also, to prevent damage to the computers and other equipment. The registrar contacts the local administration (for example, head of the village panchayat) to seek help in setting up the enrolment centre and running the enrolment process. If people live in difficult areas and villages where proper premises cannot be found, the UIDAI provides for mobile and temporary enrolment centres for the duration for which they function (UIDAI 2010e: 8).

Awareness and Publicity

The UIDAI has a strategy for spreading awareness and giving publicity so that people come in large numbers for enrolment. Registrars are made responsible for conducting awareness and publicity campaigns. The UIDAI, on its part, shares pamphlets and other advertising material with the registrars (UIDAI 2010e: 10). These advertising materials publicize both enrolment and the benefits that the Aadhaar programme would bring to people. Registrars are given the liberty of changing some of these advertisements so that they are suited to the needs of the local population, and are compatible with local conditions, and the concept of Aadhaar is communicated effectively to people (UIDAI 2010e: 10). The registrars are expected to work closely with the UIDAI in customizing the awareness and publicity material. The enrolment agencies are required to help the registrar in creating awareness among people by passing on the message about the Aadhaar programme and enrolment to the local population.

The System of Introducer

In order to help people, particularly the poor, who are unable to provide identity or proof of address, the UIDAI envisions a system in which they can be introduced by a previously designated introducer (UIDAI 2010g: 3). The UIDAI has issued broad guidelines on how to prepare a list of introducers. The guidelines stipulate:

1. The list of approved introducers should go down to the village/resident level so that the process of registration is not hampered due to lack of introducers.
2. At the ground level, people should have access to multiple introducers so that they can avoid likely harassment by a single introducer.
3. The registrars need to keep the list of approved introducers limited to their own department/organization. Village teachers, anganwadi workers, Accredited Social Health Activist (ASHA) workers, postmen, and representatives of the local NGOs could be appointed as approved introducers by registrars. For example, in MGNREGS, there are a number of NGOs involved in social

audit and registrars could nominate some of the representatives of these NGOs who work at the village level as approved introducers.

4. The introducer list should include credible organizations, which have traditionally been advocates of vulnerable communities, so as to ensure that the goal of inclusion is truly achieved. For example, in the case of migrant workers, their employers (in large industries like construction and mining) or representatives of NGOs, who work specifically for the welfare of migrant workers, could be recognized as introducers (UIDAI 2010e: 33).

The registrars need to prepare the list of introducers by following these guidelines issued by the UIDAI. The registrars can, however, include their own employees, employees of the local administration, elected members, civil society organizations, and NGOs to ensure that the poor are covered. The eligibility criteria for an introducer are stipulated as:

- Introducer should have an Aadhaar number prior to appointment.
- Introducer must be easily accessible to residents.
- Introducer must be above 18 years of age.
- Introducer must not have a criminal record.
- For inclusion of certain marginalized groups, representatives of NGOs working with the marginalized groups may be appointed (UIDAI 2010e: 34).

Ensuring Clean Enrolment Data from Registrars

Periodically, the UIDAI will carry out a process audit of information that comes from registrars in order to ensure quality of data and that the agencies are following guidelines recommended by the UIDAI (UIDAI 2010a: 20). The audit will be on a random sample of residents, carried out either directly by the UIDAI or through appointed agencies. The audit will consist of:

1. *Verification against scanned documents*: Data contained in the resident records will be verified against the scanned documents.
2. *Physical document verification*: Physical documents that are held by the registrar will be validated against electronic copies.

3. *Periodic process audits*: Periodic audits of the processes and software will be carried out at the enrolment site (UIDAI 2010a: 20).

Updating UID Details

Updating Information with the UIDAI

The Aadhaar number is a lifetime number, but the biometric information contained in the central database will have to be regularly updated. That is why the UIDAI stipulates that children may have to update their biometric information every five years, while adults have to update their information every 10 years (UIDAI 2010a: 20). From time to time, the demographic information that the CIDR holds on the resident may also become outdated. Fields susceptible to change are the present address field, as well as the resident's name (after marriage). There is also the likelihood that an error might creep into the fields at the time of enrolment.

If a service provider authenticating or enrolling a resident finds, through its KYR process, that the information required by the resident (address, name, et cetera) does not match with the UIDAI record, or that the biometrics needs to be renewed, it can ask the resident to update the information in the UIDAI database. The service provider may make the update a condition for the residents to receive service/benefit. Enrolling agencies and registrars can serve as points where the resident can update their Aadhaar fields. The resident will have to submit their new information at these updation points with the required documentary evidence. This may also include a biometric authentication prior to processing the request (UIDAI 2010a: 20).

Reaching a Steady State in Enrolment

According to the UIDAI literature, a particular challenge for full enrolment is the registration of approximately 60,000 babies that are born in the country every day (UIDAI 2010a: 23). Over the next several years, the UIDAI expects to enrol almost the entire Indian population. Once that goal is achieved, enrolment will reach a steady state, where only births (and deaths) as well as immigrants need to be recorded. There are, however, some challenges in registering new births. First, since their biometrics is not stable, they have to be scanned at a later age. Second, names are often not given in India at the time of birth registration.

Aadhaar in the Birth Certificate

According to the UIDAI, one way to ensure that all government and private agencies use the Aadhaar number is by inserting it into the birth certificate of the infant (UIDAI 2010a: 23). Since the birth certificate is the original identity document, it is likely that this number will then continue as the key identifier through the individual's various life events, such as joining school, immunization, and voting. Since the name is a mandatory field in the UIDAI database, it is essential that the child be given a name before applying for the Aadhaar number. This would ensure that the Aadhaar is allotted at birth. In the case of urban births, the municipality will be the enrolling authority, and the Aadhaar registrar can be the 'Registrar of Births, Deaths and Marriage' at the state level. In rural areas, births take place at district or block-level hospitals, in health centres, and at homes in the village. The village accountant is the registrar of rural births, and he/she also issues the birth certificate and updates the information through an enrolling agency.

Biometrics and Infants

Recording of unique individual biometrics in the UIDAI database is a challenge so far as infant records are concerned (UIDAI 2010a: 24). According to the UIDAI, the solution is to record the Aadhaar numbers and biometrics of the parents in the child's records. The child's biometrics is taken at around 5 years of age, and updated in the UIDAI system every 5 years until the age of 18 years. This is reinforced by an expiry date attached to the Aadhaar number, which becomes invalid after that date. Until the time the biometrics of the child stabilizes, any one of the parents/guardian needs to provide their biometric information for authentication.

Recording Deaths in the Aadhaar System

It is also necessary to record deaths in the country, and the Birth and Death Registration Act provides for such registration. According to the UIDAI, the same institution that records births can also be in charge of updating deaths in the UIDAI system (UIDAI 2010a: 24). The UIDAI system does not remove a record upon the person's death; it simply marks it as 'deceased' and hence renders it inactive for the purpose of authentication.

ANALYSIS OF THE UIDAI TEXT

As the UIDAI literature makes it clear, enrolment into the Aadhaar programme is totally voluntary. It is true that there is no law or regulation that mandates enrolment. The UIDAI assumes that it will be demand driven, the idea being that people would enrol in the programme only if they are convinced that the UID number is of some real use to them in getting benefits and services. In other words, people will opt for enrolment only if they choose to do so: it is a matter of their choice. This, in fact, makes the Aadhaar programme very different from run-of-the-mill government schemes and programmes, which are almost always mandated under some law or regulations that stipulate penalties for not enrolling, and in the scheme of things, the question of exercising a choice does not arise.

The NPR scheme is a case in point. Under the scheme, data is collected on citizens, which feeds into the NPR database. The database holds not just the names of persons aged over 15 years but also the names of their parents, sex, date of birth, place of birth, present and permanent address, marital status (also 'if ever married, name of spouse'), and their biometric identifiers, which include a photograph and all eight fingers and two thumbs imprinted on it (*The Hindu* 2010a: 1). For the preparation of the NPR and collection of necessary information that feeds into the database, the Registrar General of India acts under the authority of statutory provisions. The Citizenship Rules, 2003 casts an obligation on every 'individual' and 'every head of family' in the role of 'informant' to register and provide correct personal information. In addition, the individual or head of family runs the risk of incurring penalty if he does not ensure that every person gets on to the NPR. Also, it is their responsibility to keep information about themselves and their 'dependents' updated. For example, Rule 7(3) of the Citizenship Rules, 2003 provides: 'It shall be the responsibility of every citizen to register once with the Local Registrar of Citizen Registration and to provide correct individual particulars' (Ramakumar 2011a: 8).

There is a penalty in case of default. Rule 17 states: 'Any violation of provisions of rules 5, 7, 8, 10, 11 and 14 shall be punishable with fine which may extend to one thousand rupees' (Ramakumar 2011a: 8). Thus, there is an element of legal compulsion involved in the process of enrolment in the NPR scheme. In addition, the mode of collection of information in the scheme is door-to-door, while enrolment and collection of information in the Aadhaar programme is done in a camp specifically organized for the purpose. Clearly, the voluntary nature of Aadhaar enrolment and its camp-based approach, offering as they do a choice to the individual in the process, is designed to give a sense of freedom to people.

A concern has been voiced that, although according to the UIDAI literature the process of enrolment is voluntary and there is no legal compulsion, it might not actually be so in practice (Ramanathan 2010: 10). It is pointed out that if other agencies make Aadhaar number an essential requirement for their transactions, it can no longer be considered to be voluntary in nature (Ramanathan 2010: 10). It is also pointed out that, since the UIDAI has already signed MoUs with a range of agencies including banks, state governments, and Life Insurance Corporation of India to be registrars, it is possible that these agencies may insist that their customers must enrol into the Aadhaar system before they receive service or continued service (Ramanathan 2010: 10). It is, therefore, argued that, taken to its logical limit, the Aadhaar programme would make it impossible for an ordinary citizen to undertake a simple task such as travelling within the country without an Aadhaar number (*The Dayafter* 2010: 33). There is some exaggeration here, but the fact remains that the UIDAI literature acknowledges the possibility when it says, 'This [voluntary nature of enrolment] will not, however, preclude governments or registrars from mandating enrolment' (UIDAI 2010a: 3).

An important aspect of the enrolment process is that the actual enrolment is done through registrars, many of whom are private entities. The UIDAI has so far empanelled 209 registrars, most of whom are private organizations (*The Economic Times* 2011e: 13). This partnership model is the basis on which the Aadhaar programme seeks to create an ecosystem through which the UIDAI intends reaching the huge scale of enrolment that it plans to achieve. The NPR, in contrast, uses only government agencies and the Department of Information Technology (*The Economic Times* 2011e: 13). However, the overwhelming presence of private registrars in the ecosystem of UIDAI partnership is designed to give people the confidence that they are not being subjected to any government coercion or compulsion to enrol, as is typically required in other government schemes and programmes. This is meant to instil a sense of freedom in people.

Admittedly, there are risks involved in entrusting the task of enrolment to private agencies on such a large scale. First, it is possible that private enrollers would pass on the personal information gathered by them to commercial outfits: this would enable profiling of citizens by the market for commercial purposes. This aspect will be discussed more fully in the chapter on dataveillance. Second, the Ministry of Home Affairs (MoHA) has raised the data security issue associated with the responsibility of enrolment being given to private agencies (*The Economic Times* 2011a: 13). Third, the MoHA perceives a risk in the UIDAI's practice of incentivizing registrars by paying them Rs 50 per enrolment in addition to their fee (*The Economic Times* 2011a: 13). According to the ministry, this may lead to a situation in which the UIDAI's registrars, aiming to maximize numbers, would give short shrift to procedures and validation (*The Economic Times* 2011a: 13).

When it comes to private agencies, there is the added risk that these agencies, which enrol for the Aadhaar programme, may have limited or no understanding of what the job entails. It is also likely that the private agencies may get so bored with the pedestrian nature of the job that they may deal with it in a casual manner. The following incident that happened in Andhra Pradesh illustrates this point (*Deccan Herald* 2012d: 1). A coriander plant in rural Andhra Pradesh received its UID number and, in the bargain, a card for itself with the photo of a mobile phone fixed on it. An Aadhaar card with the number 4991 1866 5246 was issued in the name of Mr Kothimeer (coriander), son of Mr Palav (biryani), Mamidikiya Vuru (village raw mango), of Jambuladinne village in Anantapur district. As the card displayed the photo of a mobile phone, officials have absolutely no clue of the address to which the card has to be delivered. As an old man at the Jambuladinne panchayat office said, 'We have completed all formalities, got ourselves photographed a year ago after standing in long lines for days but have not received the card so far. The Kothimeer is lucky' (*Deccan Herald* 2012d: 1). Payyavula Keshav, a Member of Legislative Assembly (MLA) from Anantapur district, had this to say, 'It's probably the work of a young man who wanted tell us how routine the process of data collection was in villages. The private agencies entrusted with the job have no understanding of the job in hand' (*Deccan Herald* 2012d: 1).

In this context, it needs to be noted that, on the basis of complaints received in the MoHA that Aadhaar numbers have been issued in the name of fruits and vegetables in Andhra Pradesh, the Intelligence Bureau (IB) has asked all of its subsidary units to launch a security audit of Aadhaar number issued to the people in the state (Yadav 2012: 1). An official in the MoHA says:

> The letter was sent to the state unit after the Ministry of Home Affairs received complaints of misappropriation in the process. The IB message sent on June 29, 2012 directs sleuths to figure out the extent of misappropriation of cards by NGOs and private firms involved in identification process. There are issues regarding fake cards which will create problems for resident identity cards under the National Population Register. The Ministry of Home Affairs has also asked the UIDAI to conduct an internal audit to eliminate fake cards. (Yadav 2012: 1)

According to sources in the MoHA, officials of the IB, undertaking the marathon exercise of a security audit, will seek the help of *tehsildars*, village panchayats, and post offices to trace fake cards. As of April 2012, 6.46 lakh of the 13.68 crore Aadhaar cards issued were returned undelivered due to untraceable addresses (Yadav 2012: 1). Of this, as many as 45,000 cards with fake addresses are lying in various post offices in Hyderabad, and 7,000 cards with fake addresses are lying in various post offices of Karnataka (Yadav 2012: 1).

Admittedly there are risks, but one aspect of the Aadhaar enrolment process which comes across very clearly in the UIDAI literature is that it is genuinely pro-poor in its approach and orientation, with an unwavering focus on promoting the interests of the poor. This is refreshingly different from the anti-poor orientation of most government organizations implementing various welfare schemes. In the Aadhaar programme, for example, the primary consideration, while recruiting registrars, is for selecting those that have large networks among the poor and in rural communities. In addition, the UIDAI's strategy has evolved multiple approaches to reach out to frequently marginalized groups. In order to make sure that the poor are not excluded, the UIDAI has prescribed guidelines for applicants without documents and has put in place an innovative system of having introducers that is positively oriented towards the poor, vulnerable communities, and migrant workers.

On the whole, what stands out in the Aadhaar discourse on enrolment is the language in which it is couched: it is one of choice, freedom, and empathy. The process is voluntary: one gets enrolled only of one's volition. The overwhelming presence of registrars from the private sector only adds to the comfort level. The whole process of enrolment in the Aadhaar programme takes place in camps that do not compulsorily lay claim to one's attendance. Unlike the NPR exercises, there is no compulsion to part with information: nobody comes knocking on your door armed with the authority of a law or regulation, and there is no responsibility cast on the citizen to register with some local authority, and more importantly, there is no penalty to be suffered if one does not enrol for the Aadhaar programme. The Aadhaar programme has none of that coercion one normally associates with government enrolment programmes.

CHAPTER SIX

Authentication

The real test of reliability for any identity system is one of authenticating identity. Confirming 'you say who you say are' is the primary goal of all identity systems. The UIDAI claims that its approach, which consists of online authentication with biometric check, creates a very strong authentication system and gives the organization significant ability to confirm an individual's identity (UIDAI 2010a: 25). In the case of Aadhaar authentication, the number, along with other attributes such as the demographic and biometric information, is sent to the UIDAI's Central Identities Data Repository (CIDR) for verification. The CIDR verifies whether the data submitted matches the data available in the CIDR and responds with a 'yes/no'. The most important use of the data collected during enrolment is one of making online authentication (India Knowledge@Wharton 2010: 2).

TYPES OF AUTHENTICATION

There are multiple forms of authentication that the UIDAI offers (UIDAI 2010a: 26). Certain types of authentication have low to medium assurance, if there is a possibility that the card is forged. Following are the main forms of authentication that the UIDAI offers.

1. Online authentication: It is supported by the Aadhaar system and includes:

    i. Online demographic authentication where the authenticating agency compares the Aadhaar number and demographic information of the Aadhaar number holder to the information stored in the Aadhaar database. The assurance level here is medium.

ii. Online authentication where the biometrics of the Aadhaar number holder, his Aadhaar number, and key demographic details are compared to the details in the CIDR. The assurance level in this case is high.

iii. Online demographic/biometric authentication with application programming interface (API) where the registrar's back-end system makes a programmatic call to the authentication APIs exposed by the Aadhaar system to perform authentication. The assurance level here may be medium–high depending on whether the check uses demographic or biometric inputs (UIDAI 2010a: 26).

2. Offline authentication: This may be supported by the registrar and does not use the authenticating service provided by the UIDAI. This comes in two forms:

i. Photo match authentication where the photo on the card is compared with the cardholder. This is the most basic form of authentication. The assurance level here is low.

ii. Offline biometric authentication compares the scanned fingerprint of the cardholder to the biometric stored on the registrar-issued card. The assurance level here is medium (UIDAI 2010a: 26–7).

Basic Identity Confirmation

Basic identity confirmation from the UIDAI is free. In this transaction, the authenticator provides the Aadhaar number, name, and one other parameter such as date of birth of the person, and the central database confirms the identity as a 'yes' or 'no' response. This type of transaction is carried out in large numbers and needs quick response time.

Chargeable Authentication Services

These are of two types (UIDAI 2010a: 27–8):

1. Address verification: For security purposes, government agencies as well as private sector companies require address proof from Indian residents before providing them with benefits and services. The service provider usually verifies address through a physical visit, as well as an enquiry to confirm the other information provided. The process is expensive and costs between Rs 100 and Rs 500 per verification. The address verification service that the UIDAI offers to these entities is consequently a valuable one. In its transaction with the UIDAI, the agency submits the Aadhaar number, name, and address of the resident to the CIDR, which confirms the address. As a result, the agency is not called upon to do a physical verification.

2. Biometrics confirmation: Services such as issuing a credit card or granting a loan need the confirmation of the resident's identity. This process for the resident involves the submission of photographs and other documentation confirming his/her identity. In the proposed transaction with the UIDAI, the agency sends the scanned photograph or fingerprint (based on the security level required) together with other demographic details to confirm the identity of the person.

ADOPTION OF AADHAAR FOR AUTHENTICATION

The UIDAI claims that there is tremendous value for the residents from widespread adoption of Aadhaar for authentication (UIDAI 2010a: 25). While enrolment in the Aadhaar database will ensure that residents are not denied access to fundamental services and rights because they cannot present positive proof of identity, adoption in authentication would go one step further: it will ensure that residents consistently receive these services in a hassle-free manner. They would include a wide range of benefits such as education, health care coverage, National Rural Employment Guarantee Act (NREGA) payments, old-age pensions, and subsidized fuel and foodgrains, thereby fulfilling the UIDAI's pro-poor agenda.

According to the UIDAI, the adoption of Aadhaar during authentication also has a direct correlation with subsequent enrolment (UIDAI 2010a: 25). Greater enrolment comes from the value a resident derives from the Aadhaar number, which, in turn, depends on the rate of adoption. There is a positive cycle here, created from the relationship between adoption and enrolment. So, the greater the adoption, the faster is the enrolment and vice versa. The twin approaches of enrolment and adoption would result in greater traction for the Aadhaar programme among residents in the country, and would establish the UIDAI as the only genuine identity authenticator in India.

The UIDAI plans to partner with agencies involved in delivery of services and benefits, and encourage them to avail of Aadhaar authentication facilities (UIDAI 2010a: 25). If they authenticate a resident's identity against the Aadhaar database every time they carry out a service transaction, they will be in a position to deliver services more effectively. In order to avail of the authentication facility, the agencies need to change their business processes to be Aadhaar enabled. This would call for incorporating the Aadhaar method of authentication into their systems. Agencies will have to adhere to the norms and procedures specified by the UIDAI for fingerprint capture and verification, and introduce a robust biometric authentication process at every point of sale (PoS) or carrying out a service transaction.

However, as the UIDAI literature tells us, its presence is only in the identity domain. The responsibility for tracking beneficiaries and the governance of service delivery continues to remain with the respective agencies delivering services. For example, the job of tracking distribution of foodgrains and fuel among BPL families remains with the state food and civil supplies department. The adoption of Aadhaar by the department only ensures that the uniqueness and singularity of each resident is established and authenticated, thereby promoting equitable access to social services (UIDAI 2010a: 25).

ANALYSIS OF THE UIDAI CLAIMS

The UIDAI claims that it offers a strong form of online authentication in which the agencies delivering services can compare the biometric information of the beneficiary with the record stored in the central database. Residents would need to authenticate either at the time of subscribing to the service or at the time of service delivery. In that case, no one else can utilize the benefits meant for a particular resident. The idea is premised on the assumption that incentives in the Aadhaar system are aligned to a self-cleaning mechanism. This is because of the fact that existing databases in India encourage individuals to provide different personal information to different agencies, and it is assumed that de-duplication in the Aadhaar system would ensure that residents have only one chance to be in the database.

Central to the Aadhaar system is the process of de-duplication, based on biometrics. As Nandan Nilekani says:

> One of the things that struck us is that the best way to do de-duplication—to make sure that somebody is unique—is the biometric route. Biometric in the West has advanced in the last decade and has primarily been driven by a lot of applications in the surveillance and security areas...How do we then use this online authentication to provide the foundation for the reengineering of public service delivery—to make it more efficient, equitable and effective? That, to our mind, is what is so special about this project. (India Knowledge@ Wharton 2010: 2–3)

It is true that the growth of biometrics has been very rapid in the last decade. This was primarily because of the war on terror. It produced a massive surge in both research funding and implementation of biometric technology. After 9/11 in the US, biometric techniques, which were already in commercial use or on the threshold of applicability, were fast-tracked and heralded as the key to winning this new kind of war (Surveillance Studies Network 2006: para 9.7.2). The US Patriot Act, in a framework that has implications far beyond the US, established a set of practices for biometric applications that promised their unlimited use in the investigation and identification of terrorist activity (Surveillance Studies Network 2006: para 9.7.2).

For evaluating what biometric applications are capable of, we need to understand what is biometrics. Biometrics is defined as:

> The automated recognition of individuals based on their behavioural and biological characteristics. It is a tool for establishing confidence that one is dealing with individuals who are already known (or not known) and consequently that they belong to a group with certain rights (or to a group to be denied certain privileges). It relies on the presumption that individuals are physically and behaviourially distinct in a number of ways. (Ramachandran 2011: 26)

Biometrics or mathematical calculation of human features—fingerprints, facial features, and iris—is considered to be more useful than any man-made identity card in ensuring the uniqueness of an individual (*The Economic Times* 2012e: 13). Interestingly, biometrics is not really a new technology. It has been used, in some form or the other, since 29,000 BC, when the drawings made by the cavemen had their signature imprinted with their fingerprints (S. Singh 2012b: 13). In 500 BC, Babylonian business transactions were signed in clay tablets with fingerprints (S. Singh 2012b: 13). The earliest cataloguing of fingerprints dates back to 1881 when Juan Vucetich, an anthropologist and police officer, started collecting fingerprints of criminals in Argentina (S. Singh 2012b: 13). All governments, notably the police departments, use fingerprints. In over 100 years of fingerprint comparison, no two fingerprints have been found to be alike (*The Economic Times* 2012e: 13). So, one can say that a fingerprint does uniquely identify an individual.

What is it about a fingerprint that makes it such a useful anchor for establishing unique identity? Fingerprint comprises ridges and valleys that form the basis for the loops, arches, and contours seen on fingertips. Fingerprint ridges are formed in the womb—by the fourth month of foetal development—and remain constant throughout life (*The Economic Times* 2012e: 13). These ridges and valleys have different kinds of breaks and discontinuities, and are called the 'minutiae' (S. Singh 2012b: 13). From these minutiae, the unique features are located and determined. Each finger has four to half-a-dozen minutiae points and there are, in turn, two types of minutiae: ridge endings (the location where the ridge actually ends); and bifurcations (where a single ridge becomes two ridges). Based upon the unique features found in the minutiae (the location position as well as the type and quality of the minutiae), a template is created. The template is smaller in size than a raw image and is based on ISO197942-2 standard (S. Singh 2012b: 13). This standard specifies formats on how minutiae points are determined and collected. The templates thus formed are saved in a database, which, in the case of the Aadhaar programme, is located at the Bangalore technological hub of the UIDAI. To use fingerprints for authentication, the Aadhaar programme uses algorithms certified by the US-based National Institute of Standards and Technology (NIST) (S. Singh 2012b: 13).

The use of iris, the other biometric, implies capturing the patterns of the iris. Iris recognition uses camera technology with subtle infrared illumination to acquire images of the detail-rich, intricate structures of the iris (S. Singh 2012b: 13). An iris scan provides an analysis of the rings, furrows, and freckles in the coloured ring that surrounds the pupil of the eye (*The Economic Times* 2012e: 13). Digital templates encoded from these patterns by mathematical and statistical algorithms allow unique identification of an individual. Iris scan provides unique biometric data that is difficult to duplicate and remains the same for a lifetime. (*The Economic Times* 2012e: 13).

The photograph of our face is one of the most commonly employed methods of identification. Of the various biometric identification methods, face recognition is one of the most flexible (*The Economic Times* 2012e: 13). Face recognition systems work by systematically analysing specific features that are common to everyone's face. These numerical quantities are then combined in a single code that identifies each person (*The Economic Times* 2012e: 13).

The Aadhaar biometrics system, however, is a multi-modal system (Ramachandran 2011: 26). It is multi-modal in the sense that it uses data on 10 fingerprints, palm print or slap fingerprint, iris characteristics, and facial images of every person. The multi-modal approach is useful because data from different modalities—face, palm print, fingerprints, and iris—are combined. Such systems obviously require different kinds of sensors and software to capture and process each modality being used for comparison. Use of 10 fingerprints provides additional information as compared with a single fingerprint, and this improves performance, especially in very large-scale operations. Of course, this can be computationally intensive, particularly when matching is to be done from among millions of references in the database. Multi-modality, in addition, requires even greater computational resources.

The important question, however, is: how reliable is the biometric technology, particularly when it is used on a large scale like the Aadhaar programme proposes to do? Perhaps, the most objective evaluation on the reliability of biometrics comes from the report of the Whither Biometrics Committee (2010) of the National Research Council of the US, which says:

Human recognition systems are inherently probabilistic and hence inherently fallible. The chance of error can be made small, but not eliminated...The scientific basis of biometrics—from understanding the distribution of biometric traits within given populations to how humans interact with biometric systems—needs strengthening particularly as biometric technologies and systems are deployed in systems of national importance. (quoted in Ramachandran 2011: 26)

According to the Whither Committee report, the biometric system can provide only probabilistic results. This is because there are many sources of uncertainty, such as variations in biological attributes both within and between persons, sensor characteristics, and feature extractions (Ramachandran 2011: 26). Traits captured by biometric systems may change with age, environment, disease, stress, occupational factors, sociocultural aspects of the situation in which data submission takes place, and changes in human interface with the system. This is particularly true in the case of most of the poor people in India who are engaged in labour-intensive occupations such as agriculture, in which hands are put to rough use causing weathering of finger and handprints. Millions of Indians engaged in agriculture, construction work, and other manual labour have worn-out fingers due to a lifetime of hard labour, resulting in low-quality fingerprints (Ramanathan 2010: 13). That being the case, such people with low-quality fingerprints do pose a problem for the Aadhaar programme (Ramanathan 2010: 13).

R.S. Sharma, the DG and Mission Director, UIDAI, does acknowledge that there may be a problem in such cases when he says:

The challenge we face is the quality of fingerprints. Capturing fingerprints, especially of manual labourers, is a challenge. The quality of fingerprints is bad because of the rough exterior of fingers caused by hard work, and this poses a challenge for later authentication... For manual laborers, this authentication will be difficult because only one or two of the ten fingerprints may be good. It may happen that you may have very good fingerprint but the method of capturing is sloppy. That again causes problems of authentication. We will be able to ensure the accuracy in 99 per cent of the cases because of the other biometric details. Even if the fingerprints do not work, the iris scans will. Issuing a unique identity will not be a major problem.

But authentication will be, because fingerprint is the basic mode of authentication. (Srinivasan 2011: 8)

Sharma's assertion that 'even if the fingerprints do not work, the iris scans will', may not bear close scrutiny. Of course, proponents of iris scans claim that they are far better than fingerprints at differentiating people. That is because a far larger number of data points are collected in an iris scan than in a fingerprint scan. The problem with the iris biometric is that the set-up for the capture of iris biometric has to be well managed (Whitley 2011: 32). During a sudden period of good sunshine, a room brightens up very noticeably and therefore, the iris-capture device has to be potentially adjusted for these kinds of set-ups (Whitley 2011: 32). The experience with airports indicates that iris devices often have problems in operating at their full performance levels (Whitley 2011: 32).

Recent research in the field of iris scans also calls into question some of the accepted truths about iris biometrics. It has now been shown that the three accepted truths about iris biometrics involving pupil dilation, contact lenses, and template aging may not be valid any longer. Kevin Bowyer and others from the University of Notre Dame, the US, have demonstrated that iris biometric performance can be degraded by varying pupil dilation, by wearing non-cosmetic prescription contact lenses, by time lapse between enrolment and verification, and by cross-sensor operation (Ramachandran 2011: 26). All these factors can significantly alter the matching to be done to identify an individual uniquely (Ramachandran 2011: 26). In India, iris scans encounter one more serious problem. A study done in 2005 at the All India Institute of Medical Sciences estimated that 6–8 million people in India had corneal blindness, and many more people would have corneal scars. It is not possible to do iris scan of people with corneal blindness or corneal scars (Ramanathan 2010: 13). In addition, a Hyderabad-based eye institute identified cataract, which results from nutritional deficiency and prolonged exposure to sunlight and ultraviolet rays, and cataract surgery as almost certain to affect the iris (Ramanathan 2010: 13).

There are many gaps in our understanding of the nature and distinctiveness and stability of biometric characteristics across individuals and groups (Ramachandran 2011: 26). As the report of the Whither Biometrics Committee points out: 'No biometric characteristic is known to be entirely stable and distinctive across all groups. Biometric traits have fundamental statistical properties, distinctiveness, and differing degrees of stability under natural physiological conditions and environmental challenges, many aspects of which are not well understood, especially at large scales' (quoted in Ramachandran 2011: 26).

These were also the concerns raised by the report on the desirability of national ID cards prepared by the Information Systems and Innovations Group at the London School of Economics. As Dr Edgar Whitley, the Research Coordinator of the report, says:

> There was concern over whether the technology would work. No scheme on this scale had been undertaken anywhere in the world. The India project is, of course, even bigger. Smaller and less ambitious schemes had encountered substantial technological and operational problems, which may get amplified in a large-scale national system. The use of biometrics created particular concerns, because this technology had never been used on such a scale. (Whitley 2011: 30)

Even the Biometric Standards Committee, which was constituted by the UIDAI to go into the question as to what should be the type and specifications of biometrics, had some reservations on this issue. The Committee conducted a sample study of 25,000 persons. Even in such a small sample, 2–5 per cent of the respondents did not have biometric records (Ramakumar 2011a: 9). There was an increase in error rates by 2–3 per cent when the softwares were untuned to local conditions (Ramakumar 2011a: 9). For iris images, the report of the Committee did not provide estimates of error because of absence of empirical data (Ramakumar 2011a: 9). The Committee observed, 'in the absence of empirical data it is not possible for the committee to precisely predict the improvement in the accuracy of de-duplication to the fusion of fingerprint and iris scores' (Ramanathan 2010: 10). The report acknowledged 'technology risks', including the inability to guarantee biometrics of 'high quality across the thousands of enrolment points' (Ramanathan 2010: 10). According to the Committee, this kind of capture would be helpful in enrolment, but not in authentication since the equipment will not be available in most places (Ramanathan 2010: 10). So, the Committee recommended, 'for authentication, the use of fingerprinting will be sufficient' (Ramanathan 2010: 10).

Interestingly the UIDAI also had its own reservations. In its 'Notice Inviting Application for Hiring Biometrics Consultant', for a period of six months starting March 2010, it was noted:

> While NIST documents the fact that the accuracy of biometric matching is extremely dependent on demographics and environmental conditions, there is a lack of sound study that documents the accuracy achievable on Indian demographics (i.e., larger percentage of rural population) and in Indian environmental conditions (i.e., extremely hot and humid climate and facilities without air-conditioning)... The 'quality' assessments of fingerprint data is not sufficient to fully understand the achievable de-duplication accuracy. The next step is to acquire biometrics data from the Indian rural conditions in two sessions (with a time difference) and assess the matchability. (Ramanathan 2010: 13)

A biometric-based system of authentication involves the matching of measured biometric data against the previously collected data (the reference database) for a given individual. So, error rate in this biometric match becomes the important indicator of reliability. That being the case, one needs to know the number of false positive identifications and false negative identifications that can potentially arise in a situation. Recognition errors of biometric systems are stated in terms of false match rate (FMR) and the false non-match rate (FNMR) (Ramachandran 2011: 26).

Let us look at the UIDAI's record with respect to the error rate for authentication. A Proof of Concept (PoC) exercise was carried out by the UIDAI with 40,000 subjects, divided into two sets of 20,000, in rural Andhra Pradesh, Karnataka, and Bihar (Ramachandran 2011: 28). This was done to analyse the data from rural groups where the quality of fingerprints was likely to be uneven. According to the report of the POC analysis, an FNMR of 0.0025 per cent was observed, and there was an FMR of 0.01 per cent using irises alone and an FMR of 0.25 per cent with fingerprints alone (Ramachandran 2011: 28). So, the report said, 'by doing analysis as shown in the examples above on real data captured under typical Indian conditions in rural India, we can be confident that biometric matching can be used on a wider scale to realise the goal of creating unique identities' (quoted in Ramachandran 2011: 28).

Is the conclusion of the report of the POC analysis sustainable? It is true that the order of magnitude of cases of misrecognition is small, but this small order may magnify into much larger numbers when the programme is done for a population of 1.2 billion (Ramachandran 2011: 28). As the Whither Biometrics Committee report points out:

> Even very small probabilities of misrecognition—the failure to recognize an enrolled individual as another—can become operationally significant when an application is scaled to handle millions of recognition attempts. Thus, well-articulated processes for verification, mitigation of undesired outcomes, and remediation (for misrecognitions) are needed, and presumptions and burdens of proof should be designed conservatively, with due attention to the system's inevitable uncertainties. (quoted in Ramachandran 2011: 26–7)

These observations of the Whither Biometrics Committee become relevant when we look at the results of exercises carried out by the UIDAI on a wider scale. Subsequent to the PoC exercises in Andhra Pradesh, Karnataka, and Bihar, eight pilots were taken up by the UIDAI, which covered 50,000 individuals across five states (S. Singh 2012a: 13). These eight pilots sought to test the ease and accuracy of doing several kinds of transactions using a 12-digit UID number and fingerprints in real time. These transactions included opening bank accounts, delivering LPG subsidy, and paying manual workers under MGNREGS.

What happens in these transaction pilots is that a beneficiary states his/her Aadhaar number and places a finger on a small fingerprint reader. The device sends the print to the UIDAI server in Bangalore, via mobile Internet, for real-time authentication. Once the server confirms that the number and fingerprints belong to the same person—a process that the UIDAI does in 0.2 seconds—the authentication is completed and the transaction proceeds.

The results of these pilots were declared in March 2012 and they reveal gaps in authentication (S. Singh 2012b: 13). Authentication of identity could not be done for all the people merely by their putting a finger on a scanner (S. Singh 2012b: 13). All scanned prints did not match the ones stored in UIDAI server in Bangalore (S. Singh 2012b: 13). According to UIDAI, 80 per cent of these transactions in these pilots needed fingerprints (S. Singh 2012a: 13). Of these, 93.5 per cent were completed in the first attempt and by using just one finger, which is the ideal (S. Singh 2012a: 13). When two fingers were used and up to three attempts were allowed, which indicates iteration, the success rate was 99 per cent (S. Singh 2012a: 13). These figures varied across areas, with the pilot for payment of wages to MGNREGS workers in Jharkhand showing only 60 per cent success in the first try and about 90 per cent in the third (S. Singh 2012a: 13).

Mysore district of Karnataka state was chosen for a transaction pilot project for distribution of LPG under the PDS because of the fact that it was among the first few districts in the country to finish with over 90 per cent enrolments (*The Hindu* 2012b: 4). Three oil companies had, as a part of the pilot, successfully enrolled around 70,000 consumers in six months. But just a few months after the union government announced that the pilot would be scaled up to 50 districts, the part of the pilot in Mysore district that involved using PoS devices to authenticate identity as a prerequisite to making the transaction was withdrawn (*The Hindu* 2012b: 4). According to the oil companies, the proposal to authenticate identity at every transaction was withdrawn because there were problems with authenticating fingerprints (*The Hindu* 2012b: 4). The rate of success in authenticating fingerprints was reported to be only 67 per cent (*The Hindu* 2012b: 4).

According to the UIDAI, the shortfalls in these transaction pilots can be attributed to multiple factors. The main reasons are the breaking of the mobile Internet connection between the fingerprint reader and the central server, the machine operators placing the finger incorrectly on the scanner, a dirty scanner, dirty fingers, and fingerprints not being taken properly during enrolment (S. Singh 2012a: 13). So, while fingerprints are unique, authentication accuracy depends on a multiplicity of factors, ranging from cleanliness of fingers to size of fingerprint scanners, leading to mixed results. Anil Jain, an authority on biometrics who teaches at the Michigan State University and holds six patents in fingerprinting technology, lists several factors that can affect the authentication accuracy (S. Singh 2012b: 13). First is the condition of the finger itself, that is, whether the fingers have cuts, abrasions, and whether they are wet, too dry, dirty, and so on. The second is the quality of fingerprint image acquired by the fingerprint scanner. The quality of the acquired image will depend upon the first factor, namely, the condition of the finger, but it also depends on how the user is interacting with the sensor (finger placement on the sensor and the applied pressure) and the condition of the sensor plate or surface (could be dirty). Third is the robustness of the fingerprint matcher. So, Jain says: 'Given these confounding factors, we cannot guarantee that fingerprint authentication will be 100 per cent accurate. However, for a reasonable quality fingerprint image and a high grade fingerprint matcher, we can be assured that authentication accuracy will be very close to 100 per cent (say, over 99 per cent). Field deployments and testing support this' (quoted in S. Singh 2012b: 13).

The UIDAI has initiated several steps to fix these errors (S. Singh 2012a: 13). It is planning to buy machines with a larger scan area. It is putting in place alternative authentication mechanisms like demographic details (name, address, and date of birth) and a one-time password (currently used for credit card payments on e-commerce sites). However, the UIDAI cannot do anything about the mobile Internet connection between the fingerprint reader and the central server (that depends on the general packet radio service [GPRS] connectivity), but the authorities in the UIDAI are very confident of success. Ashok Pal Singh, the DDG of UIDAI, says, 'These are early days and things will only get better. The idea is to take the success rate to 99.999999 per cent' (S. Singh 2012a: 13). That will be possible only if everything is in place and functioning—scanners, processors, networks, and connectivity.

CHAPTER SEVEN

The Organization

❧

The UIDAI proposes to assign Aadhaar numbers to half of India's population by 2014. For doing that, 600 million Indians are to be photographed; 1.2 billion irises are to be scanned; 6 billion fingerprints are to be collected; and 600 million addresses and many other personal particulars would have to be duly recorded. When the 600 millionth person is given the Aadhaar number, the UIDAI system would have done it only after comparing it with 599,999,999 photographs, 1,199,999,998 irises, and 12,999,999,990 fingerprints so as to make sure that the number is indeed unique (Jayashankar and Ramnath 2010: 1). When in full flow, the UIDAI system is expected to add a million names to its database every single day until the task is completed (Jayashankar and Ramnath 2010: 1). No system in the world has handled anything on such a mind-boggling scale.

The scale of the programme is a big technological challenge (India Knowledge@Wharton 2010: 3). As noted earlier, globally, biometric technology has advanced a lot in the last decade, but it has been driven by applications in the surveillance and security areas. What distinguishes the Aadhaar programme from the application programmes of biometric technology in the Western countries is that it is the first instance of the use of biometric technology on a huge scale for ensuring efficient, equitable, and effective delivery of public services. So, the technological challenge is not merely to provide unique identities to 1.2 billion people but also to use the process of authentication of that identity to provide the foundation for re-engineering of public services. As Nandan Nilekani, the chief programmer, says:

The second thing...has been the technological challenge. This scale of the use of biometrics has not been done anywhere in the world. So, in many ways you are at the frontiers of technology—something like a moon shot. You are saying you want to do something and then you are digging out all the possible ways to get there. (India Knowledge@Wharton 2010: 3)

The other challenge is the managerial challenge. This has three aspects. The first one is to create an ecosystem of partnerships and align all the partners in that ecosystem to the objectives of the Aadhaar programme (India Knowledge@Wharton 2010: 3). It calls for delineating a clear vision; articulating that vision forcefully; and making the partners see that it is beneficial for all the parties to be in a constructive partnership for realizing that vision.

The second aspect of the managerial challenge is to enlist registrars as partners from a wide variety of backgrounds and professions to enrol people for Aadhaar and convince them that a successful process of enrolment is something that would be in the best interests of their respective organizations. These partners have to be persuaded that when they enrol people into the Aadhaar system, they would get tangible benefits in return. The benefits would include tidying of their databases; removing ghosts and duplicates so that their systems work more efficiently; getting online authentication so that they can streamline the process of service delivery; and being inclusive so that the poor can avail of these services. In essence, the challenge is one of bringing about change management by articulating the value proposition and convincing the partners that it is mutually beneficial (India Knowledge@Wharton 2010: 3).

The third aspect of the management challenge is the process of enrolment itself. The challenge is one of ensuring logistics, process efficiency, and data quality while enrolling people. This would mean that, while enrolment has to be carried out at a high volume and low cost, it should also be of the highest quality. The scalability is an important consideration here. The technology has to be there in the right place, and the operators have to be trained. The challenge is also one of putting processes in place, refining the process, refining the software, putting in more quality checks and quality control, and debugging. Last but not the least, the technology needs to be proved in the field, while ensuring that it is foolproof (India Knowledge@Wharton 2010: 3).

In sum, the execution of the Aadhaar programme poses complex challenges of technology and management because it is the world's most ambitious and biggest social inclusion programme with wide-ranging objectives and multiple stakeholders; a programme that calls for leveraging a massive array of public and private entities, sophisticated biometrics, and IT. The successful execution of this programme requires an organizational set-up that is capable of meeting these challenges and assembling a team that has the expertise to drive all the managerial and technology issues. The organizational set-up needs to function in a manner that has the flexibility to take quick decisions and the autonomy to carry them out. The composition of the team calls for a diverse yet eclectic mix of knowledge and skills, ranging from domain-specific knowledge on business issues and managing large organizations to specialized skills in domains such as technology design, vendor development and informed buying, contract facilitation and monitoring, law, relationship building, and communication and outreach.

ORGANIZATIONAL SET-UP

The UIDAI began on a modest scale. It was set up as an attached office of the Planning Commission with a core team of 115 officers and staff. To start with, three posts of DG, DDG, and Assistant Director General (ADG) were sanctioned for headquarters, along with 35 UID commissioners in each of the states. It was later decided to have regional offices in Bangalore, Chandigarh, Delhi, Hyderabad, Guwahati, Lucknow, Mumbai, and Ranchi, with their jurisdiction covering specific states across the country. In September 2009, 268 additional posts were created. The UIDAI, at present, has a total sanctioned strength of 383 officers and subordinate staff (UIDAI 2012a: 3).

Headquarters

The UIDAI is headquartered in Delhi, with Nandan Nilekani as the Chairman and R.S. Sharma as the DG and Mission Director. The DG and Mission Director is assisted by seven DDGs (officers of the level of Joint Secretary to Government of India) who are in charge of various divisions. The DDGs are supported by 21 ADGs, 15 deputy directors, 15 section officers, and 15 assistants. The headquarters has a total sanctioned strength of 146 officers and staff. All the officers and staff have been appointed on deputation either under the Central Staffing Scheme or through the bilateral route. At the headquarters, there are seven divisions functionally arranged along thematic lines. The divisions are: (i) Onboarding, Enrolments, Media, Monitoring, and Audits Division; (ii) Logistics, Contact Centre, Financial Inclusion, Strategic Planning, and Project Management Division; (iii) IT and Technology Procurement Division; (iv) Enrolment, Training, and Testing and Establishment Division; (v) Finance, Authentication, and Updation Process Division; (vi) Administration, Volunteer/Sabbatical, and Interns Division; and (vii) Aadhaar Applications and Accounts Division. Each division is headed by a DDG (UIDAI 2012a: 3).

Regional Offices

Each of the regional offices is headed by a DDG. The support structure consists of four ADGs, three deputy directors, three section officers, one senior accounts officer, one accountant, and personal staff (UIDAI 2012a: 3).

Technology Development Unit

A Technology Development Unit consisting of experts in various areas of operation, including technology, legal framework, procurement of hardware and software, etc, has been established. Volunteer resources and sabbatical candidates support this unit (UIDAI 2012a: 5).

Project Management Unit (PMU)

The PMU was set up with a core team of experts to kick-start the Aadhaar issuance process and provide guidance in areas of technology, legal matters, procurement of hardware and software, preparation of detailed project reports, awareness building, et cetera. These experts brought to the organization, rich experience in their respective domains, and they worked with consultants and service providers on various aspects of the Aadhaar programme, including development of prototypes, testing the PoC, building the technology platform, and designing communication and awareness programmes. The PMU team was created with the assistance of National Institute of Smart Governance. There are 20 experts now in the PMU with expertise in technology, legal matters, communications and procurement, capacity building, and process and operations (UIDAI 2012a: 5).

UIDAI Biometrics Centre of Competence

The UIDAI Biometrics Centre was set up to help deliver on the mandate of issuing Aadhaar to all residents of India. The Centre specified the initial biometric system as also the improvements required to introduce new technologies and best practices. The Centre evaluates and characterizes technology, devices, and algorithms. It also indicates scope for revision or enhancement of specifications for processes. The Centre has attracted world-class biometrics talents, and has built a key group of exceptional scientists and engineers. The idea is that, with its expertise, the Centre would push the state-of-the-art in biometrics to achieve the objectives of UIDAI. The Centre is considered a national resource in biometrics, and other departments in the government take its help for implementing Aadhaar-compatible biometrics systems (UIDAI 2012a: 5–6).

THE AADHAAR TEAM

Nandan Nilekani heads the Aadhaar team. His credentials for the top job are impeccable. He has been a key player in India's growth story. Apart from his pioneering contribution as the Chief Executive Officer (CEO) of Infosys (2002–7), and later as its Co-Chairman, he co-founded India's National Association of Software and Services Companies (NASSCOM). In January 2006, he became one of the youngest entrepreneurs to join 20 global leaders on the prestigious World Economic Forum Foundation Board. The *Time* magazine listed him as one of the 100 most influential people in the world. He was named among the world's most respected business leaders in 2002 and 2003, according to a global survey by *Financial Times* and PricewaterhouseCoopers. In recognition of his contribution, he was awarded the *Fortune* magazine's 'Asia's Businessmen of the Year 2003' award. He also received Joseph Schumpeter Prize for innovative services in economy, economic sciences, and politics in 2005. In 2007, he was named *Forbes* Businessman of the Year for Asia. In 2009, he was presented the 'Legend in Leadership Award' by Yale University.[1]

Nilekani, a graduate of the Indian Institute of Technology (IIT) Mumbai, has been India's most visible new-age entrepreneur. But he is an entrepreneur with a social conscience. As Nilekani says in his book:

> My years as an entrepreneur have specially brought home to me how much India, despite its recent tremendous growth, is straining against the challenges that hold it back. Today, we are a nation that has barely scratched its potential. Almost two decades after liberalization, the absence of critical reforms means that for a majority of Indians daily life continues to be a struggle—for the millions of marginal farmers unable to find alternatives to bare, hard livelihoods; for people living in slums for want of cheaper housing; for families cobbling together their savings to send their children to private schools because our government schools are in a mess. (Nilekani 2008: 4)

This shows, on the one hand, Nilekani's great concern for the poor, and on the other, an enviable sense of public-spiritedness. As Nilekani himself explains: 'Apart from my business interests, I have an interest in public policy issues...I grew up in an environment where my family members, specifically my father and uncle were very public-spirited people. Perhaps that rubbed off on me' (India Knowledge@ Wharton 2010: 4).

Moreover, he has a very sound public policy background. As he says, 'in general, I have been on the fringe of public policy for the last 10 years' (India Knowledge@Wharton 2010: 4). Nandan Nilekani is being modest when he says that he has been on the fringe. In fact, for many years now, he has had a ringside view of how the government works, as a member of many important advisory panels (*The Economic Times* 2011e: 13). He has also contributed immensely to public policy issues. As the head of Bangalore Action Task Force (BATF), he had a big role in improving Bangalore city's governance systems. Based on his experience at the BATF, he pushed for a national focus on urban renewal through an appropriate project, and was instrumental in getting the Jawaharlal Nehru National Urban Renewal Mission (JNNURM) put in place. This is what Nilekani has to say about it:

When the task force ended, I and other members went on a road show around Delhi's government offices to push for a broader, national focus on urban change. We had interested politicians from the left and right, all of whom thought that the urban issue was an urgent one. And we went through the whole trip without being labeled as out-of-touch elitists! The national mission on urban change eventually took shape with the JNNURM, and our experience with the BATF helped us a great deal while helping shape reforms towards improving disclosure laws for urban bodies, strengthening citizen participation, introducing more effective financial accounting and aligning city organizations better. (Nilekani 2008: 228)

Nilekani's various stints in the public space have groomed him for his assignment as the Chairman of the UIDAI. He now says, 'An important lesson that I have learnt is that in the public space, there are a lot more stakeholders with different views. We have to work with them and build consensus, and that is what we are doing' (India Knowledge@Wharton 2010: 3).

Nandan Nilekani is Aadhaar team's prime driving force and also, its chief evangelist (India Knowledge@Wharton 2010: 1). As the CEO of Infosys for many long and difficult years, he has an impressive track record of executing complex technology projects competently. He brings loads of technological prowess to the Aadhaar team. He has been the chief technology policy adviser to the government for many years. Now, in his capacity as the Chairman of the UIDAI, he brings all his varied experience to the implementation of the Aadhaar programme.

When the prime minister called him personally in early 2009 to head the UIDAI, he agreed to take the job. He says that he responded to an inner calling and the public-spirited family trait when he accepted his five-year assignment with the UIDAI. He was given the status of a cabinet minister. Nilekani's appointment as Chairman of the UIDAI was given top billing in the news and print media at the time. When the news of his appointment went viral, it was not only welcomed universally but also got the old schoolboy network cracking (Jayashankar and Ramnath 2010: 1).

Raj Mashruwala is now the Chief Biometric Coordinator at the UIDAI. In that capacity, he has authored biometric standards for Aadhaar applications, and also for India's various e-governance programmes. Before Mashruwala joined the UIDAI in 2009, India could not boast of having any biometric standard worth its name. Mashruwala had a difficult task on hand. For the UIDAI to achieve its objectives, it had to develop consensus on a national standard, adopt it, utilize it, and provide reference implementation for all other civilian applications. Mashruwala and his team did full justice to all these tasks.[2]

At the UIDAI, Mashurwala's accomplishments have been commendable. He was responsible for designing, building, and implementing a multi-modal, multiple Automated Biometrics Identification System (ABIS) vendor and capture device agnostic system on an open-source private cloud platform. With the help of global IT/biometric community, his design produced new Indian standard for: (i) capture device interface; (ii) ABIS interface; and (iii) use of multiple ABIS' without partitioning of gallery.[3]

Mashruwala was Nilekani's senior at IIT Bombay. He moved to the US in 1976 to pursue a Masters in engineering at the University of California at Berkeley. After finishing his Masters, he stayed on in the US, and as a software entrepreneur, executive, and investor, he founded several successful companies, including Consillium and TIBCO Software. When Mashruwala heard that the prime minister had appointed Nandan Nilekani as the head of UIDAI, he sent a congratulatory letter to Nilekani and offered to assist him. Nilekani wrote back, asking Mashruwala and a number of other people from various parts of the world to discuss a broad framework for the UIDAI project. When Mashruwala joined the discussions in Bangalore in July 2009, he found bankers, professors from American Ivy League colleges, technology professionals, people from NGOs, representatives from the insurance sector, and also, Nachiketa Mor, the Co-President of the ICICI Foundation. Mashruwala was so impressed by the diversity of the participants that he decided to stay on in India and work for the UIDAI (Jayashankar and Ramnath 2010: 1).

Nilekani and Mashruwala had a common friend in Srikanth Nadhamuni (Jayashankar and Ramnath 2010: 1). Nadhamuni, an engineer from the University of Mysore, had, like Mashruwala, pursued a Masters in the US. After his Masters, he spent almost 14 years in California's Silicon Valley, working for several global companies. He started with Sun Microsystems as part of the Sparc central processing unit (CPU) design team, including its most successful CPU—the Spitfire. He followed this up by a stint at Intel Corporation in Santa Clara on the development of the P6 and P7 CPUs. Next, he was at Silicon Graphics on the interactive television project to stream video on demand from Time Warner. He was also a part of the initial team set up by Jim Clark—the founder of Netscape and Silicon Graphics—to create an Internet health care company, the WebMD. At WebMD, he was Director, Engineering, and developed some of the key products and was also part of the business development involved in merger and acquisitions. Later, he founded Globe Trades Inc., an Internet start-up focusing on Internet marketplaces for apparel and construction industries.[4]

Apart from being a successful entrepreneur, Nadhamuni is a brilliant technologist with over 23 years experience in the chip design, Internet technologies, and e-governance industries. He moved back to India in 2002 to focus on social development initiatives. In 2003, Nandan Nilekani and Nadhamuni co-founded eGovernments Foundation, a non-profit organization, to help municipalities deliver better services to citizens by using Information Technology (IT). The idea was to provide municipal e-governance tools for Indian cities to improve their service delivery. The organization has successfully deployed municipal enterprise resource planning (ERP) solutions in over 250 cities across the country. Nadhamuni is also a member of the e-governance core committee of Government of Karnataka.[5]

Nilekani now invited Nadhamuni to join the UIDAI. Nadhamuni has been the Head of Technology for the UIDAI since it inception in 2009, right from the conceptual stage to designing and building the biometric-based Aadhaar system that will uniquely identify 1.2 billion residents of India. He helped set up the Technology Centre at Bangalore which has developed the Aadhaar system with the help of technology development partners/vendors as well as sabbatical and volunteer members from the corporate sector.[6]

Michael Foley is the famous designer who created the baton for the Commonwealth Games 2010. As the design head of Titan Watches, Foley has created watches, sunglasses, and other lifestyle products. His most celebrated product is the Titan Wedge, the world's slimmest watch. He later founded FoleyDesigns, which designs lighting systems and waste disposal. Foley was asked by Nilekani to join the UIDAI. Working for the UIDAI, Foley designed the portable kit that houses a laptop, camera, and iris and fingerprint scanners (Jayashankar and Ramnath 2010: 2).

Govindraj Ethiraj is a veteran journalist who has specialized in economic and corporate matters. He has worked for *The Economic Times*. He has also been a television journalist, spending time with the CNBC-TV18. He has worked as the editor of Bloomberg-UTV. Accepting Nilekani's invitation, Ethiraj joined the UIDAI as the Head, Industry Outreach (Jayashankar and Ramnath 2010: 2).

People from the Government

The UIDAI's team has wide-ranging talents from across the government: it has not only people from the elite Indian Administrative Service (IAS) but also from the railways, postal services, income tax, audit and accounts, and even, Bharat Sanchar Nigam Limited (BSNL) (Jayashankar and Ramnath 2010: 2). The diversity is really amazing. But what is striking about the government people in the UIDAI is that they are not the archetypal, run-of-the-mill, dyed-in-the-wool bureaucrats with stiff upper lips and matching ambivalence, but committed people who have been missionaries in public service.

R.S. Sharma, the DG and Mission Director of the Aadhaar programme, did his Masters in IIT Kanpur, in mathematics, in 1976; and in 2000, he did his Masters in computer science from the University of California, Riverside. He joined the IAS in 1978 and he brings with him the valuable experience of working in various challenging assignments in the governments of Bihar, Jharkhand, and the central government.[7]

Interestingly, in all the assignments he has had in the government, Sharma has tried to incorporate technology in the various processes of governance in order to make them more efficient and people friendly. In 1986, he wrote a programme in DBASE: a programming language that keeps a record of all stolen firearms in a crime-prone district. As soon as a firearm was found, the programme would run a search query among thousands of age-old records. The successful working of the DBASE programme managed to capture the attention of the government as it solved 22 cases in just 30 days. He was the first civil servant in Bihar to introduce a DCM 10-D computer in Begu Sarai where he was the Collector. He introduced computerization in the Department of Treasury in Purnia district, and a public grievance system in the MGNREGS in Bihar. Sharma received the Prime Minister's Award for Excellence in Public Administration in 2008.[8] He is a civil servant with a difference: the engineers from MindTree, the Bangalore-based IT company which created the enrolment application for UIDAI, are constantly amazed that even at 4 a.m., the DG personally reviews their software code (Jayashankar and Ramnath 2010: 3–4).

K. Ganga, who is from the Indian Audit and Accounts Service, has worked as the Financial Adviser to the President of India. She brings to the UIDAI the perspective of a government auditor. When Nilekani, who was introduced to her through a mutual friend, asked her if she could give five years of her life to the project as DDG in charge of finance, Ganga agreed but with one caveat. She did not want her role to be limited only to handling the finance department. She wanted to be part of the team that created the project ground up. She got what she wanted (Jayashankar and Ramnath 2010: 2). She was not only appointed as the DDG in charge of Finance, Authentication, and Updation Process Division, but is also in charge of the Delhi Regional Office.

Ashok Pal Singh is from the Indian Postal Service. He is an alumnus of Mayo College, Ajmer, and St Stephens College, Delhi. He was DDG in the Department of Posts, where he had nurtured the dream of giving every Indian a bank account and an email ID. When the Aadhaar programme was announced, he sought a meeting with Nilekani to discuss how the Aadhaar programme could fulfil these two objectives. Nilekani ended up by taking Ashok Pal Singh into the programme as a DDG (Jayashankar and Ramnath 2010: 2). He is in charge of Logistics, Contact Centre, Financial Inclusion, Strategic Planning, and Project Management Division.

Volunteers, Sabbatical/Secondment, and Interns

The UIDAI has a very well-crafted scheme of volunteers, sabbatical/secondment, and internship. The tenure of volunteers ranges from a few months to a year; those in the PMU stay longer. The volunteer is a person with expertise who wants to give services to the UIDAI, either on a part-time or full-time basis, without any remuneration. When an expert in a particular field applies for becoming a volunteer, the UIDAI assesses if the volunteer's services are required in his/her area of expertise. The UIDAI, then, conducts an interview. If the UIDAI is satisfied that the applicant possesses requisite specialized skills, experience, and qualifications; has relevant professional/ volunteer experience; has satisfactory background and references; and there is no conflict of interest between the applicant working as a volunteer for the UIDAI and any other work the volunteer may be doing either for gain or as a volunteer, then the UIDAI issues an offer letter along with specific role for the volunteer and the reporting structure (UIDAI 2011a: 1–5).

Sabbatical/secondment scheme is meant for experts who want to give their services to the UIDAI, on a full-time or part-time basis, while on sabbatical from their parent organizations, without seeking any remuneration from the UIDAI. It was considered necessary to have the scheme of sabbatical/secondment because a project of Aadhaar's scale had not been executed anywhere in the world, and the UIDAI needed to attract talent from technology, law, policy, marketing, social sciences, and administrative spheres. Under this scheme, UIDAI could take people from industry and academia to work with the UIDAI on sabbatical or secondment from their parent organization (UIDAI 2011b: 1–6).

Several academic institutions and young scholars expressed their desire to contribute to the Aadhaar programme—the biggest social inclusion programme in the world. That being the case, the UIDAI started an internship programme to ensure interaction of the UIDAI with young Indian scholars from reputed academic institutions in the country and abroad with brilliant academic background. The idea was that interactions with young scholars would bring in fresh new ideas and research support from the academia; it would also provide an opportunity to young scholars to contribute to a project of national importance and provide insight into how the government works (UIDAI 2012b: 1–5).

Since the time the Aadhaar programme was announced, the UIDAI has received more than 1,000 applications from people across the world. Twenty-three applicants have come in as unpaid volunteers, 14 persons have taken sabbaticals from their jobs, and 23 persons have taken massive pay cuts to join the PMU of the UIDAI. Sanjay Swamy is a volunteer in the Authentication and Payments Division. He studied at the Ecole Nationale Superieure de l'Aeronautique et de l'Espace, France, and then, at the University of Washington, Seattle. He is at present the CEO of mCheck, a mobile payments start-up. He had written an email to Nilekani on how the UIDAI should evolve, and then realized that he did not know what Nilekani's email ID was. So, he posted the text of his proposed email on a blog and this caught Nilekani's attention. When they finally got in touch, Nilekani asked him to help the UIDAI with the micropayment module. Sanjay Swamy joined the UIDAI. He now works in the area of financial inclusion and strategy, and uses his entrepreneurial skills to convince banks, insurance companies, and telephone companies to use Aadhaar numbers for verification and reduce customer acquisition costs.[9]

Raju Rajagopal got his BTech degree from IIT Chennai in 1968 and worked in the US. He retired as the Chief Operating Officer of a public company after 30 years of professional career. After retirement, he returned to India to work in the development sector. He was involved in rural development projects and advocacy work on governance issues. After the 2002 communal disturbance in Gujarat, he spent a lot of time on the issue of communal harmony, including the Promise of India Global Initiative. He also played a major role in post-disaster relief and rehabilitation in Gujarat earthquake and Tamil Nadu tsunami. He now works in the UIDAI as a volunteer in the area of civil society outreach, helping the organization to form partnerships with NGOs around the country in order to ensure that the weakest sections of the society (migrant workers, nomads, and children) are enrolled in the Aadhaar programme.[10]

D. Subhalakshmi is a graduate of Indian Institute of Management (IIM) Ahmedabad. She has worked with Genpact in the area of human resources development and operations. Her boss at Genpact, Promod Bhasin, recommended her name to Nilekani. She now works in the UIDAI as a volunteer and is in charge of the volunteer and sabbatical programme (Jayashankar and Ramnath 2010: 5).

Sahil Kini graduated from IIT Chennai and has worked in DSP Merrill Lynch and Larsen & Toubro. He now works in McKinsey

& Company in the area of process and operations. On a sabbatical loan from his parent company, he joined the UIDAI and helped it to set up its contact centre. During his stint, he managed to scale up operations of the contact centre. He also created and executed multiple tenders for the UIDAI, worked on the UIDAI telco policy, and did research on UIDAI authentication as a platform for application development.[11]

Ajit V. Rao received his BTech degree in electronics and communication engineering from IIT Madras, and his Masters and Doctorate from University of California, Santa Barbara. After his graduation, he joined SignalCom in Santa Barbara. In 2000, he moved to Microsoft where he worked on Windows Media. In mid-2002, he returned to India to join the Imaging and Audio Group of Texas Instruments and worked there for 12 years. His areas of interest and research include compression of speech, audio and video for packet and wireless networks, speech recognition, and statistical pattern recognition. He quit his job in Texas Instruments to work in the UIDAI as a volunteer and help the organization with biometrics.[12]

Samant Veer Kakkar got his LLM in European Law and Practice from the University of Rouen, France, and did further studies in law in University Catolica in Portugal. After his studies, he worked for the Council for European Social Organizations (Community Economic Development Assistance Corporation [CEDAC]) and later, at Lefebvre Hanneman Consultancy, Brussels. He gave up his lucrative legal career to come and work in the UIDAI. He works as a volunteer on the communication team at the UIDAI.[13]

Jagadish Babu did his Masters in engineering from the Indian Institute of Science, Bangalore. He then joined Intel and worked as the Asia Pacific Regional Engineering Manager. The areas he worked in include application performance optimization, 3D graphic application design and optimization, and sizing and optimization of large e-business infrastructures. He is currently on a sabbatical assignment and is a volunteer in technology hardware platforms with the Technology Centre of the UIDAI. His role is to lead the enrolment and authentication devices ecosystem for UIDAI's programmes.[14]

These volunteers and those on sabbatical, who are experts in their specific domains, have been responsible for creating many of the systems in the UIDAI, working with other experts in the organization. For example, the scaling-up system in Aadhaar authentication was created and put in place by a team of about 70 people, in which there were 40 volunteers from the UIDAI and the rest were from Ernst & Young and companies like Google and Genpact on sabbatical (S. Singh 2012a: 13). These volunteers are experts in new-age computing or are data management experts drawn from banking, finance, manufacturing, retail, among other sectors (S. Singh 2012a: 13).

On the whole, it is a fantastic team of experts who have excelled in their respective domains. As Jayashankar and Ramnath (2010: 4) point out:

> The team includes some of the fine minds in the world, from academic institutions, the private sector, and hand-picked candidates from the government who have done remarkably well for themselves, entrepreneurs who can build business applications around the UID number so that it evolves into a viable, self-sustaining model. They deal with complex technical problems, biometrics, models of financial inclusion, privacy laws and communication. At various times, different roles took priority. In the run up to the projects, it was the technologists. Once enrollment picks up steam, it will need people to work with regulators and businesses to find ways in which the UID number can be used.

What attracts such exceptionally bright people with tremendous expertise to the UIDAI? After all, the UIDAI is a government organization. There is certainly no big money to be made in the UIDAI. Even if the UIDAI succeeds in creating and putting in place an identity infrastructure for all Indians, it will not fetch bounties of private profits or stock options for all these experts. Ashok Pal Singh, the DDG of the UIDAI, says, 'In terms of perks, privileges and pay, this place has nothing more to offer than any other job in government. In many respects, it is worse off. And yet everyone is here, because they want to be' (Jayashankar and Ramnath 2010: 2). As Jayashankar and Ramnath (2010: 1) say:

> The only tangible gain most of the team on the project will have the pleasure of knowing they worked on the most complex data management project the world has ever known. And perhaps the warm glow that comes with knowing they wanted to change the

world. After which they will go back to wherever it is they came from. How many people do you know who'd have the spunk to be in full-time on an assignment like this?

Nandan Nilekani, Aadhaar's chief evangelist and the magnet that draws all these talented experts to the 'world's most ambitious and biggest social inclusion programme', says, 'Some of the best minds in the country are working at very low fees on solving all the complex issues involved in setting up something like this. And they are doing it because they are engaged with the future of this country and believe this will help it' (*Tehelka* 2010: 29).

On the whole, what comes across clearly is that the UIDAI is an organization of experts. The experts in the UIDAI represent some of the finest minds in the world in their respective areas. Their awesome expertise ranges from domain-specific knowledge on complex business issues and management of large organizations to specialized skills in diverse domains such as technology designs, vendor development and informed buying, contract facilitation and monitoring, and communication and outreach. They work for very low remuneration or no remuneration at all, and they have made huge sacrifices because they believe that they are doing something for the good of the community and the country. Such an eclectic mix of expertise and public-spiritedness establishes the credentials and credibility of the UIDAI as an organization of expertise that can be relied upon to deliver socially relevant outcomes.

FUNCTIONING OF THE ORGANIZATION

Going by how the UIDAI has functioned so far, it is rather difficult to cast the organization in the typology of conventional government structures. Let us look at how government organizations are structured in India. A 'department' is one that is responsible for formulation of policies of the government in relation to business attached to it and also, for the execution and review of those policies (*Swamy's Manual of Office Procedure* 2004: 7). Where the execution of the policies of the government requires decentralization of executive action and/or direction, a department may have under it executive agencies called 'attached' and 'subordinate' offices (*Swamy's Manual of Office Procedure* 2004: 7).

Attached offices are generally responsible for providing executive direction required in the implementation of policies laid down by the department to which they are attached. They also serve as repository of technical information and advise the department on technical aspects of question dealt with by them. Subordinate offices generally function as field establishments or as agencies responsible for the detailed execution of the policies of the government. They function under the direction of an attached office, or where the volume of executive direction involved is not considerable, directly under a department. In the latter case, they assist the departments concerned in handling technical matters in their respective fields of specialization. There is a system of checks and balances built into this hierarchical ordering of a department, attached office, and subordinate office (*Swamy's Manual of Office Procedure* 2004: 7).

It is true that the UIDAI was set up as an attached office of the Planning Commission and notified as such. Its operations are fully funded by the government. But, if one goes by how it has actually functioned, the UIDAI does not exactly correspond to the prototypical attached office in the government. As a matter of fact, the UIDAI functions like a seamless combination of a department, an attached office, and a subordinate office. It formulates policies of the government in respect of the business allocated to it (like a department); it provides executive direction for implementation of policies and is the repository of technical information (like an attached office); and it functions as the field establishment for the detailed execution of policies (like a subordinate office). It is as if all the carefully differentiated and hierarchically ordered government formations have been rolled into one omnibus structure in the case of the UIDAI.

The difference between the UIDAI and conventional governmental structures is not merely in terms of official typologies but also with respect to ambience and setting. The ambience in the UIDAI is very different from that of a run-of-the-mill government office. In UIDAI's offices, there is an informality that is conspicuous by its absence in a government office. Even the setting, particularly in the UIDAI's Bangalore office where most of the technical work gets done, is very unlike a government office. The doors and partitions are of gleaming glass. People rush around energetically with a determined, purposeful look (Jayashankar and Ramnath 2010: 3). Even as late as 8 p.m. in the evening, there are blazing lights; visitors stream in; and impromptu meetings take place in the corridor (Jayashankar and Ramnath 2010: 3). Everybody is on a first-name term and the ambience is absolutely collegial, to say the least (Jayashankar and Ramnath 2010: 3).

Institutionally, the UIDAI functions differently from a conventional government organization, particularly when it comes to compliance with mandatory government procedures. Its functioning has been so unconventional that the Planning Commission, its host department, has raised serious questions about the administrative structure of the UIDAI. It has gone to the extent of calling for the appointment of an independent financial adviser to monitor the finances and transactions of the UIDAI. As the Planning Commission wrote in a letter to the Ministry of Finance in September 2011, 'UIDAI's present system represents a major departure from the Government of India procedures and removes all in-built checks and balances. We need a re-look at UIDAI's administrative structure' (*The Economic Times* 2011f: 1). The Planning Commission complained to the Ministry of Finance that, though the UIDAI was set up as its attached office in January 2009 and derives its budget from the Ministry of Planning, it never got to examine any of the Authority's financial proposals till date. The letter pointed out that the expenditure proposals of the UIDAI needed to be normally seen by the Planning Commission's secretary and financial adviser, 'but neither the secretary nor the financial advisor are in the loop' (*The Economic Times* 2011f: 1).

In a subsequent letter sent to the Ministry of Finance, the Planning Commission asked for 'a full-time financial advisor' to be placed in the UIDAI tasked with the 'responsibility of looking into the authority's financial sanctions and clearances' (*The Economic Times* 2011f: 1). The Planning Commission objected to the decision-making structure in the UIDAI that delegated the powers of a financial adviser to a DDG who was also responsible for UIDAI's programmes and projects (*The Economic Times* 2011f: 1). Typically, financial advisers of government departments are not entrusted with any discretionary policymaking powers so that they can take a fair and independent view of financial proposals. As the Planning Commission's letter pointed out, the financial adviser in the UIDAI had been charged with a slew of executive responsibilities: she even prepared several memos and cabinet notes for the authority (*The Economic Times* 2011f: 1).

The Planning Commission also questioned the expenditure of Rs 30,000 crore incurred by the UIDAI to collect fingerprints, iris scans, and photographs of a section of the population (Ramakrishnan 2011: 11). The deputy chairman of the Planning Commission and the Commission's member secretary had serious objections to the UIDAI's proposal to raise the implementation costs and to the methods adopted by the UIDAI to collect biometrics. In his letter dated 30 August 2011, the deputy chairman requested the home minister to 'kindly see the note below with the duplication in the rollout of Aadhaar numbers by the UIDAI and the ongoing exercise of the national population register by the Registrar General of India' (Ramakrishnan 2011: 11). The member secretary of the Planning Commission pointed out that 'a reasoned decision is missing [on] whether iris [scans] really needs to be collected' (Ramakrishnan 2011: 11). She also pointed out that the Planning Commission was keen to avoid the duplication of data and expenditure (Ramakrishnan 2011: 11). What is important to note is that these are the views of the Planning Commission, the department to which the UIDAI is attached as an attached office, and as we noted earlier, in terms of normal functioning of the government, it is the department which is responsible for formulation of policies and also for the execution and review of these policies, and the attached office functions under the direction and superintendence of the host department.

These letters and the proposed rejection of the outlay proposed by the UIDAI show that the host department did not exactly approve of the ways in which its attached office was functioning. As if to compound matters, the Comptroller and Auditor General (C&AG) had already declared its intention to do a 'pilot' performance audit of the UIDAI's operations and finances with a view to ascertaining whether the UIDAI has, as is expected of all government departments, achieved its intended outcomes at the lowest possible cost (*The Economic Times* 2011i: 13). Conducting of such audit was rather unusual because, at that time, the UIDAI had been functioning only for a short period of time. According to the C&AG's office, while the audit of the UIDAI was a part of its plan, the timing had been advanced because of the risk perception (*The Economic Times* 2011i: 13). An official from the C&AG's office said, 'We initiated the process after we considered the audit risk involved', adding that the risk in UIDAI's case was enhanced by recent reports about duplication of expenditure and questions raised by several government departments about some of UIDAI's decisions (*The Economic Times* 2011i: 13). Audit risk is a factor relied upon by the C&AG to determine which offices needed to be audited on a priority basis.

Several political observers, including some Members of Parliament (MPs), were of the view that the C&AG report could raise some questions on UIDAI's expenditures, especially in the context of the financial autonomy that has been provided to the UIDAI (Ramakrishnan 2011: 12). The financial autonomy accorded to the UIDAI was perceived as improper by a number of high government functionaries, including the C&AG and member secretary of the Planning Commission (Ramakrishnan 2011: 12). The style of functioning of the UIDAI also rankled several people in the government, both politicians and bureaucrats. As a senior official told the *Frontline* magazine: 'Technically the UIDAI is supposed to be under a...Ministry, but there have been several occasions when the authority dealt directly with the Finance Ministry, giving the clear impression of bypassing the designated reporting Ministry. This has not been taken lightly by many in the Ministry' (Ramakrishnan 2011: 12).

Nandan Nilekani was quick to counter these charges. He pointed out that the proposed C&AG audit is unwarranted since the UIDAI had been functional barely for a year. He also pointed out that the UIDAI is a government department and functions under all the norms and rules of the government (*The Economic Times* 2011g: 5). 'We are accountable,' he said as he reacted to the Planning Commission's criticism about the structure and functioning of the UIDAI, 'to the CAG, CBI, CVC, RTI, media and the Parliament' (*The Economic Times* 2011g: 5). Regarding the autonomy enjoyed by the UIDAI, Nilekani said that he, holding the rank of a cabinet minister as he does, derives his powers from the prime minister, while the powers of the UIDAI's DG are notified by the Planning Commission's deputy chairman and UIDAI's financial adviser has been delegated powers by the expenditure secretary (*The Economic Times* 2011g: 5). 'What could be in dispute is whether we should have these powers, but that's a different issue,' he said (*The Economic Times* 2011g: 5).

Nilekani vigorously defended the UIDAI against criticism from various government departments and dismissed concerns about the lack of checks and balances in its functioning. He said, 'Our website has instant information on all the tenders we issue, quarterly updates of our expenditure, enrollment data is available real-time' (*The Economic Times* 2011g: 5). He declared that the UIDAI follows the highest standards of government and there is total transparency in its activities and procurements. Speaking at a function organized to mark the first anniversary of the launch of the Aadhaar programme, Nilekani, the former CEO of Infosys Technologies, said, 'I have worked for 30 years in a company that followed very high corporate governance standards, so you cannot expect me to transcend the norms of good governance' (*The Economic Times* 2011g: 5).

Six months after the imbroglio, things took a positive turn for the UIDAI. The budget of 2012 was a huge validation for the UIDAI (*The Economic Times* 2012d: 13). The budget speech of the finance minister categorically endorsed the Aadhaar programme and declared that the government would issue identity cards with Aadhaar numbers to all residents above 18 years of age, and drive welfare measures like subsidies, pensions, and PDS benefits through the Aadhaar platform. The 2012 budget speech was, in fact, a political and operational statement endorsing both the UIDAI and the Aadhaar programme, and indicated that the government was throwing all its weight behind the UIDAI.

All said and done, the UIDAI is a government department, but with a big difference. It has been given much greater autonomy as compared to other government departments that are required to function in a very tight, often constricting, framework of government rules and regulations, punishing budgetary constraints, and rigid compliance with procedural requirements. In fact, the UIDAI is so different from a run-of-the-mill government department or organization that it has often been called a 'private' organization, and the Aadhaar, a private project (*The Hindu* 2012a: 1). *The Economic Times* (2012d: 13) calls it 'the state entity with a private-sector soul'. This allusion to the privateness of the UIDAI is prompted by the fact that, in general perception, the organization works like a private sector company and its functioning is not at all like that of a routine government organization implementing a fully funded government programme.

The government has allowed the UIDAI to function as an autonomous organization even though it is a direct-line government unit as an attached office of the Planning Commission. This autonomy had been given to Nilekani by the top political leadership of the government. In fact, the UIDAI was so close to the top ruling political leadership of the time that Nandan Nilekani was the only person to be mentioned by name in the finance minister's budget speech of 2012 (*The Economic Times* 2012d: 13). Incidentally, in the same budget speech, Aadhaar was mentioned 11 times; a very handsome tribute, indeed (*The Economic Times* 2012d: 13).

As *The Economic Times* (2011e: 13) observed:

Nandan Nilekani has had a free run at the UIDAI, with the Congress high command shielding him from red tape and civil society. So, at the outset, when the UIDAI said it wanted to create a new database to allot UIDs because the existing ones were unreliable, the government agreed. When the National Advisory Council opposed UID, citing privacy and profiling concerns, Congress President backed Nilekani over the council she heads. To keep the Cabinet out of UIDAI's hair, a nine-member cabinet committee on UIDAI was formed in October 2009. When UIDAI said it didn't want to wait for biometrics from the National Population Register under the home ministry, to issue Aadhaar, the government let it collect 100 million biometrics by March 2011. When the UIDAI sought to add iris scan as a third biometric, along with photographs and fingerprints, the government agreed, despite the costs doubling. In November 2010, when it bypassed the PM's council and the cabinet committee on UIDAI, and asked the Finance Minister Pranab Mukherjee to extend the March 2011 deadline, the FM gave them another year; he also allowed UIDAI to double its biometric collection target, to 200 million by March 2012. It's done about 35 million so far.

Nandan Nilekani says: 'Politically we have a very broad based, bipartisan support; every state government in the country has signed up with us—of all political hues. We have support from parliamentarians, chief ministers, banks, etc. Otherwise, we could not have come so far' (India Knowledge@Wharton 2010: 3).

Both Nilekani's compatriots and critics acknowledge the fact that he, as the head of the UIDAI, has received overwhelming political support. But we should not lose sight of the fact that Nilekani has worked hard to get this support. Nilekani has met, made presentations, and signed up for support from every chief minister and chief secretary in 28 states and seven union territories. He visited 24 states in 87 whirlwind days after he accepted the Aadhaar job in July 2009. Nilekani has political support, but not exactly the broad-based, bipartisan political support that he claims to have. The Parliamentary Standing Committee on Finance, which is chaired by Bharatiya Janata Party (BJP) leader Yashwant Sinha, has criticized the Aadhaar programme as a directionless project, and has raised serious questions about the ethics, feasibility, and purpose of the project (*The New Indian Express* 2012a: 8). Nilotpal Basu of the Communist Party of India (Marxist) (CPI(M)) has raised several concerns about the objectives that the UIDAI proposes to pursue, especially in the way the project is being channelled to become an instrument for effecting changes in the subsidy regime (Ramakrishnan 2011: 12).

It is a fact that the UIDAI has found a great deal of political support from the ruling politicians. The then Prime Minister, Manmohan Singh, said, 'Aadhaar…is symbolic of the new and modern India' (Ramakumar 2011a: 4). For Rahul Gandhi, the General Secretary of the Congress Party, Aadhaar is the key to 'bridging the two Indias', where you 'take some' from the 'India of opportunity' and 'put them' into the 'India without opportunity' (Ramakumar 2011a: 4). Abhishek Manu Singhvi, the then spokesperson of the Congress Party, said, 'What needs to be seen is that the UID is likely to transform the face of India by effectively dealing with the scourge of leakages in public welfare development projects and providing a uniform model of verification for one of the largest populations in the world' (Ramakumar 2011: 12).

Why was there such overwhelming support for Aadhaar from the ruling politicians? This is for two reasons. One is that the political government is using the UIDAI to legitimate and operationalize its new political rationality. The government wants to make fundamental changes in the existing system by which subsidies are provided to the poor at present. The instrument through which the government wants to achieve this is the Aadhaar programme. The government expects the UIDAI to identify certain shortcomings in the existing system of delivery of public services as problems, translate them into the vocabulary of technology and management, and propose knowledge-based solutions, which are aligned with this new political rationality that the government seeks to propagate.

The UIDAI has been chosen for this catalytic role for a very special reason. This is because the UIDAI is seen as an organization of experts, consisting of a team that includes some of the finest minds in the world drawn from reputed academic institutions and the private sector, from the ranks of technologists with domain specialization and entrepreneurs. In popular perception, the UIDAI is viewed as embodying technical knowledge and skill. Therefore, it can claim to speak the truth in the name of technology and knowledge. That is why people see it operating according to an ethical code, which is beyond self-interest, good and evil, and which represents total objectivity. In popular perception, this removes the UIDAI from the murky and self-interested terrain of politics and government, and locates it in the disinterested territory of technology, knowledge, truth, and objectivity.

That is also the reason why people find it credible when the UIDAI says that, by using state-of-the-art technology, it would provide unique identities to millions of poor people who do not have an identity and also, give them the right to an acknowledged existence. People trust the UIDAI to provide knowledge-based solutions to re-engineer the public services so that they can get better services. The hassles of public service delivery in provision of food and fuel, wage employment, health care, and school education constitute the minutiae of daily existence of the poor, and the UIDAI promises to make delivery of these services efficient and hassle free. Now, these are also the objectives of the government aligned to its political rationality, and what the UIDAI does, through the Aadhaar programme, is linking the new political rationality of the government to the elimination of hassles faced by the poor. In the process, it helps the government by identifying certain shortcomings in delivery of public services as problems and promising to provide technology-based solutions to address these problems in a manner that introduces a range of techniques and tactics to realize the new political rationality of the government.

It so happens that the technology-based solutions offered by the UIDAI carry credibility for the poor: partly because these solutions promise to free them from the hassles they face, on a quotidian basis, to access public services; and partly because the UIDAI offers these solutions using a language that claims the power of truth, knowledge, and objectivity. As far as the poor are concerned, they find the pro-poor Aadhaar discourse appealing and convincing. They see the UIDAI as an organization of experts, which is capable of doing things for them based on its technical expertise. Their perception is that it will give them an identity with which they will become visible to the state, and it will also plug leakages in public service delivery and make it more effective and efficient. They see Aadhaar as a triumph of expertise that can deliver socially relevant outcomes. The expertise that the UIDAI institutionalizes is viewed as embodying neutrality and skill, and as a potent force that can be harnessed to do good things for the poor. What UIDAI does in the process is to translate the trials and tribulations of the poor into a language of freedom by claiming to empower them with the basic right to an acknowledged existence, emancipate them from their namelessness and ignominy, and free them from the hassles of accessing their benefits and entitlements in the public space. The credibility of the UIDAI in the eyes of the poor is enhanced by the fact they see it as a benevolent organization far removed from the intrusive, rent-seeking bureaucracy that is bent upon harassing them for promoting its selfish ends.

The other reason is that it helps the government to govern the poor from a distance. In fact, it makes sense to view the extent of autonomy that the political government has given to the UIDAI from this perspective. As noted earlier, the UIDAI has been exempted, de facto, from compliance with mandatory government procedures and the in-built checks and balances applicable to other attached entities of government departments. Its budget does not come under the scrutiny of the Planning Commission, the UIDAI's host department, and neither the secretary of the Planning Commission nor its financial adviser have any visible control over the financial dealings of the UIDAI. By granting such unusual yet unconditional autonomy to the UIDAI and empowering it to function as a fully autonomous organization, the government plans to be in position to divest itself of many of its welfare responsibilities and devolve them to the poor. This is an instance of the government governing from a distance, and the complete autonomy given to the UIDAI, which makes it look like an autonomous, benevolent organization embodying expertise, makes this shift of responsibility possible.

NOTES

1. Available at http://en.wikipedia.org/wiki/Nandan_Nilekani, accessed 23 September 2012, pp. 1–3.

2. Available at http://biometrics.org/bc2010/biographies/Standards/mashruwala-raj.pdf, accessed 25 December 2011.

3. Available at http://biometrics.org/bc2010/biographies/Standards/mashruwala-raj.pdf, accessed 25 December 2011.

4. Available at http://www.nasscom.in/upload/events2011/NGSD_June 2011/Srikanth_Nadhamuni.pdf, accessed 25 December 2011.

5. Available at http://www.nasscom.in/upload/events2011/NGSD_June 2011/Srikanth_Nadhamuni.pdf, accessed 25 December 2011.

6. Available at http://www.nasscom.in/upload/events2011/NGSD_June 2011/Srikanth_Nadhamuni.pdf, accessed on 25 September 2011.

7. Available at http://en.wikipedia.org/wiki/Ram_Sewak_Sharma, accessed 3 October 2011.

8. Available at http://en.wikipedia.org/wiki/Ram_Sewak_Sharma, accessed 3 October 2011.

9. Available at http://in.linkedin.com/in/sanjayswamy, accessed 14 October 2011.

10. Available at http://raju-rajagopal,sulekha.com, accessed 14 October 2011.

11. Available at http://in.linkedin.com/pub/sahil-kini/4/a00/618, accessed 14 October 2011.

12. Available at http://www.tenet.res.in/ncc2003/bio.html, accessed 14 October 2011.

13. Available at http://www.em-a.eu/en/home/newsdetail-ema-members-report/ema-alumni-profile-and-int, accessed 14 October 2011.

14. Available at http://www.nasscom.in/upload/events2011/NGSD_June 2011/Jagdish_Babu.pdf, accessed 14 October 2011.

Legal Framework

♞♞

The National Identification Authority of India Bill was introduced in the Rajya Sabha on 3 December 2010. The Bill seeks to:

> provide for the establishment of the National Identification Authority of India for the purpose of issuing identification numbers to individuals residing in India and to certain other classes of individuals and manner of authentication of such individuals to facilitate access to benefits and services to such individuals to which they are entitled and for matters connected therewith and incidental thereto. (PRS Legislative Research 2010c: 1)

KEY FEATURES OF THE BILL

The Bill provides for the establishment of the National Identification Authority of India to issue UID numbers (called Aadhaar) to residents of India (Clause 11) (PRS Legislative Research 2010c: 3–4). The National Identification Authority shall have a chairperson and two part-time members. Each member shall have experience in matters relating to technology, law, or public administration. The tenure of each member shall be three years with an age limit of 65 years.

Every person residing in India is entitled to obtain an Aadhaar number after furnishing relevant demographic and biometric information (Clause 3). No information pertaining to race, religion, caste, tribe, ethnicity, language, income, or health shall be collected (Clause 9) (PRS Legislative Research 2010c: 3). The Aadhaar number shall serve as sufficient proof of identity, but it shall not confer any right to citizenship or entitlement. Clause 8, however, requires that the Aadhaar number holder may be required to update his biometric and demographic information in a manner to be specified (PRS Legislative Research 2010c: 3).

The Aadhaar number shall be a random number and the number itself shall bear no information of the individual (PRS Legislative Research 2010c: 3). The collected information shall be stored in the Central Identities Data Depository (CIDR) and shall be used to authenticate the identity of each person. The process of authentication will consist of either a positive or negative response and will not divulge demographic and biometric information.

The Bill describes the powers and functions of the Authority (Clause 23) (PRS Legislative Research 2010c: 7). The Authority shall develop the policy, procedure, and systems for issuing Aadhaar numbers to residents and perform their authentication. The functions of the Authority include: (i) specifying, by regulation, the demographic and biometric information to be collected during enrolment, and the processes for collection and verification of the information; (ii) assigning Aadhaar numbers to individuals; (iii) authenticating Aadhaar numbers; (iv) specifying the usage of Aadhaar numbers; (v) omitting and deactivating of an Aadhaar number; (vi) specifying the use and applicability of the Aadhaar number for delivery of various benefits and services as specified in regulations; and (vii) setting up grievance redressal mechanisms.

The Authority shall establish and operate the CIDR (Clause 23). The Authority is also given the responsibility of maintaining and updating the information of individuals in the CIDR in a manner to be specified by regulations. The Authority can appoint one or more entities to operate the CIDR. The Authority is empowered to call for information and records, and conduct inspections, inquiries, and audit of operations of the CIDR. The Authority may require the Aadhaar number holders to update their demographic and biometric information so as to ensure continued accuracy of their information in the CIDR (Clause 8) (PRS Legislative Research 2010c: 3).

The Authority shall appoint registrars and enrolling agencies to collect demographic and biometric information for the purpose of issuing Aadhaar numbers. The purpose of these numbers is to facilitate access to benefits and services. Special measures are to be taken to issue Aadhaar numbers to women, children, senior citizens, people with disability, migrant unskilled and unorganized workers, nomadic tribes or to such other persons who do not have any permanent dwelling house, and such other categories of individuals as may be specified by regulations (Clause 10).

The Bill empowers the Authority to specify, by regulations, the terms and conditions for appointment of registrars, enrolling agencies, and service providers, as well as revocation of their appointments (Clause 23) (PRS Legislative Research 2010c: 7). The Authority is also authorized to set up facilitation centres and grievance redressal mechanisms for redressal of grievances of residents, registrars, enrolling agencies, and service providers (Clause 23).

The Bill provides that the Authority may enter into MoU or agreement with the central government, or state governments, or union territories, or other agencies for the purpose of performing any function in respect of collecting, storing, securing, or processing of information or performing authentication. Power is given to the Authority to appoint such number of registrars, and engage and authorize such agencies to collect, store, secure, and process information or do authentication (Clause 23).

The Authority is required to ensure security and confidentiality of identity information and authentication records of individuals (Clause 30) (PRS Legislative Research 2010c: 10). The Authority is enjoined to take measures (including security safeguards) to ensure that the information in the possession or control of the Authority (including information stored in the CIDR) is secured and protected against any loss, or unauthorized access or use, or unauthorized disclosure. Sharing of data is prohibited except with the consent of the resident, by a court order, or for national security, if directed by an authorized official of the rank of joint secretary and above in the central government. However, the Authority may share information of Aadhaar number holders, based on their written consent, with agencies engaged in delivery of public benefits. The Authority or any agency, which maintains the CIDR, is forbidden from revealing any information stored in the repository. However, an Aadhaar number holder may request the Authority to provide access to his own identity information. He may also ask for information on authentication requests of his Aadhaar number as well as the responses provided (Clause 32) (PRS Legislative Research 2010c: 10).

The central government is required to constitute an Identity Review Committee to analyse the extent and pattern of usage of Aadhaar numbers across the country (Clause 28) (PRS Legislative Research 2010c: 9). The Committee is required to prepare a report annually on the extent and pattern of usage of Aadhaar numbers and submit its recommendations to the central government (Clause 29) (PRS Legislative Research 2010c: 9). The report of the Committee is to be laid before each House of the Parliament.

The Bill lists several offences such as unauthorized collection of information, impersonation, manipulation of biometric information, and unauthorized access or damage to the CIDR (Clause 35) (PRS Legislative Research 2010c: 11). Penalties vary from three years imprisonment and a fine of Rs 10,000 (for impersonation) to a fine of Rs 1 crore (for unauthorized access to the CIDR). Penalties have also been prescribed for offences committed outside India by a person of any nationality. The Bill states that no court shall take cognizance of any offence except on a complaint made by the Authority.

Is a Law Necessary?

As noted in Chapter 3, the central government had decided to issue UID numbers to all residents in India as early as November 2008. Accordingly, the UIDAI was constituted and notified by the Planning Commission on 28 January 2009, by a notification (number A-43011/02/2009-Admin.I), as an attached office under the aegis of the Planning Commission. The role and responsibilities of the UIDAI were clearly laid down in the notification dated 28 January 2009. The UIDAI started functioning by virtue of this notification, and the first set of Aadhaar numbers was rolled out at Tembhli in September 2010. The notification dated 28 January 2009 was by way of exercise of executive functions of the government. Acting in pursuance of this notification, the UIDAI has so far issued as many as 21 crore Aadhaar numbers (as of October 2012) (*The Economic Times* 2012f: 10). So, the question arises: what is the need for a legislation when the UIDAI is already issuing Aadhaar numbers?

This can perhaps be explained by the fact that it was realized by the government that the act of issuing UID numbers involved certain issues, which could only be addressed by a statute (PRS Legislative Research 2010c: 17). The issues are:

1. security and confidentiality of information, imposition of obligation of disclosure of information so collected in certain cases;
2. impersonation by certain individuals at the time of enrolment for issue of UID numbers;
3. unauthorized access to the CIDR;
4. manipulation of biometric information;
5. investigation of certain acts constituting offences; and
6. unauthorized disclosure of information collected for the purposes of issue of the UID numbers, which are to be addressed by law and could thus attract penalties (PRS Legislative Research 2010c: 17).

That being the case, it was considered necessary to make the UIDAI a statutory authority. What happens to the ID numbers already issued by the UIDAI? A provision to regularize actions already taken by the UIDAI is made in Clause 22 of the National Identification Authority of India Bill 2010 (PRS Legislative Research 2010c: 7). Clause 22 provides that all data and information collected during enrolment; all details of authentication performed; debts, obligations, and liabilities incurred; and all contracts entered into and all matters and things engaged to be done by, with, or for the UIDAI shall be deemed to have been incurred, entered into, or engaged to be done by, with, or for the National Identification Authority of India (PRS Legislative Research 2010c: 6–7). In addition, Clause 57 provides that anything done or any action taken by the central government under the Resolution of the Government of India, Planning Commission, bearing notification number A-43011/02/2009-Admin.I, dated the 28 January 2009, shall be deemed to have been done or taken under the corresponding provisions of the National Identification Authority of India Act, 2010 (PRS Legislative Research 2010c: 16).

THE AADHAAR NUMBER IS NOT MANDATORY

The Bill does not make it mandatory for an individual to obtain an Aadhaar number. However, it does not prevent any service provider from prescribing the Aadhaar number as a mandatory requirement for availing services. We need to look at this aspect against one of the avowed objectives of the Aadhaar programme: weeding out ghost beneficiaries in government schemes and programmes, and in particular, in the context of the Public Distribution Scheme (PDS). In fact, the success of the Aadhaar prgramme in weeding out ghost beneficiaries will depend upon mandatory enrolment (PRS Legislative Research 2010b: 3). If enrolment is not mandatory, ghost beneficiaries and persons/households with multiple ration cards will choose to opt out of the Aadhaar system.

Sharing of Information

The Bill provides that the information collected by the Authority may be shared with agencies engaged in delivery of public services and benefits with prior written consent of the Aadhaar number holder. However, the Bill does not specify whether the consent should be taken only once or at each instance a person avails of a new service. A one-time consent may be prone to misuse and this may affect an individual's privacy. There is a need to look at whether the safeguards provided in the Bill are adequate for preventing such misuse and protecting an individual's privacy. This will be discussed more fully in the next chapter.

Parliamentary Standing Committee on Finance

The National Identification Authority of India Bill was referred to the Standing Committee on Finance on 12 December 2010. The Committee has rejected the biometric data-based identification as proposed by the Aadhaar project. The Committee has criticized Aadhaar as a directionless project, and has raised questions about the ethics, feasibility, and purpose of the project, as well as its legality (*The New Indian Express* 2012a: 8). The Committee observed that the scheme was 'built up on untested, unreliable technology and several assumptions' (*The New Indian Express* 2012a: 8), and large-scale involvement of private agencies in collection of biometric data about the citizens of India was not only unconstitutional but a threat to national security (*The New Indian Express* 2012a: 8). The Committee has recommended that the government should reconsider the Bill.

The government has already started the process of redrafting the National Identification Authority of India Bill and placing it for the consideration of Parliament (M.K. Singh 2012: 11).

CHAPTER NINE

Dataveillance

୶ఆఞ

There is a joke making the rounds of party circles in most metropolitan cities. It goes something like:

When ordering a pizza

Operator: 'Thank you for calling us. May I have your...'

Customer: 'Heloo, can I order..?'

Operator: 'Can I have your Aadhaar number first, Sir?'

Customer: 'It's the...hold on...889861356102.'

Operator: 'OK...You're Mr Singh and you're calling from 17, Jala Vayu...Your home number is 2x2xxxx, your office 250xxxxx and your mobile is o9xxxxxxxx. Which number are you calling from now, Sir?'

Customer: 'Home! How did you get all my phone numbers?'

Operator: 'We are connected to the system, Sir.'

Customer: 'May I order your Seafood Pizza...'

Operator: 'That's not a good idea, Sir.'

Customer: 'How come?'

Operator: 'According to your medical records, you have high blood pressure and even higher cholesterol level, Sir.'

Customer: 'What?...What do you recommend then?'

Operator: 'Try our Low Fat Pizza. You'll like it.'

Customer: 'How do you know for sure?'

Operator: 'You borrowed a book entitled "Popular Dishes" from the National Library last week, Sir.'

Customer: 'OK I give up. Give me three family-size ones then, how much will that cost?

Operator: 'That should be enough for your family of five, Sir. The total is Rs. 500.00.'

Customer: 'Can I pay by credit card?'

Operator: 'I'm afraid you have to pay us cash, sir. Your credit card is over the limit and you owe your bank Rs 23,000 since October last year. That's not including the late payment charges on your housing loan, Sir.'

Customer: 'I guess I have to run to the neighbourhood ATM and withdraw some cash before your guy arrives.'

Operator: 'You can't, Sir. Based on your records, you've reached your daily limit on machine withdrawal today.'

Customer: 'Never mind, you send the pizzas, I'll have the cash ready. How long will it gonna take anyway?'

Operator: 'About 45 minutes, Sir. But if you can't wait you can always come and collect it in your Nano car.'

Customer: 'What!'

Operator: 'According to the details in your system, you own a Nano car...registration number GZ-05-AB-1107.'

Customer: '?'

Operator: 'Is there anything else, Sir?'

Customer: 'Nothing...By the way, aren't you giving me that three free bottles of cola as advertised?'

Operator: 'We normally would, Sir, but based on your records, you're also a diabetic...'

Customer: #$$^%&$@$%^

Operator: 'Better watch your language, Sir. Remember on July 15, 2010, you were convicted of using abusive language on a policeman?'

Customer: [Faints]!!! (*Frontline* 2011: 15)

The joke would have been funny if it were not so morbid. But, even in its morbidity, it captures the essence of the process that Roger Clarke calls 'dataveillance'. The collection, use, and communication of large stores of personal data held on citizens are now central to the functioning of public service and private business. Different data sets are matched against each other to identify persons and patterns of activity. The data is also mined and analysed in great depth by sophisticated technologies to reveal patterns of activity. This process can be usefully thought of in terms of dataveillance. Roger Clarke (1991: 2) defines dataveillance as 'the systematic use of personal data systems in investigation or monitoring of the actions or communications of one or more persons'.

Dataveillance is made possible by the storage capability, which is certainly the most significant change brought about by the IT revolution: the ubiquity of the computer database (Surveillance Studies Network 2006: para 9.6.1). Multiple data can now be gathered, tabulated, and cross-referenced much faster and more accurately than with a paper file that was the key to the bureaucratic way of functioning (Surveillance Studies Network 2006: para 9.6.1). In dataveillance, databases are important, not the visual or auditory means of watching over people. This is because databases, in tandem with other systems, allow algorithmic processes, the use of software to work on captured images or data and compare them to those in the database (Surveillance Studies Network 2006: para 9.6.3). This, in fact, has been the key to the development of biometrics.

The idea of dataveillance is not a new one. Max Weber had talked about it almost a hundred years ago. Weber had, in fact, viewed this process (keeping detailed records, collating information, limiting access to certain eligible persons) as evidence of progress towards efficient administration; and a benefit for the development of Western capitalism and the modern nation state (Gerth and Mills 1964). But Weber had enough sense to say that the benefit the process yielded was mixed. At its worst, this made the efficient but soulless world of bureaucratic organization into an iron cage. As Weber pointed out, oversight of subordinates and creation of records within the system is essential to a bureaucracy, and the process of governing has always embodied this. But the process has now become highly technological, and has even spilled over into the society and private sector.

Watching over people has always been there in history as people watched over each other to discover information covertly. We can break down the elements of this process of watching over as follows:

1. *The attention is first purposeful*: the watching has a point that can be justified in terms of control, entitlement, or some publicly agreed goal.
2. *It can be routine*: it happens as we go about our daily business. It is in the weave of life.
3. *But it can also be systematic*: it is planned and carried out according to a schedule that is rational, not merely random.
4. *It can be focused*: it gets down to details. While some of this watching depends on aggregate data, much refers to identifiable persons, whose data are collected, stored, transmitted, received, compared, mined, and traded (Surveillance Studies Network 2006: para 3.2).

The personal details may be of many kinds, including closed-circuit television (CCTV) images, biometrics such as fingerprints or iris scans, communication records or the actual content of calls, or most commonly, numerical or categorical data. Much of the data is of the last type referring to transactions, exchanges, accounts, and so on (Clarke 2006). In the private sector, the decreasing cost of databases and the increasing ability to extract actionable knowledge and value from data has resulted in the creation of a personal information economy in which private sector companies seek to gather as much consumer data as possible (Dyson *et al.* 1996). Consumer data can generally be divided into four categories:

- *Geographic data*: they describe features of place, demarcated by telephone area codes, postal codes, Internet uniform resource locators (URLs), and domain names.
- *Demographic data*: they give information about individuals.
- *Psychographic data*: they give information about the social aspects of consumers in terms of class, values, lifestyle stages, and personality.
- *Consumer behaviour data*: they provide data about consumer behaviour (Michman 1991).

Creation and collection of data is done in many ways. Every transaction provides a data trail, which can be linked to an individual or type of person. These transactions include the use of credit cards, mobile phones, the Internet, a purchase, search, or a phone call. Additional data is often generated through customer surveys, focus groups, promotional contests, product information requests, consumer feedback forums, and credit transactions (Surveillance Studies Network 2006: para 9.6.5). This internal data is overlaid with external data from government agencies (for example, census data), civil society bodies, or specialist data collection organizations. Thanks to technology, such simple matching techniques are now augmented by sophisticated processes of data mining, often referred to as knowledge discovery in databases (KDD) (Surveillance Studies Network 2006: para 9.6.5). This helps in discovering previously unknown and non-obvious relationships within sets of information. The product of these systems is most visible as the basis for Web personalization systems, which use multiple sources of data to predict the likely preference of shoppers. Private sector companies use such data to target their marketing to a narrower band of customers, thereby decreasing marketing costs and increasing response rates. This is the preferred mode now because this is much more economical than mass marketing channels of television, radio, or print marketing. Application of real-time geographic data to consumer profiles can generate yet another layer of data to assist private sector companies in targeting marketing campaigns to particular consumers (Surveillance Studies Network 2006: para 9.6.5).

TECHNOLOGICAL SYNERGY AND FUNCTION CREEP

There are also increasing instances of technological synergy, or convergence, of surveillance technologies (Surveillance Studies Network 2006: para 9.9.1). This is driven by considerations of creating economies of scale as well as of achieving interoperability. The trend is to add such interoperability and technological synergy to the common idea of 'function creep' since several new uses are found for technologies, and as information collected for one purpose, or in one domain, leaks through into others. That is why there is an increasing tendency to have IDs that work for several purposes: fraud control; access to government information; and commercial and semi-commercial purposes. But, once these systems are established, they acquire a life of their own which is difficult to halt, and it becomes extremely difficult to control the means of identification.

Interestingly, these technologies are at their productive best when they become ubiquitous, taken for granted, and largely invisible. As Mark Weiser (1991: 94) argues, 'the most profound technologies are those that disappear. They weave themselves into the fabric of everyday life until they are indistinguishable from it.' Pervasiveness is now a common feature of digitized, networked technology. Pervasive or ubiquitous computing (ubicomp) creates the conditions for such pervasiveness or ubiquity (Surveillance Studies Network 2006: para 9.10.1). One of the fundamental building blocks of ubicomp is the concept of URL (Surveillance Studies Network 2006: para 9.10.1). We know about URL through Internet addresses. This enables continuous software sorting of people and their life chances. In urban areas, such software sorting is made possible through numerous electronic and physical 'passage points' or 'choke points', negotiated through code words, passwords, Personal Identification Numbers (PINs), user names, access controls, and electronic cards (Surveillance Studies Network 2006: para 9.10.2). The task now is to create some means of such continuous software sorting of people and their life chances in rural areas where such passage points or choke points are either limited or do not exist. So, they have to be organized, and this is where biometric scans combined with demographic information come in handy.

INFORMATION SHARING

With liberalization, private sector companies have been given a big role in government activities, and there is a trend towards more integrated public services, often through partnerships with private sector companies. This means that personal data about citizens now flow into new channels through private sector companies that never before had access to them. Consequently, as government agencies and private sector companies share personal information about citizens, there is now a distinct possibility of personal information about citizens, which is routinely collected by government with different purposes in mind, being used by private sector companies to profile citizens as consumers for their own commercial purposes.

DATA PROTECTION

In order to safeguard privacy, governments have put in place mechanisms to ensure that personal information of citizens is not used for a purpose other than the one for which it was collected. The mechanisms so far tried are regulation, law, and self-regulation.

Regulation

Regulation means adopting either legal means to control systems and practices or techniques that have a regulatory effect (Baldwin and Cave 1999). Typically, these regulations apply rules to the processing of data by setting limits and controls. This usually consists of two aspects: (i) controlling activities within a framework of principles, rules, and required safeguards; and (ii) banning activities that do not submit to the technique of regulatory regimes. The question is: how effective are regulations in protecting data? The experience of almost all countries which have introduced regulations has not been particularly rewarding. This is because regulations have suffered from the following common drawbacks:

1. Regulations have tended to be reactive. What it means is that, while putting these regulations in place, it has been done as a response to technological development, implementation, and practice after the fact.
2. Most regulations have a largely technical and managerial focus, based on codes of practice, the fulfilment of standard legal requirements, and the application of privacy-protective technologies, leaving little room for anticipation.
3. Generally, regulations are based on a narrow conception of personal privacy and of its value to the individual alone, reflecting the current thinking of policymakers who often implement a restricted view of what is in public interest.
4. Regulation is often seen as a burden unfairly placed on the private sector as well as the state, inhibiting initiative, risk-taking, and productivity. Because of this, it has become difficult for governments

to design and implement regulations that involve stringent requirements (Surveillance Studies Network 2006: para 41.1).

These are the reasons why regulations have not been effective in protecting data and checking privacy invasions in the private sector. On the whole, the current position is that, though many countries have introduced regulations for controlling information processes concerning personal data, even the best of efforts has not succeeded fully.

Law

Starting in the 1970s, many countries have enacted laws to control personal information processing. These laws have stipulated certain principles and created enforcement and supervisory machinery in the form of privacy commissioners to safeguard privacy. While Universal Declaration of Human Rights, covenants, and conventions have provided the basis for these domestic privacy laws, the approaches of countries in enacting them have varied with respect to scope of the law, emphasis put on different elements of protection, exceptions provided in the law, and the machinery of enforcement. While most European countries have opted for heavy-handed enforcement, countries in Southeast Asia have preferred the light-handed self-regulator. However, the common points covered by these privacy laws are:

1. *Choice and consent*: securing consent of the individual before his personal information is collected.
2. *Collection limitation*: only that information is to be collected which is essential for the purpose.
3. *Use limitation*: information is to be strictly used for the purpose for which it was collected.
4. *Access and correction*: an individual should be allowed access to his personal information and he/she should be enabled to correct/update his/her information.
5. *Security*: data is to be secured against accidental loss or theft.
6. *Disclosure to third party*: individual's consent is required for disclosure of his/her personal information to third parties.
7. *Openness*: data controller should be transparent in his/her working in respect of collection and use of personal data.

8. *Accountability*: data controller and his/her agents need to be accountable for the safety of personal data and its use.
9. *Preventing harm*: harm to the individual whose personal information is being stored by private or governmental entity should be prevented (Government of India 2010: 8).

In the UK, for example, the UK Data Protection Act of 1998 lays down the principles and establishes a hierarchy of data controllers and places them under the jurisdiction of the information commissioner. The Act states:

Data controllers must also abide by the data protection principles. They are, in brief,

a) the data must be processed fairly and lawfully and only for one of the prescribed purposes. For data concerning sensitive matters, there is a narrower group of specified purposes;
b) it must be adequate, relevant and not excessive for the purpose;
c) it must be accurate, and where necessary, kept up to date;
d) it must not be kept for longer than is necessary;
e) it must be processed in accordance with the rights of data subjects;
f) appropriate technical and organizational measures must be taken against unauthorized or unlawful processing and against accidental loss or destruction of or damage to the data;
g) it must not be transferred out of the EEA (European Economic Area) unless the country to which it is taken or sent gives adequate protection for the rights of data subjects.

The Commissioner can serve an enforcement notice if she is satisfied that a data controller has contravened any of these principles. An individual who suffers damage because a data controller has contravened any requirement of the Act is entitled to claim compensation. The special provisions for journalistic material give exemption from: the data subjection principles (except those concerning security of data); data subject access rights; the rights of data subjects to prevent data processing; the rights of data subjects to correct inaccuracies; and rights concerning automated decision-making. (Noorani 2011: 14)

The UK Data Protection Act is based on what is called the 'privacy paradigm', and this is exemplified in the approach of most countries in enacting their data protection laws. The privacy paradigm consists of enunciating a set of principles, which are known as the 'fair information principles' (FIPs) (Surveillance Studies Network 2002: para 43.2.2). The approach is to prescribe a set of procedural requirements for data controllers for their processing activities, the idea being that once there is formal compliance with these procedural requirements, data would have been protected. This encourages a kind of box-ticking mentality, and the emphasis is on limiting the uses to which personal data can be put and the length of time it can be stored (Surveillance Studies Network 2002: para 43.2.2). As Noorani (2011: 15) says, 'However, this is not to say that statutes on the subject do not exist. They do in Canada as well as in the U.S. But the experience is not particularly inspiring.' On the whole, these data protection laws have not been particularly effective in controlling personal information processing.

Self-regulation

Industries, private sector companies, and specialist bodies have developed a variety of codes and conduct, or practices, in order to put in place a process of industry self-certification. In most cases, self-regulation consists of various industry verticals appointing independent certifying agencies to prescribe data standards and to oversee compliance with data protection principles (Government of India 2010: 2). The system is voluntary but relies on peer pressure to ensure that industries or private sector companies remain compliant with their obligations so that they can continue to be accepted by their customers and business ecosystem. In fact, self-regulation is generally regarded as a better way of regulation, given the failure of laws and the need for fostering a less-regulated business climate (Government of India 2010: 2). However, the credibility and efficacy of self-regulation has not yet been generally demonstrated. More generally, it is debatable whether the framework of self-regulation will ever be in a position to regulate the conduct of agencies that are most likely to indulge in dataveillance (Surveillance Studies Network 2006: para 43.4.1).

In sum, although there has been a lot of activity to check dataveillance by way of regulation, law, and self-regulation, these instruments have not been particularly effective. One reason for this is that the governments are now called upon to share vast amounts of personal information of their citizens with private sector companies in order to implement a number of government schemes and programmes (Surveillance Studies Network 2006: para 10.4.1). The other reason is the increasing sophistication of privacy invasions in the commercial sector through the use of state-of-the-art technologies (Surveillance Studies Network 2006: para 44.9). The data protection regulations and laws have not been able to keep pace with the advance of dataveillance technologies, practices, and purposes, and therefore, with the sheer ingenuity of those trying to sidestep these regulations and laws. The advent of many new information and communication technologies (ICTs), and the environment of AmI (Ambient Intelligence) and ubicomp that integrates many and varied dataveillance devices, poses serious challenges to the effectiveness of regulations and laws that were designed to handle issues in the age of mainframe computer, or even the laptop, and the mobile telephone. Each generation of technology makes obsolete the regulatory strategies that were devised for earlier ones (Surveillance Studies Network 2006: para 44.9). With the advent and spread of Internet, the convergence of technologies, and interaction of online and offline information practices, information collection and further processing, including transmission, is literally everywhere, and this has made the existing laws and regulatory frameworks totally inadequate for controlling dataveillance.

Another problem in protecting data with the advent of newer and newer technologies is the question of defining who exactly is responsible for it. For example, when it comes to storing data in the cloud, it is not clear who is in charge of ensuring security of the data (*The Economic Times* 2012c: 4). The biggest threat to data stored remotely, it turns out, may be the failure to understand who is responsible for keeping it protected. One challenge to standardizing cloud security practices is the sheer variety of cloud offerings. The term refers to a wide variety of computing—from buying server space from a start-up to using software applications and getting them delivered over the Internet from a provider such as Salesforce.com (customer relationship management [CRM]) (*The Economic Times* 2012c: 4). The servers may be housed in a nearby city, another state, or even another country governed by different data regulations.

According to a 2011 report by consultants Frost and Sullivan in Mountain View, California, about 74 per cent of security providers say that more training is needed for cloud security issues (*The Economic Times* 2012c: 4).

For example, Adventist Health System, which operates 43 health facilities and needs to follow strict regulatory requirements for safeguarding health data, is looking to move at least its email system into IBM's cloud (*The Economic Times* 2012c: 4). Sharon Finney, the Corporate Data Security Officer for Adventist Health System, says that she will lean heavily on IBM to keep the information secure. Finney says:

> If I want to retain all of that liability, all of that control, then there's no cost benefit to me putting data in the cloud. It's the cloud provider's infrastructure, I will look to them for security. Even so, Adventist Health might still have to take responsibility if one of our employees caused a breach. (*The Economic Times* 2012c: 4)

With nobody in charge of security for these new technologies, it is very likely that dataveillance is likely to flourish. In fact, one of the reasons why people are not in a hurry to jump into the cloud fray is because of information security worries (Scaria 2012: 14). As H.R. Srinivasan, founder of Take Solutions, says:

> It is normal buyer behaviour to be cautious of adopting any new technology and that applies to cloud adoption as well. The cloud can be penetrated, and to that extent, it is difficult answering an audit query whether one is in complete control of one's information on the cloud. All of these have slowed down cloud development. (Scaria 2012: 14)

On the whole, intensified dataveillance seems to be a normal feature of the functioning of the modern times (Surveillance Studies Network 2006: para 11.5.6). It is very difficult to control such intensified dataveillance because it involves the manipulation of large quantities of personal data in ways that technologically defy the reach and grasp of the existing data protection regulations and laws (Surveillance Studies Network 2006: para 11.5.6). As far as citizens are concerned, they are not in a position to comprehend what happens to their personal data. That being the case, it is almost a certainty that consumer dataveillance will continue to be a feature of the modern society, and citizens will continue to be profiled as consumers based on their presumed economic value in spite of the operation of laws and regulatory instruments (Gandy 1993).

AADHAAR AND DATAVEILLANCE

In India, dataveillance was never viewed as a concern because it was difficult for private sector companies to get hold of personal information from a unified source in a form that could be used for commercial profiling purposes. While many agencies of the government collected personal data, this information was stored in silos with each agency of the government using different fields and formats. Government databases did not talk to each other and given how differently they were organized, the information collected by various departments could not be aggregated or unified. That is why data privacy and the need to protect personal information was never a concern when data were stored in a decentralized manner. Data that is maintained in silos is largely useless outside that silo and consequently, has a low likelihood of being used for other purposes. However, this scenario is likely to change with the implementation of the Aadhaar programme.

In fact, the UIDAI document acknowledges this concern. It states:

Data Security and Fraud: Protecting personal information of residents

Even as the UIDAI stores resident information and confirms identity to authenticating agencies, it will have to ensure the security and privacy of such information. By linking an individual's personal, identifying information to a UID, the UIDAI will be creating a transaction identity for each resident that is both verified and reliable. This means that the resident's identity will possess value, and enable the transfer of money and resources. The UIDAI envisions storing basic personal information, as well as certain biometrics. However, limiting its scope to this, and not linking this information to financial/other details does not make the resident records in the database non- sensitive. Biometric information, for example, is often linked to banking, social security and passport records. Basic personal information such as date of birth is used to verify owners of credit cards/bank accounts and online accounts.

Such information will therefore, have to be protected. (UIDAI 2010a: 33)

How serious is this concern about protection of personal information collected by the Aadhaar programme? For that, we need to know what kind of personal information is being collected by the Aadhaar programme.

What Kind of Information Is Collected?

According to the UIDAI literature, and as mentioned earlier, Aadhaar collects the following data fields from those who seek an Aadhaar number (UIDAI 2010a: 10):

* Name
* Date of birth
* Gender
* Father's/Husband's/Guardian's name and UID (optional for adult residents)
* Mother's/Wife's/Guardian's name and UID (optional for adult residents)
* Introducer's name and UID (in case of lack of documents)
* Address
* All 10 fingerprints, photographs, and both iris scans.

This is what the UIDAI literature states but, in practice, it does not appear to be so. We need to sample the following report that appeared in the media when people in Bangalore city queued up for being enrolled in the Aadhaar programme.

Inquisitive UIDAI wants all details about you and I

The Unique Identification Authority of India (UIDAI), Karnataka, which is all set to begin its ambitious 'Aadhaar' enrolment in Bangalore from August 17, has kicked up a row even before its formal launch by surreptitiously widening the scope of the ID card beyond the officially stated position. On the second day of the special enrolment for media persons and their families in the City— as a precursor to the launch for the general public—there were heated arguments between applicants and officials, as the enrolment forms distributed by the officials did not match the forms put out by the UIDAI on its website and seemed to be far wider in scope, seeking personal details.

Several applicants for enrolment objected to the columns asking for details of bank account numbers and the LPG gas connection numbers. Some people who had not brought their passbooks or gas connection receipts were turned away, leading to protests. The officials later clarified that the submission of the information they sought was voluntary and continued registering others who had left the columns in the application forms unfilled. In fact, there is wide disparity between the form specified by the UIDAI on its official website and the one being used...It (the one being used) is a long list, starting from 'availing any social security pension' to 'Sandhya Suraksha', 'physically handicapped person', 'destitute/widow pension', 'ration card', 'NREGA job card', 'member of milk cooperative society', and so on...The form requires the assignee to put his signature to the clause, 'I have no objection to my identity being authenticated for delivery of services from time to time to whom I present the UID number and I am aware that information provided by me for securing UID number shall be used for authenticating my identity.' (*Deccan Herald* 2011a: 1)

The incident sparked off quite a bit of uproar in the garden city; so much so that *Deccan Herald*, the local news daily, wrote the following editorial on 15 August 2011.

Tainted by deceit

Even as registration for the unique identification number (UID) or Aadhaar is set to begin in Bangalore, there is very little clarity about it. The Aadhaar website sets out a picture that seems at odds from the reality unfolding on the ground. The information being sought is far more intrusive than that is officially claimed. Not surprisingly, Aadhaar is raising questions, suspicions and unease in the minds of the public. Its website says the 12 digit unique number to be issued to all residents, which will be stored in a centralised database, will be linked to basic demographics and biometric information—photographs, ten fingerprints and iris—of each individual. It goes on to clarify that getting the number is not mandatory, neither will it replace other IDs such as ration cards, for instance. It also reassures the public about confidentiality.

A special registration done for media persons a few days ago laid bare a rather different Aadhaar. People were asked to provide bank account numbers, LPG gas connection numbers and so on. Significantly, the form they were asked to fill was different from the one available for the download on the official website. Officials have said provision of bank information etc is voluntary and indeed, they did register those who refused to divulge this information. Yet, why is this information being sought in the first place? Does the government intend pushing people who refused to divulge this information now, to divulge it subsequently by linking the number to availability of banking services, LPG and so on? The objectives of Aadhaar are unclear. The UID has been touted as a tool that will empower the poor in accessing services such as the formal banking system. As far as security is concerned, it is naïve to think that people with criminal intent will come forward to register themselves.

In any case, biometrics is not fool-proof, say experts. Critics are also drawing attention to possible misuse of information gathered. It could facilitate cyber crime. It is hard to dispel the feeling too that UIDAI will eventually force us to volunteer all information about ourselves, our bank accounts and so on. A large amount of public money is being invested in Aadhaar. The government owes the public honest answers. It must clarify what information it is gathering and why. If the Aadhaar juggernaut is more of a bane than a blessing, it must be stopped now. (*Deccan Herald* 2011b: 10)

These are strong words from a conservative newspaper like *Deccan Herald*. This is presumably because of the impression that the UIDAI will eventually force people to volunteer all information about themselves, their bank accounts, and so on. As the editorial in *Deccan Herald* points out, the government owes honest answers to the public about what personal information the UIDAI is collecting, and why. That being the case, there is a need to study the mind of the programmer. Nandan Nilekani says in an interview with the *Tehelka* magazine:

Question: There are many questions around the project—about efficiency, privacy, danger of profiling, etc...but we'll come to that later. First of all, what information do people have to give to get a UID?

Nandan Nilekani: Let's talk about the information we are keeping in our system. We keep the name, date of birth, sex, address and father's or mother's name and the biometrics. Apart from this, we are, in fact, by law forbidding listing things like caste and religion. Broadly, there are three methods of getting a number. It's all on our website. First is the classic document method. The second is that the National Population Register is going to collect information and put it on public boards. If no one objects, they will deem that information to be accurate about you. The third, created specifically for the purpose of inclusion, is the introducer method. If the person does not have any documentation, there will be approved introducers—they could be employees of the state or an NGO. If these introducers are willing to vouch for the person's identity and address, it will be basis for giving a number. This is a very important inclusion method to facilitate the poor and marginalized to get a UID. (*Tehelka* 2010: 26–7)

Nandan Nilekani's interview does not really clarify why the UIDAI is collecting information on bank account numbers, LPG gas connection numbers, details of social security pension, ration card, NREGA job card, membership of milk cooperative society, etc. It also does not say anything about the possible misuse of the data, invasion of privacy, and danger of profiling. In another interview, Nandan Nilekani says:

Question: Data security and privacy concerns have been raised by Aadhaar's critics who worry about how it can avoid leaks, duplication, fraud, etc. How well are you prepared for all that?

Nandan Nilekani: There are certain design features which enhance our ability to do that. The first thing is when the data comes from the enrolling agency, it comes fully encrypted. Nobody in the chain of enrollment really has access to the data because it is encrypted at the point of collection, and only we can decrypt it when it comes to us. There is nobody in the middle who can do that. So that is one way of protecting the data. The second feature is, once the data comes to us and the numbers are assigned to people, the data doesn't go out again. The only further use of this data is online authentication. You come to us and say, 'I am so and so, my number is 123 and here is my authentication token'—it can be biometric or a pin [number] or whatever—that packet is sent to our server and it will come back with a response that this set matches this number and name or that they don't match. So the only answer you can get from our system is a 'Yes' or a 'No.' You can't read our database. We have made the database into a sort of black box. (India Knowledge@Wharton 2010: 2)

Nandan Nilekani repeats the same in his interview to *Tehelka* magazine, but with a caveat. He says:

Question: The other big area of concern is data protection and privacy. The fact that you are using many other registrars to enroll people is causing a lot of concern.

Nandan Nilekani: Let me be clear. These registrars are already engaging with you and me. The bank today is already taking a lot of information from you. If you take a loan, they ask so many questions about your credit history. If you take an insurance policy, they ask intimate details about your health. So let's be clear: a lot of registrars are already collecting a lot of information about you...

Question: Yes, but so far these were islands of information held in different silos. With the UID, the fear is all this data can be centrally converged. Shouldn't there be strict protocols under which information will be protected under the UID?

Nandan Nilekani: First of all, when a registrar collects data for us, there are clear rules on how what data is to be used. When it reaches us, it goes into a black hole. Let's say you are enrolling in Aadhaar. You give your biometric, the data is captured, the record is encrypted. It can't be intercepted by someone, because it'll all be encrypted and scrambled. When it comes to our database, we do scan to de-duplicate and see if there's another person with the same biometric. If it matches, it means you have already got a number from somewhere else. That is against the law. If you're not registered, we give you a random number. In other countries, you can tell a person's year of birth and place of domicile because of the way the numbers are serialized. We are trying to improve on all that by generating a completely random number so you cannot make out anything about a person by looking at his UID. So our number doesn't give away anything. It is only used to authenticate your identity if you're a participant in a transaction.

Question: But that means the State—or big corporations—can track every one of us at the click of a button. There are great fears about the misuse of data.

Nandan Nilekani: There are protocols in place under the UID Act. The fact is, we raised the issue of privacy long before anyone else. What India needs is a comprehensive data protection and privacy framework. The problem is not just unique to the UID. We have

700 million mobile phone users in the country where the same logic applies. You have PAN numbers. When you use Gmail or Google, targeted advertisements hit you. You are sharing intimate information on Facebook. Why should the anxiety only arise when one is trying to draw the poor into the benefits of technology? Our point is that as we become more electronically dependent, we need to legislate as a society based on a privacy framework that cuts across functions. We ourselves suggested this to the government in May (2010). It has come out with an approach paper on creating a privacy and data protection law. (*Tehelka* 2010: 28)

On the whole, Nilekani emphasizes the need for a comprehensive data protection and privacy framework. More specifically, he talks about the approach paper on creating privacy and data protection framework, and the UIDAI Act and the protocols that would be there in the Act. Let us look at these instruments.

Approach Paper for Privacy Legislation

The Government of India (2010: 1) constituted a Group of Officers to develop a conceptual framework 'that could serve the country's balance of interests and concern on privacy, data protection and security and which also responds to domain legislation on the subject'. This Group of Officers prepared an approach paper, which proposed a framework for privacy legislation. The approach paper, while noting that data privacy and the need to protect personal information was almost never a concern when data was stored in a decentralized manner, pointed out that data maintained in silos was largely useless outside that silo and consequently, had a low likelihood of causing any damage (Government of India 2010: 2). The paper further said:

> However, all this is likely to change with the implementation of the UID Project. One of the inevitable consequences of the UID Project will be that the UID Number will unify multiple databases. As more and more agencies of the government sign on to the UID project, the UID Number will become the common thread that links all those database together. Over time, private enterprise could also adopt the UID Number as an identifier for the purpose of delivery of services or

even for enrolment as a customer. Once this happens, the separation of data that currently exists between multiple databases will vanish.

Such a vast interlinked public information database is unprecedented in India. It is imperative that appropriate steps be taken to protect personal data before the vast government storehouses of private data are linked up and the threat of data security breach becomes real.

Similarly, the private sector entities, telecom companies, hospitals etc are collecting vast amount of private or personal information about individuals. There is tremendous scope for both commercial exploitation of this information without the consent/knowledge of the individual and also for embarrassing an individual whose personal particulars can be made public by any of these private entities. The IT Act does provide some safeguards against disclosure of data/ information stored electronically, but there is no legislation for protecting the privacy of individuals for the information that may be available with private entities.

In view of the above, privacy of the individual is to be protected both with reference to the actions of government as well as private sector entities. (Government of India 2010: 2)

The approach paper also examined whether there was a need for enacting a law on privacy. It pointed out that there was an influential argument contending that, given the technical and highly dynamic nature of personal data, a heavy legislative approach was unwarranted; instead, industry self-certification could achieve the same results without the downsides of putting in place a legislative and regulatory framework (Government of India 2010: 2). However, the approach paper suggested that the industry self-certification model did not give the individuals, whose data was at risk, any form of legal remedy in case of a breach of their personal privacy, and that was why a legislation was needed that spelt out the nature of rights available to individuals and the consequences that an organization would suffer if it breached those rights (Government of India 2010: 3). On the whole, the approach paper recommends a hybrid approach in which a statute is to be enacted to provide the contours within which all organizations, private and public, are to conduct themselves with regard to personal information that they collect, and industry associations could then define more detailed guidelines and practices that member organizations would need to follow with specific reference to the specific needs of that industry (Government of India 2010: 3).

In effect, what the approach paper suggests is that the proposed legislation should be in the form of a framework rather than detailed prescriptions. It should highlight the basic principles that data controlling authority will need to subscribe to and how the privacy rights of an individual would be protected. Thereafter, the sector-specific or industry-specific detailed guidelines will be prepared and approved by the regulator who will also be responsible for enforcing the legislation. By way of final recommendation, the approach paper states:

> In the Indian context, it is advisable to establish a regulator under the proposed data protection legislation. The role of the regulator would be to ensure that the legislation responds dynamically to the changing digital environment and fulfills the principle upon which the legislation is based. To this end the regulator should have the power to prescribe standards both technological and operational that could mould the manner in which the legislation is implemented. It is particularly important to develop the concept of accountability so that it should no longer be sufficient for organizations to meet applicable data protection requirements—they should demonstrate their willingness and ability to take on data responsibility and ensure compliance on an ongoing basis. The regulator should also have the power to require subsidiary regulators who operate under the provisions of legislations that include reference to data protection principles, to conform to the broad principles of the data protection legislation. (Government of India 2010: 20)

In sum, the approach proposed by the approach paper is based on the Fair Information Principles (FIPs). In this respect, as noted earlier, the approach essentially follows the box-ticking mentality in order to ensure that all the items in the box of FIPs are included. To that extent, the approach is procedural in its orientation: it enjoins upon the data controllers a set of procedural requirements for their processing activities, thereby conveying the impression that formal compliance with these requirements is enough to legitimize their activities. Consequently, the regulator is given the task of applying more substantive considerations.

The approach suggested in the approach paper places a great deal of reliance on choice and consent of the data subjects (Government of India 2010: 11–12). The underlying principle is that citizens have a right to know what information is held about them and how it is being used. It so happens that choice has played a major role in debates about data protection. It is argued that, like in medicine, 'informed patient consent' to the use of personal data can work as a safeguard (Surveillance Studies Network 2006: para 11.3.2). However, the fact remains that a large number of people do not know their rights, fail to exercise them, and receive little help from others in doing so. We need to remember that personal information gathered by these technologies flow around computer networks. Many people may consent to giving personal information in one setting, but what happens if the personal information is then transferred to another setting? There is very little knowledge among data-sharing agencies about where exactly the personal information travels.

Laws protecting privacy have proved to be weak because of the increasing sophistication of technologies that move personal information from one setting to another. That is why it is surprising that the approach paper does not even raise the issue of questioning, examining, and checking the processes that involve information flow from one setting to another. Such information flows require description and analysis. For the purpose, the approach paper should have asked questions like: how secure are databases from unauthorized access or leakage?; and to what extent should personal information be permitted to move from one sphere to another? It is necessary to ask these questions in order to get a proper understanding: technologies need to be analysed and monitored in an ongoing way. We have to understand how they work (what the software and hardware do), how they are used (this is an interactive process, involving the organization's own personnel as well as technology consultants, service providers, and those who operate the systems), and how they influence the working of the organization. That being the case, the approach proposed by the approach paper does not appear to be adequate for controlling dataveillance.

NATIONAL IDENTIFICATION AUTHORITY OF INDIA BILL, 2010

Chapter VI of the Bill (Clauses 30–3) relates to protection of information, while Clauses 53 and 54 deal with the power of the National Identification Authority of India to make regulations (PRS

Legislative Research 2010c: 8–9, 14–15). Clauses 34–46 talk about offences and penalties (PRS Legislative Research 2010c: 10–11). It will be useful to enumerate what these clauses provide in order to attempt a thematic analysis.

Clause 30 provides for security and confidentiality of information (PRS Legislative Research 2010c: 10). It enjoins that the National Identification Authority shall ensure the security and confidentiality of identity information and authentication records of individuals, and take measures (including security safeguards) to ensure that the information in the possession and control of the Authority (including the information stored in the CIDR) is secured and protected against any loss, or unauthorized access or use, or unauthorized disclosure. The clause also provides that the Authority, or any of its officer, or other employee, or any agency, which maintains the CIDR, shall not reveal any information stored in the repository to any person, but an Aadhaar number holder may request the Authority to provide access to his/her identity information.

Clause 31 provides for alteration of demographic or biographic information (PRS Legislative Research 2010c: 10). It stipulates that in case any demographic information relating to an Aadhaar number is found to be incorrect or it changes subsequently, and in case any biometric information of Aadhaar number holder is lost or changes subsequently for any reason, then the Aadhaar number holder shall request the Authority to alter such demographic or biometric information in his record in the CIDR. The clause also provides that when such a request is received, the Authority, if it is satisfied, may make such alteration in the record and intimate such alteration to the concerned Aadhaar number holder.

Clause 32 is about giving access to own information and records of requests for authentication (PRS Legislative Research 2010c: 10). It provides that the Authority shall maintain details of every request for authentication of the identity of every Aadhaar number holder and the response provided thereon by it in such manner and for such time as may be specified by regulations. It further provides that every Aadhaar number holder shall be entitled to obtain details of request for authentication of his Aadhaar number and the response provided thereon by the Authority in such manner as may be specified by regulations.

Disclosure of Information

Clause 33 provides for disclosure of information, including identity information or details of authentication in certain cases (PRS Legislative Research 2010c: 10). These cases include an order of a competent court or a direction issued by designated officers specifically authorized. The Bill provides:

1. The National Identification Authority of India shall be responsible for the security and confidentiality of information. It is required to take measures to protect information against loss or unauthorized access.
2. The National Identification Authority of India or any agency, which maintains the CIDR, is forbidden from revealing any information stored in the repository.
3. There are four exceptions to this rule.

    i. An Aadhaar number holder may request the National Identification Authority to provide access to his own identity information. He may also ask for information on authentication requests of his Aadhaar number.
    ii. The National Identification Authority may share information of Aadhaar number holders, based on their written consent, with agencies engaged in delivery of public benefits and services.
    iii. The National Identification Authority may reveal information in response to an order of a court.
    iv. Information may be revealed in the interest of national security, if directed by an authorized official of the rank of joint secretary and above in the central government.

Adequacy of Safeguards

We start with the assumption that personal information collected is likely to be used for commercial purposes if safeguards are not adequate. That is why we need to examine whether the Bill has sufficient safeguards: (i) if information is shared with agencies engaged in delivery of public benefits and services; (ii) if the information is used to identify consumer behaviour patterns through data mining;

and (iii) if the penalties for unauthorized disclosure of personal information are rigorous enough to act as a disincentive.

Sharing of Information with Agencies Engaged in Delivery of Public Benefits and Services

Clause 23(1)(k) of the Bill allows the National Identification Authority to share the information of an Aadhaar number holder (based on his/her written consent) with agencies engaged in the delivery of public benefits and services (PRS Legislative Research 2010c: 7). However, the Bill does not specify whether consent should be taken only once or at each instance a person avails of a new service. A one-time consent is very likely to be misused (PRS Legislative Research 2010b: 4).

Potential to Profile Individuals

The Bill does not specifically prohibit agencies from using the Aadhaar number as a link while running computer programmes across various databases in order to recognize patterns of consumer behaviour (PRS Legislative Research 2010b: 4). For example, as a safeguard against misuse of personal information, the US had introduced (not passed) a legislation that required each agency that was engaged in data mining to submit an annual report to Congress on all such activities (PRS Legislative Research 2010b: 4).

Penalties for Unauthorized Disclosure of Information

Clauses 30, 37, 38, 39, and 40 of the Bill require all persons with access to Aadhaar-related information to keep it secure and confidential, and prescribe penalties for unauthorized access or intentional disclosure of information (PRS Legislative Research 2010c: 10–11). However, it does not penalize any negligence that leads to leakage of information. Also, it does not have a specific provision to compensate an individual in case his personal information is misused. This differs from the Information Technology Act, 2000, which stipulates that a company handling 'sensitive personal data' is liable to pay a compensation up to Rs 5 crore if it is negligent in implementing and maintaining reasonable security practices and procedures with respect to such data (PRS Legislative Research 2010b: 4).

Conflict of Interest

Clause 46(1) of the Bill stipulates that no court shall take cognizance of any offence punishable under the Act, except on a complaint by the National Identification Authority (PRS Legislative Research 2010c: 12). Such a provision is usually included to ensure that the regulatory body verifies all complaints before a criminal charge is filed. However, unlike regulatory bodies such as the Securities and Exchange Board of India (SEBI) or the Reserve Bank of India (RBI), the National Identification Authority is an implementing body and its employees have been assigned duties related to data security (PRS Legislative Research 2010b: 4). If the offence were to be committed by an employee of the National Identification Authority, it could result in a conflict of interest situation (PRS Legislative Research 2010b: 4).

Discretionary Powers Given to the Authority

Regulation of Demographic Information to be Recorded

The Bill empowers the Authority to specify demographic information that may be recorded. The only restriction imposed on the Authority is that it shall not record information pertaining to race, religion, caste, language, income, or health of the individual. By asking the Authority to specify demographic information, the Bill gives the Authority the power to collect additional personal information, without prior approval from the Parliament (PRS Legislative Research 2010b: 5). As noted earlier, the enrolment form currently being used contains fields for capturing information such as mobile number and bank account number. Though these fields are labelled optional, it is unclear why this additional information is being asked for and recorded.

Storage of Authentication Information

The National Identification Authority is required to maintain details of every request of authentication and the response provided (PRS Legislative Research 2010b: 5). The Bill does not specify the maximum duration for which the National Identification Authority can store authentication data. This has been left out of regulations.

Authentication data provides insights into usage patterns of an Aadhaar number holder. Personal information, if kept for a long duration of time, is likely to be used for activities such as profiling an individual's consumer behaviour (PRS Legislative Research 2010b: 5).

Different Dates for Notification of Different Clauses

Some provisions in the Bill provide the National Identification Authority with the power to collect and maintain data. Some other provisions provide safeguards against misuse. Clause 1(3) of the Bill contains a blanket provision that allows the central government to notify different provisions to come into effect on different dates (PRS Legislative Research 2010c: 2). There is no requirement that the safeguard provisions should come into force by the time provisions enabling collection of data is notified (PRS Legislative Research 2010b: 5).

To sum up, the safeguards provided in the Bill are not adequate to prevent dataveillance. The Bill also gives certain responsibilities to the National Identification Authority in Clauses 23 and 53. Clause 23(m) provides that the powers and functions of the Authority may include 'specifying, by regulation, various processes relating to data management, security protocols and other technology safeguards under this Act' (PRS Legislative Research 2010c: 7).

Nandan Nilekani, in the course of one of his interviews, had specifically mentioned about the protocols in place under the UID Act. This is mentioned in Clause 53(q). Clause 53(q) gives the power to the Authority to make regulations covering 'various processes relating to data management, security protocol and other technology safeguards' (PRS Legislative Research 2010c: 15). Right now, it is the UIDAI which has to put the regulations in place. Right now, there is no Act and the UIDAI has no statutory authority to make regulations. As a result, there are no legally mandated regulations in place. In any case, there is nothing in the public domain about what kind of protocols the UIDAI has in mind and what these protocols would contain. And, this is in spite of the fact that a large volume of personal information has already been collected and recorded by the UIDAI.

On the whole, these instruments—the framework for the proposed legislation on data protection and privacy; and the

National Identification Authority of India Bill—do nothing much by way of providing safeguards to prevent dataveillance. The UIDAI claims that it has framed information security policy and other guidelines to ensure safety of individual data being collected in the form of a security handbook (*The New Indian Express* 2012c: 10). The guidelines, the UIDAI says, were framed for authentication of user agencies, data centre service providers, logistic service providers, registrars, UIDAI employees, and for enrolment agencies (*The New Indian Express* 2012c: 10). We do not have any idea of what these guidelines are because they are not in the public domain, but the fact remains that without any statutory cover, these guidelines are ineffectual to establish the necessary deterrence.

The experience with the SSNs in the US is instructive in this context. As noted in Chapter 3, though the SSN was never conceived as an identity document, service providers (both government organizations and private firms) did manage to mandate the SSN in order to deliver services, and in the 2000s, it began to be used widely for proving one's identity at different delivery and access points. As a result, the SSNs of individuals were exposed to a wide array of private players, which identity thieves used to access bank accounts, credit accounts, utilities records, and other sources (*The Hindu* 2011a: 8). In fact, in 2006, the Government Accountability Office of the US noted, 'over a 1-year period, nearly 10 million people—or 4.6 per cent of the adult U.S. population—discovered that they were victims of some form of identity theft, translating into estimated losses exceeding $50 billion' (*The Hindu* 2011a: 8). Following public outcry, the President of the US appointed a Task Force on Identity Theft in 2007 (*The Hindu* 2011a: 8). Acting on its report, the President notified a plan, 'Combating Identity Theft: A Strategic Plan'. This plan directed all government offices to 'eliminate unnecessary uses of SSNs' and reduction and, where possible, elimination of the need to use SSN to identify individuals (*The Hindu* 2011a: 8).

As noted in Chapter 3, Tony Blair had proposed issuing of identity cards and creation of a National Identity Register through the Identity Cards Act, 2006. Under the proposed provisions of this Act, while the identity cards were supposed to serve the traditional Home Office functions regarding law enforcement, immigration and asylum, national security, and counterterrorism, they were also intended to secure the efficient provision of public services. A key element in the scheme was the provision of a unique reference number for each person, facilitating the integration of a vast number of data sources. The proposal ran into controversy, one of the issues being the potential of dataveillance through the process of interaction between the public and private sectors in the use of identity cards, including access to the National Identity Register. In fact, it was also advertised that the UK identity card system was to guard against 'identity theft'. Then, this suggests that commercial data as well as data relating to government departments would have been accessible.

The experience of these two countries indicates that there is a distinct possibility for dataveillance once the provision of a unique reference number for each person facilitates the integration of a vast number of data sources containing personal information of individuals. In fact, the Technology Advisory Group for Unique Projects did observe that there is such a risk. The Technology Advisory Group, which was chaired by Nandan Nilekani, submitted its report to the Ministry of Finance in January 2011. The report has a chapter, 'Protection of the Individual' (Ministry of Finance 2011a: 52–3). The chapter points out:

> As IT systems become commonplace in governance, issues related to the protection of the individual's right to privacy come to the fore. With paper records, the risk of unauthorized access of large quantities of data has been limited due to the difficulty of aggregating and accessing the data. When data is stored in electronic format, the risk is greater. (Ministry of Finance 2011a: 52)

As the Advisory Group's report points out, the risk of unauthorized access to large quantities of personal data is real when the data is stored in electronic format. The personal data has tremendous value for the market. Such information has, as the 'Approach Paper for Legislation on Privacy' says, 'tremendous scope for commercial exploitation' (Government of India 2010: 2). In fact, it has been pointed out that it is the government which actually intends such sharing of personal information of individuals with private companies. For example, the discussions that took place in the government about unique IDs favoured sharing of personal information with private sector companies. As noted in Chapter 3, the concept of UID had been mooted for the project, 'Unique ID for BPL Families', in March 2006. In July 2006, a Processes Committee was set up to suggest processes for updation, modification, addition, and deletion of data fields from the CDB to be created under the Unique ID for BPL Families project. At that time, a Working Group of the Planning Commission examined the possibilities of improving upon this scheme and introducing smart cards linked to unique IDs of citizens (*The Hindu* 2011a: 8). The report of this Working Group observed:

> [U]nique ID could form the fulcrum around which all other smart card applications and e-governance initiatives would revolve. This could also form the basis of a public–private partnership wherein unique ID-based data can be outsourced to other users, who would, in turn, build up their smart card-based applications...In the context of the unique ID, part of the database could be shared with even purely private smart card initiatives such as private banking/financial services on pay-as-you-use principle... (*The Hindu* 2011a: 8)

WHO COULD POSSIBLY LEAK PERSONAL INFORMATION IN THE AADHAAR SYSTEM?

It is quite possible that the leakage of personal information of individuals to private sector companies could take place through registrars, user agencies, data centre service providers, logistic service providers, and UIDAI employees.

Registrars

In Aadhaar programme, registrars have been charged with the responsibility of collecting biometric and demographic information. The UIDAI has empanelled 209 registrars, and most of these registrars are private organizations (*The Economic Times* 2011b: 13). It is very likely that these registrars, particularly those from the private sector, may leak the information collected to the market for the purpose of consumer profiling. In fact, the registrars have been given authority to collect additional information relating to their business requirements. If a bank is a registrar for Aadhaar enrolment, it can collect additional information for its banking requirements. The UIDAI literature specifies:

If a bank is a Registrar for Aadhaar enrolment, then they can capture additional data fields as per their requirements. The same UIDAI client application that will be used for Aadhaar enrolment, allows additional fields to be captured by the Registrar (E.g. Bank) for their internal use (referred to as KYR+). Additionally the Registrar can also decide to keep the resident's biometric information if they so wish. (UIDAI 2010c: 21)

In such cases, it is very likely that the personal information collected by Aadhaar will ultimately find its way for being used for profiling individuals for marketing purposes. In fact, a note by the Planning Commission says, 'The issue of data security and invasion of privacy when multiple registrars are engaged is a serious concern' (UIDAI 2010c: 21). The matter is compounded by the fact that, as the evidence from the field suggests, the registrars are neither responsible nor subject to any meaningful control (*Deccan Herald* 2012d: 1).

As mentioned in Chapter 5, the IB has taken up a security audit to figure out the extent of misappropriation of Aadhaar cards by NGOs and private firms involved in the process of Aadhaar identification. This social audit was ordered following several complaints that were received in the MoHA.

User Agencies

The leakage of personal information could be through agencies engaged in the delivery of public services. In India, there is now great encouragement given to promotion of private players in the provision of social services such as education, insurance, and health. With the privatization of social services, there is a distinct possibility that the personal information of individuals stored in the Aadhaar system would be passed on to private sector companies. This could also happen through business correspondents, through telecoms, and others who are now coming into the system to deliver last-mile inclusion services.

Data Centre Service Providers and Logistic Service Providers

It is also likely that the leakage of personal information could be through the data centre service providers and the service providers for logistics.

UIDAI Employees

This can even take place through insiders in the UIDAI. In fact, threat to information security from insiders is very real. As the *Report of the Technical Advisory Group for Unique Projects* points out:

> Projects that depend upon mission-critical IT systems may have a number of employees, and an order of magnitude larger number of employees. Employees are given privileges within the system to enable them to carry out their daily functions. It has been observed in a number of cases that security is often at risk due to insiders having authorized access, but use this authority in ways that are malafide. (Ministry of Finance 2011a: 46)

One instance of when the Aadhaar information could be penetrated and used for dataveillance is when the information is put on the cloud. In fact, the UIDAI has already declared its intention of putting the Aadhaar-enabled MIS of the PDS, which will host online food accounts, on the cloud. As the UIDAI document on PDS states: 'Aadhaar would make it possible to implement an online food account through which entitlements would be delivered to the poor. The Aadhaar-enabled MIS can host online food accounts on the cloud, which are linked to Aadhaar numbers of Fair Price Shop (FPS) owners as well as each individual beneficiary' (UIDAI 2010c: 13).

Interestingly, the first complaint of misuse of personal data was reported in September 2011. The UIDAI is looking into a complaint of misuse of personal data while issuing Aadhaar numbers to individuals, its first case of breach of privacy (*Deccan Herald* 2011c: 8). The UIDAI stated in a reply to a query under the Right to Information (RTI) Act:

> The contact centre of the UIDAI is handling the grievances and complaints of all stakeholders. They have not received any specific complaint related to privacy concerns while collecting individual data. However, a complaint regarding the misuse of address proof was received…The contact centre has registered a complaint and forwarded the same to the concerned department. (*Deccan Herald* 2011c: 8)

There are several other complaints of misuse of personal data and duplication of cards. In reply to a query under the RTI Act, the UIDAI clarified:

UIDAI has received six complaints regarding errors or use of address documents. Four were received on UIDAI help line on May 7, 13 and 23 last year [2011] and March 9 this year [2012]. The rest were by emails on February 27 this year and August 10 last year. The complaints were forwarded to respective authorities. Of these, four were sent to the authorities concerned in Delhi and one each to registrars in Maharashtra and Karnataka. (*The New Indian Express* 2012c: 10)

The analysis here shows how these two instruments—the framework for the proposed legislation on data protection and privacy; and the National Identification Authority Bill, 2010—do not provide any meaningful safeguard against dataveillance. In fact, the National Identification Authority Bill, 2010 gives the power to the UIDAI to make regulations covering various processes relating to data management, security protocols, and other technology safeguards. Since the Bill is still under scrutiny, it means that there are no legally mandated regulations in place. The UIDAI claims that it has framed information security policy and other guidelines to ensure safety of individual data being collected in the form of security handbook. But, in the absence of any statutory cover, the security handbook, by itself, does not create the necessary deterrence. That being the case, there is a distinct possibility of the Aadhaar programme enabling dataveillance.

Some commentators on the Aadhaar programme have written extensively about this aspect of the programme. For example, Usha Ramanathan (2010: 11) comments: 'This convergence of information may be efficient for business and meet standards of efficiency, but there are those who would argue that it profiles individuals and exposes them to market and other forces in ways which are intrusive, and which could make them insecure, and unsafe.' Usha Ramanathan gets it right when she says that the convergence of information that the Aadhhaar programme enables will profile individuals for the purposes of the market and expose them to the market. But she gets it wrong when she says that the exposure to the market will be in ways which could make the individuals insecure and unsafe. As argued in the last chapter of this book, the dataveillance which the Aadhaar programme enables would have given an opportunity to India's poor for being profiled as consumers for the market, and this will eventually bring the market into their lives. It is also argued that India's poor stand to gain considerably in the process.

CHAPTER TEN

Aadhaar and the PDS

৵৩৵

The Public Distribution System (PDS) provides subsidized food and fuel to the poor. While affordable food is a source of sustenance for India's poor, they use subsidized kerosene for cooking and lighting extensively. India has a network of more than 4.62 lakh fair price shops (FPSs) distributing food and fuel valued at more than Rs 30,000 crore annually, to about 180 million families. India's PDS is the largest distribution network of its kind in the world. Of all the social safety net programmes of the government, the PDS is considered to be the most important because it provides food and fuel to the poor for sustenance. The subsidies given out in the PDS (Rs 60,750 crore for food and Rs 3,050 crore for kerosene and LPG, annually) account for the single-largest item in the list of subsidy expenditure of the Indian government (*The Economic Times* 2012f: 10).

THE AADHAAR BLUEPRINT

The UIDAI has a 16-page document that lists out how the Aadhaar programme can streamline the PDS (UIDAI 2010c: 1–16). According to the document, several deficiencies have plagued the PDS. In many cases, the true beneficiaries have suffered due to wholesale problems such as pilferage and diversion, and retail-level problems such as duplicates and ghost beneficiaries, wrongful exclusion and inclusion, availability and quality of commodities, as well as pilferage at the level of the FPSs. The document suggests that the Aadhaar number could be the foundation over which the government can build more effective PDS processes (UIDAI 2010c: 3).

According to the document, the greatest value of Aadhaar for the PDS stems from how easily it can be integrated into the existing infrastructure (UIDAI 2010c: 3). It is suggested that Aadhaar presents governments with a highly flexible solution in the sense that states can choose to implement Aadhaar within the PDS in stages, beginning with Aadhaar-based identification, progressing towards Aadhaar-based authentication and an Aadhaar-enabled MIS. The eventual nature of an Aadhaar-linked approach to PDS, it is suggested, would depend upon the particular benefits that the government hopes to gain. Using Aadhaar only for identification would enable clear targeting of PDS beneficiaries, inclusion of marginal groups, and expansion of the coverage of the poor through elimination of fakes and duplicates. Implementing Aadhaar-based authentication across PDS would enable the government to guarantee food delivery to the poor. An Aadhaar-enabled MIS would streamline PDS processes, make possible a more transparent and flexible system, and enable the government to fulfil the objective of food security in times of crises. The Aadhaar programme would thus be a powerful tool in fulfilling the government's overall objectives for the PDS and ensuring food security for the poor (UIDAI 2010c: 3).

AREAS FOR PDS REFORM

The UIDAI document identifies the following critical elements in the implementation of the PDS that need reform:

1. beneficiary identification, and addressing inclusion/exclusion errors;
2. addressing diversions and leakages;
3. managing foodgrain storage and ensuring timely distribution;
4. effective accountability and monitoring, and enabling community monitoring;
5. mechanisms for grievance redressal; and
6. ensuring food security (UIDAI 2010c: 4).

A ROLE FOR AADHAAR WITHIN THE PDS

According to the UIDAI document, Aadhaar can be a powerful tool for the government in making the PDS more effective across these identified areas of reform (UIDAI 2010c: 4). The document suggests that the following features of the Aadhaar programme will be instrumental for delivering entitlements to the beneficiary:

1. *One Aadhaar, one beneficiary*: Aadhaar is a unique number and no resident can have a duplicate number since it is linked to his/her individual biometrics. Using Aadhaar to identify beneficiaries in the PDS databases will eliminate duplicate and fake beneficiaries from the rolls and make identification for entitlements far more effective.

2. *Portability in identification*: Aadhaar is a universal number, and agencies and services can contact the central UID database from anywhere in the country to confirm a beneficiary's identity. The number thus gives individuals a universal, portable form of identification.

    a) *Aadhaar-based identification to confirm entitlement delivered to the beneficiary*: Aadhaar enables remote, online biometric and demographic authentication of identity. Such Aadhaar-based authentication can take place in real time, and can even be performed through a mobile phone. Using Aadhaar for real-time identity verification at the FPS, when beneficiaries collect their entitlements, will help governments to verify that the benefits have reached the person they were meant for.

    One challenge here is ensuring that such authentication is carried out at the FPS. Governments can ensure that Aadhaar-based authentication is implemented by the owner of the FPS by linking future foodgrain allocations to authenticated offtake by beneficiaries. The fewer the number of Aadhaar-based authentications at the outlet, the less grain the FPS should receive from the government. This will give the owner of the FPS a strong incentive to ensure that Aadhaar-based authentication is carried out, and that the authentication devices are working.

    Implementing such authentication while leveraging the portability of Aadhaar can bring significant benefits. Today, beneficiaries in a particular block or district can collect their rations only from their allotted FPS. However, since Aadhaar would be recognized across outlets, the Aadhaar number will help residents to collect their entitlements from any FPS within the state. Governments would then replenish stocks in the FPSs based on authentication-linked offtake, which would give them real-time information on how many beneficiaries have collected their entitlements and from which outlet.

These two aspects of the Aadhaar-enabled system—linking grain allocation to authenticated offtake and choice of the FPS for the beneficiary—would enable a significant shift from the present approach, in which foodgrain allocations within the PDS are static, supply led, and divorced from beneficiary demand and choice. The Aadhaar-enabled approach would instead help create a demand-led, dynamic system, one that gives power and choice to the beneficiary.

3. *Aadhaar-based authentication to track foodgrain movement:* Aadhaar-based authentication can be implemented across the supply chain, which will enable governments to track foodgrain as it is exchanged between PDS intermediaries. This will curb diversions and help identify bottlenecks in delivery.

4. *Aadhaar-enabled cloud computing infrastructure:* The use of Aadhaar-based authentication across the supply chain gives governments the opportunity to link such authentication to a cloud-based MIS within the PDS. An Aadhaar-linked MIS would enable the PDS to address broader procurement, storage, and monitoring challenges. Registration and procurement orders could be managed online, enabling decentralized and more local procurement. Inventory management could be streamlined and handled online in real time. This would also enable the PDS to implement statewide information systems that link all FPSs in a state, and also give beneficiaries more flexibility in how they collect their entitlements and from which FPS.

5. *Electronic benefit transfers* (EBTs): Aadhaar-based authentication at the delivery point (the FPS) would enable governments to transfer entitlements to residents through an electronic system. Beneficiaries could have an online food account on the PDS system, which would enable governments to directly communicate details of food entitlements to residents (UIDAI 2010c: 4–5).

According to the UIDAI document, these features of the Aadhaar number would give governments the opportunity to empower PDS beneficiaries. The use of the portable Aadhaar number and Aadhaar-based authentication would give beneficiaries choice in collecting their rations from any FPS in the state. Tracking the offtake of entitlements through authentication and an Aadhaar-linked MIS would enable governments to make entitlements collection-flexible (beneficiaries would be able to collect their entitlements on a weekly and monthly basis, and also claim entitlements left over from previous months). And, finally, EBTs linked to Aadhaar would give beneficiaries the flexibility in the kind of foodgrain they have access to, particularly in times of shortage; it would also enable governments to tailor food entitlements to pregnant women, infants, and young children (UIDAI 2010c: 5–6).

Choices in Aadhaar Implementation

According to the UIDAI text, the government can determine which Aadhaar-linked features to implement within the PDS, depending on priorities, cost, and feasibility of the intervention. Governments may choose to rapidly implement Aadhaar implementation across the system, and establish an MIS across the PDS infrastructure; other states may prefer to first implement identification-related features and roll out other measures over a period of time (UIDAI 2010c: 6).

AADHAAR-ENABLED REFORMS IN THE PDS

The UIDAI claims that Aadhaar can play an important role in the core areas outlined for reform within the PDS.

Aadhaar for Beneficiary Identification and Addressing Inclusion/Exclusion Errors

According to the UIDAI, the PDS has, for a long time, faced challenges in effectively identifying beneficiaries for food entitlements and limiting exclusion of the poor. The issues that the PDS has identified include:

1. *Omission of poor families*: A problem in reaching benefits to BPL families is that the poorest families often lack identification documents that they need to receive ration cards. They are, as a result, excluded from the PDS.

2. *Fake and duplicate ration cards which do not correspond to real families*: The PDS has pointed out the problem of large number of duplicate and fake cards in both the BPL and Antyodaya Anna Yojana (AAY) categories, which results in significant leakage of food subsidies from the PDS system. The Wadhwa Committee corroborated the problem of duplicate cards, noting that the problem of 'multiple ration cards under a single name' is widespread nationally. In Delhi alone, RTI petitions uncovered 901 ration cards issued in the name of one woman, 'Manju', in Badarpur.

3. *Individual versus household benefits*: A key step which the government has considered for ensuring right to food for every citizen in India is guaranteeing an individual-based entitlement, rather than the PDS approach of a household-based entitlement. While the household-based entitlement reduces food availability in large families (particularly for women and children), the household-defined benefit also limits access to the PDS for certain groups such as single women (UIDAI 2010c: 6).

The UIDAI claims that Aadhaar-based identification will help the government to address the following challenges:

1. *Clear identification of beneficiaries*: Since Aadhaar guarantees uniqueness, linking each beneficiary listed on the ration card to their Aadhaar number would ensure that only unique individuals are present in the PDS database. This would eliminate duplicates, ghosts, and fake identities.

2. *Ensuring inclusion of the poor*: Savings from eliminating duplicates and fakes through Aadhaar-based identification will enable governments to expand benefits to more poor residents. In addition, the UIDAI will issue Aadhaar numbers to residents through multiple registrar agencies as well as through focused outreach efforts. This means that marginal groups that have lacked a proof of identity will receive their first identification through the Aadhaar initiative. Once the PDS accepts Aadhaar as sufficient proof of identity and proof of address, these individuals will be provided ration cards. Aadhaar can help address another significant source of exclusion of the poor: the denial

of applications for a ration card as well as prolonged delays in processing the application, once the individual applies for a card. To address this, the government can implement a centralized, Aadhaar-enabled registration system for the whole state, where a poor person can log a request for a ration card through SMS. The request would be published on the system once the Aadhaar is verified. Governments could subsequently process the logged request and verify the eligibility of the individual. Governments would also be able to track delays in processing applications and identify bottlenecks in issuing ration cards. In addition, civil society groups could track the progress in processing of the applications and take up the cases of these applications on behalf of the individuals.

3. *Enabling individual entitlements*: Linking Aadhaar to ration cardholders enables the government to provide individual, rather than household, entitlements. This would make allocations more transparent, and also address the challenge of larger households receiving insufficient foodgrain (UIDAI 2010c: 7–8).

Addressing Diversions and Leakages

According to the UIDAI, high rates of leakages take place in the PDS while delivering food subsidies to beneficiaries. Diversions take place both at the FPS point and en route, before subsidies reach the FPS. The UIDAI claims that Aadhaar-based identification can help curb both these kinds of diversion. There are two options in Aadhaar authentication:

1. Aadhaar-based authentication at the FPS comes with distinct advantages.

   i. *Ensuring zero proxy withdrawals*: A key source of leakage identified in the PDS is subsidized food drawn from the FPS in the names of eligible families by someone else. In such cases, the ration card has usually been issued and distributed without the knowledge of the eligible beneficiary. When the beneficiary does have the ration card, owner of the FPS does not open the ration shop, or opens it without warning, so that beneficiaries are unable to claim their rations. Rations are then diverted through proxy withdrawals through duplicate cards. Through Aadhaar-based authentication at the FPS, the government can ensure that rations are not collected without the beneficiary's knowledge, and that only entitled beneficiaries collect rations.

ii. *Providing beneficiaries with portable entitlements*: Since Aadhaar is a universal, mobile number that can be verified across ration outlets, beneficiaries would be able to withdraw their entitlements from any ration shop in the state, using Aadhaar authentication. Such choice will give beneficiary more negotiating power with FPS owners. If one FPS owner, for instance, refuses to honour the beneficiary's entitlement or does not provide him with the authenticating device to withdraw rations, the beneficiary can go to another FPS to collect his benefits. Aadhaar-based authentication would also enable the government to allocate foodgrain to ration shops based on the amount of authentication-linked offtake. The approach of portable entitlements can be first implemented in parts of the country (for example, urban centres) where PDS supply can be managed more dynamically.

2. Aadhaar-based authentication across the supply chain: Implementing Aadhaar authentication at every exchange point would enable governments to track the movement of food entitlements across the PDS chain and identify bottlenecks and diversions in real time. In the case of centralized procurement, such authentication would begin at the Food Corporation of India (FCI) point (UIDAI 2010c: 8–9).

Managing Foodgrain Storage and Ensuring Timely Distribution

According to the UIDAI, the expense of grain storage is a significant aspect of the PDS costs. Also, storage availability limits the amount of grain that the PDS can procure and distribute. Storage limitations also increase grain spoilage, resulting in losses and additional cost. Once Aadhaar-based authentication is in place across the PDS infrastructure, it can be linked to an MIS to ensure efficient grain management and storage. Governments would then be able to track and manage Aadhaar-linked procurement, storage, and movement of foodgrain in real time. The UIDAI literature points out that such an Aadhaar-based system would have the following features:

1. *Online registration of farmers through Aadhaar*: Farmers, anywhere in the country, supplying grain to the PDS could first register online through their Aadhaar number. They would be officially registered after PDS officials verify their details.
2. *Electronic order management*: The Aadhaar-based system would enable the government to issue procurement orders online, which would mean immediate visibility for farmers on requirements and reduction of delays. Authentication through Aadhaar at every exchange point would also enable inventory management to be reconciled online, and payments could be seamlessly processed into suppliers' Aadhaar-linked bank accounts. This system would also enable the government to predict and manage local storage requirements. Electronic registration and order management would encourage local, decentralized procurement, as close to storage facilities and demand points as possible.
3. *Portability*: The use of an MIS linked to a universal identifier such as Aadhaar would enable governments to match supply and demand across districts, and, in the longer term, across states.
4. *Focus on efficiency*: Online registration and management would improve the efficiency of the system and enable timely distribution of foodgrain to beneficiaries. Delays in movement and offtake of grain could be identified by delays in Aadhaar authentication and immediately flagged on the system.
5. *Tracking grain offtake*: Tracking of individual offtake through Aadhaar-based authentication would enable beneficiaries to collect their entitlements in instalments, and also collect leftover quota from previous months (UIDAI 2010c: 9–10).

According to the UIDAI, building an Aadhaar-enabled MIS within the PDS would require process changes across various organizations, including the FCI, state food and civil supplies corporations, and food and civil supplies departments. These changes would have to accompany MIS implementation in order to ensure that the system works effectively across PDS procurement, storage, movement, and distribution (UIDAI 2010c: 10).

Enabling Effective Accountability and Monitoring

According to the UIDAI, although the PDS has put in place vigilance groups and monitoring systems to ensure that food subsidies reach the poor, a limitation that the programme faces is lack of transparency and accountability: the government and the public have no means of verifying whether vigilance checks and inspections were carried out, and who is accountable for the delays and leakages. The UIDAI claims that Aadhaar authentication will be a tool for the government to implement high levels of accountabilities across the system as follows:

1. *Accountability in foodgrain movement*: The use of Aadhaar authentication at subsidy exchange points would ensure that the responsibility of each individual—supplier, transporter, FPS owner, inspector—is traceable, and clearly visible across the PDS infrastructure.

2. *FPS accountability*: Requiring Aadhaar authentication every time the beneficiary collects the entitlement from the FPS would ensure that the FPS owner must clearly account for the offtake claimed by his outlet.

3. *Beneficiary accountability*: Aadhaar authentication by the beneficiary would ensure that proxy withdrawals of entitlements are no longer possible. Beneficiaries would also not be able to withdraw more subsidies than they are entitled to through duplicate ration cards.

4. *Community participation in monitoring*: Communities in both rural and urban India have turned to the RTI, as well as public activism, in order to access FPS records and monitor the functioning of the FPSs. However, these community-monitoring efforts by individuals and civil society organizations have been constrained by the limited access they have to records across the PDS supply chain, before the foodgrain arrives at the FPS (UIDAI 2010c: 11).

The UIDAI literature claims that Aadhaar-based authentication and MIS would bring transparency to a currently opaque system. Clear accountability through Aadhaar authentication as well as use of electronic records would make data available for community monitoring and would strengthen the use of RTI in PDS. In addition, the Aadhaar-enabled infrastructure would enable governments to take additional steps for effective public monitoring, such as sending SMS alerts and making information public. An SMS alert can be sent to the resident's Aadhaar-linked mobile number when the truck leaves from the warehouse for the FPS. The SMS can contain information such as the time when the truck left, the quantity of grain it is carrying, and grain prices. An MIS system across the PDS infrastructure would mean that data would be easily accessible across the supply chain. Government can share this information with beneficiaries. This would also create new spaces for the civil society to engage and monitor delivery of entitlements to the poor (UIDAI 2010c: 11).

Mechanisms for Grievance Redressal

According to the UIDAI, a particularly powerful use of Aadhaar would be in the tracking of grievances and complaints from PDS beneficiaries. The UIDAI claims that Aadhaar number will enable:

1. *Individual recognition*: Aadhaar ensures that PDS beneficiaries are individually recognized and easily verified as beneficiaries, without fear of duplicates. Aadhaar can enable the government to implement a central system which automatically publishes grievances submitted by beneficiaries online or through a toll-free number. The complaint would be published once the system verifies the beneficiary's Aadhaar.
2. *High visibility*: An Aadhaar-enabled IT grievance system could ensure that complaints are visible publicly and across different levels of government. As a result, there would be a strong incentive to address complaints quickly.
3. *Ensuring impartiality in addressing grievances*: The advantage of an IT-enabled grievance system is that the complaints of all beneficiaries are treated the same. This is often not the case today, when grievances are channelled through village or local administration.
4. *Pre-empting grievances in food delivery*: The PDS has typically been highly reactive in responding to challenges in delivering food, and weaknesses are addressed once complaints and problems reach a

threshold. An Aadhaar-based MIS, however, would create new opportunities for governments to identify and address problems in real time (UIDAI 2010c: 12).

Fulfilling Food Security Goals

According to the UIDAI, Aadhaar can help the PDS ensure food delivery to beneficiaries without loss and leakage. The number offers benefits in identification of beneficiaries, confirmation in delivering entitlements, and accountability across the delivery infrastructure. Aadhaar would also make it possible to implement an online food account through which entitlements could be delivered to the poor in the following manner.

1. The Aadhaar-enabled MIS system can host online food accounts on the cloud, which are linked to Aadhaar numbers of FPS owners as well as each individual beneficiary.
2. The online account of the beneficiary could be updated monthly with the details of their entitlements—which foodgrains, how much, and at what price.
3. When the beneficiary authenticates himself with his Aadhaar number at the FPS to collect benefits, the authentication confirmation would appear against the FPS owner's food account. The government can thus track offtakes of foodgrain in real time.
4. If the subsidized goods were provided to the FPS at market price, the FPS owner can then claim their reimbursement from the government. The system, on receiving the Aadhaar-linked confirmation that the entitlement was delivered, would electronically issue a cheque to the FPS owner, or transfer money to the FPS owner's bank account (UIDAI 2010c: 13).

The UIDAI claims that online food account would have none of the disadvantages of offline food coupons/vouchers. The FPS owners would not be able to collude with officials to accept photocopies of food coupons or fake coupons, since reimbursements would be carried out electronically. This approach could streamline benefit transfers and give both governments and residents flexibility in food delivery and access. The government could, for instance, immediately tailor entitlements in response to local shortages, such as temporarily providing higher allocations of rice when wheat is not available. It would also help improve government responses to crises and disasters, as governments can provide higher allocations, as well as temporarily increase the number of outlets within a particular area from where subsidized grain can be claimed (UIDAI 2010c: 13).

INCENTIVES FOR IMPLEMENTING AADHAAR ACROSS THE PDS INFRASTRUCTURE

Incentives for Residents

According to the UIDAI literature, the following are the incentives for residents:

1. *Ease in identity verification*: With Aadhaar, residents can easily establish their identity, wherever they are in the country. Identity verification will be simpler while getting a ration card.
2. *Expanded coverage*: Ease in identity verification will allow poor residents, who have so far been shut out of food subsidies, to access food entitlements
3. *Address exclusion of eligible poor*: A centralized, Aadhaar-enabled registration system for PDS applicants would encourage governments to respond more quickly to applications, and also limit the exclusion of eligible individuals.
4. *Portability and choice in accessing benefits*: A universal identification number gives governments the chance to offer portable food entitlements, which beneficiaries can claim wherever they are in the state.
5. *Improved services through increased transparency*: Clear accountability and transparent monitoring would significantly improve access and quality of entitlements to beneficiaries.
6. *Better grievance redressal*: Transparent, centralized system of grievance redressal would encourage rapid responses from governments on complaints (UIDAI 2010c: 13–14).

Incentives for Distributors and FPS Owners

1. *Focus in food entitlements shifts to commercial viability*: As leakages decrease, the focus will shift to making the FPS viable as an

outlet. This would follow the current trend in reformist states: the states that have implemented reforms to curb PDS leakages also increased commissions to FPS outlets in order to ensure that these shops were not forced to close.

2. *Growth based on monthly offtake*: The portability enabled by Aadhaar and choice for beneficiaries will give FPS owners opportunities to expand the number of beneficiaries they cover and the amount of foodgrain they sell.

3. *Fewer delays and efficient allocations*: The implementation of Aadhaar-based authentication and an Aadhaar-enabled MIS will create more efficiencies within the system and lower delays for FPS owners in receiving supplies (UIDAI 2010c: 14).

Incentives for Governments

1. *Elimination of ghosts/duplicates/fakes*: Aadhaar-linked identification would help address the long-standing problems of duplicates, ghosts, and fakes in the PDS system.

2. *Effective targeting*: Aadhaar can enable individual entitlement. It can also enable tailoring of benefits to beneficiaries.

3. *Lower costs in procurement and storage*: Use of an Aadhaar-enabled MIS in farmer registration, foodgrain movement, delivery, and payment can ease costs and complexity within the PDS infrastructure.

4. *Ease in capacity additions*: By easing registration of suppliers as well as distributors, an Aadhaar-enabled MIS can make capacity additions and changes more convenient for the government to implement.

5. *Effective monitoring*: Aadhaar would greatly improve the power of vigilance committees and overall monitoring, as it would enable the government and public to track delays and diversions.

6. *Expansion to other schemes*: A variety of programmes, including the ICDS and the mid-day meals, offer food entitlements to the poor. These multiple benefits can eventually be delivered to beneficiaries through online food accounts (UIDAI 2010c: 14–15).

NEXT STEPS

The UIDAI claims that Aadhaar offers a highly flexible solution, which governments can implement depending on their priorities surrounding the PDS. According to the UIDAI, the following steps are necessary to make Aadhaar-enabled solutions a reality.

Use of Aadhaar for Identification

1. Require every ration card to contain Aadhaar numbers of every household member, including children.
2. Recommend Aadhaar as sufficient proof of identity and proof of address in the PDS.

Use of Aadhaar for Authentication and Tracking

1. Require authentication at FPS each time a beneficiary withdraws his entitlement.
2. Require Aadhaar for every stakeholder in the system—every wholesaler, FPS owner, inspection officials, etc.
3. Recommend authentication infrastructure across the PDS supply chain. The Aadhaar authentication system could be as simple as demographic authentication through a mobile phone.
4. Recommend a cloud-based, Aadhaar-linked IT infrastructure for PDS in each state, to enable online procurement and inventory management.
5. Recommend linking Aadhaar authentication to online tracking of food across the supply chain.

Use of Aadhaar for Monitoring and Grievance Systems

1. Link Aadhaar authentication to vigilance and inspection processes.
2. Recommend a central Aadhaar-enabled grievance system, where complaints are publicly available and accessible across government levels (UIDAI 2010c: 15).

According to the UIDAI, the Aadhaar-based solution will be strengthened by the expanding mobile and Internet connectivity across India (mobile connectivity is now available in over 3 lakh villages, and remaining shortages are expected to be resolved over the next few years). The UIDAI literature points out that Aadhaar's success across states will depend on specific PDS reforms adopted by different state governments and how they link these reforms to Aadhaar-enabled solutions. At the state level, for example, the Aadhaar-based approach would be more effective when augmented by an online food account system, rather than an offline food coupon/voucher approach. Similarly, state decisions on incentives for FPS owners, the use of electronic procurement and movement orders within the MIS, etc, will determine how Aadhaar functions within the PDS infrastructure. According to the UIDAI, Aadhaar can be a powerful tool for the government intent on making the PDS more effective: it will help transform India's oldest, most well-established welfare programme into an initiative that is potent, effective, and that empowers India's poor; one that the poor can trust will deliver their entitlements to them (UIDAI 2010c: 15–16).

ANALYSIS OF THE UIDAI CLAIMS

The UIDAI document on the PDS puts forth several claims. These claims relate primarily to six areas: (i) addressing exclusion/inclusion errors; (ii) portability in identification; (iii) authentication in the supply chain; (iv) enabling effective accountability and monitoring; (v) developing an MIS; and (vi) establishing mechanisms of grievance redressal.

Addressing Exclusion and Inclusion Errors

It is a fact that a large number of poor people are excluded from the purview of welfare programmes. There are two reasons for this (Khera 2011a: 39). First, the coverage of welfare programmes depends upon the budgetary allocations made for them for a particular financial year. For most welfare schemes, the money provided in the budget is never adequate to make these schemes universal in their coverage. That is why there is almost a compulsion to make most of these schemes targeted. When a programme is made targeted in its coverage, the benefits flowing from it are limited to the poor and therefore, their inclusion in the programme is conditional upon a particular family being classified as a BPL family in the official census conducted for the purpose. Second, quite often, there are cases of misclassification of people because of corruption or wrong interpretation of guidelines issued by the government from time to time.

Targeted Public Distribution Scheme

To start with, the PDS was a programme with universal coverage. In 1997, the government made it a targeted programme and called it the Targeted Public Distribution System (TPDS). The TPDS introduced two changes in the scope of the universal coverage of the earlier programme. One was that the population was divided into two card-holding categories: the population above the poverty line (APL); and the population below the poverty line (BPL). For the APL category, the prices charged were stipulated at 80 per cent of the economic cost, whereas the prices charged for the BPL category were half of the economic cost. From March 2000 onwards, the APL prices were set at the economic cost, thereby taking away the subsidy altogether from the APL beneficiaries, while the prices for the BPL beneficiaries were continued at 50 per cent of the economic cost (Government of India 2000). As a result of these pricing changes made in 1997 and 2000, there was a sharp fall in the offtake and purchases of PDS commodities for APL beneficiaries. The second change made in 1997 was that entitlements under the TPDS were limited to 10 kg per month per card for both APL and BPL categories.

The TDPS was introduced with the avowed objective of providing subsidized foodgrains primarily to poor families (Khera 2008: 53). This made it imperative that the poor households be identified. Towards this end, the approach was to conduct a BPL census that would identify households based on various correlates of poverty such as landlessness and education. For example, the official guidelines issued in 1997 for selection of BPL households have two sections. The first section deals with those assets and consumer durables (such as more than 5 acres of operational landholdings, television sets, refrigerators, fans, two- or four-wheelers, threshers, tractors, and power tillers), the ownership of which automatically disqualifies the household from eligibility under the BPL category. In addition, families living in *pucca* houses or with a member of the household who has a regular job are automatically disqualified. The second section, which looks at consumption expenditures, is for those households that are not already disqualified by the criteria set in the first section of the guidelines (Khera 2008: 53).

Faulty and Inadequate Guidelines The criteria laid down in the first section of the 1997 guidelines have been critiqued on the ground that they are faulty and inadequate (Khera 2008: 53). It has been pointed out that the landownership criterion does not take into account the differences that might exist in quality and productivity of land. In most arid and semi-arid districts of the country, land is often of poor quality, and ownership of 5 acres of such marginal land does not take a family above the poverty line (Khera 2008: 53). There are problems with the other criteria too. For example, landless widows have been denied BPL cards because they live in pucca houses, even though these houses were built under Indira Awas Yojana (Khera 2008: 54). There are implementation errors, too (Khera 2008: 54). Because the guidelines were not properly communicated to investigators who conducted the BPL census, the investigators interpreted the guidelines incorrectly and there were errors. This was compounded by the fact that most people in the villages were unaware of the criteria for the selection of BPL households, and this allowed misclassification to creep into the preparation of the BPL list. Some of the errors in the selection process can also be attributed to acts of favouritism on the part of the officials in charge.

Caps The more serious reason as to why there are large exclusion errors in the list of beneficiaries is due to the prevailing practice of arbitrarily striking off names from the proposed list. This is done because of a system of what is euphemistically called 'caps'. The central government imposes 'caps' on the number of BPL families allowed for each state (Khera 2011b: 38). The proportion of BPL families that the central government is prepared to subsidize in each state is fixed in accordance with the Planning Commission's poverty estimates; and 1993–4 poverty estimates are still used for this purpose, on account of a Supreme Court order in the PUCL *vs* Union of India case (Khera 2011b: 38). The proportion of BPL families that the central government is prepared to subsidize in the state becomes the 'cap' for that state. The state governments divide and allocate the quota to districts and in turn, the district authorities distribute quotas to talukas and blocks. As a result, names are struck off arbitrarily from the BPL list in order to make it correspond to the quota allocated to the state, district, taluka, or block.

So, both in its conception and implementation, the TPDS has proved to be problematic. Conceptually, some of the criteria prescribed by the government guidelines are faulty and inadequate. The implementation is defective because of lack of public awareness regarding the selection criteria, distortion in the selection criteria due to poor communication to the actual investigators, acts of favouritism, and arbitrary deletion of names from the proposed lists to meet central caps. As a result, there are large exclusion errors in the list that is operated by the PDS for distributing food and fuel. Such exclusion is not because these poor families lack identification documents to receive ration cards. So, the Aadhaar number that provides unique identity to residents may not have a role to play in redressing such exclusion errors.

Updating the BPL List One important source of exclusion error can be attributed to the fact that the government does not regularly update the BPL list (Khera 2011b: 40). Two BPL censuses have been conducted in 1997 and 2002. Lists prepared on the basis of the 2002 census were held up because of the stay order from the Supreme Court in the case of PUCL *vs* Union of India. The Supreme Court vacated the stay in 2005 after stipulating that: (i) names of the households in the 1997 BPL list should not be struck off the 2002 list; and (ii) effective appeal procedures should be put in place for all households. Even after the stay was vacated, a number of states did not adopt the new BPL list because of confusion over which survey the BPL list should correspond to, and as a result, the exclusion errors continue to persist.

Interestingly, Andhra Pradesh and Tamil Nadu did not adopt the BPL caps put by the central government, and these two states do not have a BPL category for the PDS. In Andhra Pradesh, persons who are entitled to PDS commodities are given 'white cards'. In Tamil Nadu, these persons are given 'rice cards'. In fact, many states have found the BPL caps imposed by the central government to be very stringent. As a result, some of these states have initiated their own schemes (for example, the Mukhya Mantri Khadya Sahayog Yojana in Chhattisgarh, Rajasthan, and Madhya Pradesh) to issue ration cards (Khera 2011b: 38). Household entitlements of these cards are the same as that of the regular BPL households (Khera 2011b: 38).

Can the Aadhaar programme set right these exclusion errors? The answer is in the negative. Inclusion of families that have been excluded is possible only if they are included in the BPL list by a fresh census, and that too, if the numbers included are within the BPL caps imposed by the central government. In the alternative, the state governments can include them by formulating their own schemes. In either case, the Aadhaar will not have any role to play.

Eliminating Duplicates, Ghosts, and Fake Identities

The UIDAI literature claims that using the Aadhaar number to identify beneficiaries in PDS databases will eliminate duplicate and fake beneficiaries from the rolls and make identification for entitlements far more effective. Obviously, what the UIDAI has in mind is weeding out what is known as bogus ration cards in popular parlance. There can be three types of bogus cards in the PDS: (i) ghost cards; (ii) duplicates; and (iii) misclassified cards (Khera 2011b: 38). Ghost cards are those that exist in the names of non-existent persons or in the names of persons who are dead and gone. In case a person or a family entitled to one ration card gets hold of more than one card through unfair means, these are duplicates. In case the non-poor is classified as poor, thus enabling ineligible persons or families to claim benefits from the PDS, there is misclassification.

Admittedly, Aadhaar has the capability to weed out ghost ration cards and duplicates. But for that to happen, the Aadhaar number has to be made mandatory. As noted earlier, since enrolment in Aadhaar is not mandatory, ghost beneficiaries and persons/households with multiple ration cards would obviously choose to opt out of the Aadhaar system (PRS Legislative Research 2010b: 3).

Impact of Weeding out Ghosts and Duplicates Let us assume for a moment that the Aadhaar programme is made mandatory in some form or the other for the PDS and succeeds in weeding out the ghosts and duplicates. What will be its impact on the PDS in terms of numbers? To answer the question, we need to find out the proportion of these bogus ration cards. Rough estimates based on newspaper reports put the number of bogus cards in 2–13 per cent range (Khera 2011a: 40). Let us take the cases of Tamil Nadu and Karnataka.

As a Planning Commission report puts it, only 2 per cent of the cards in Tamil Nadu are bogus (Khera 2011a: 40). It was not always like this in Tamil Nadu. In fact, the existence of bogus cards used to be a recurring phenomenon. Even at the time of statutory rationing, there were bogus cards. In the 1967 budget session of the Legislative Assembly in Tamil Nadu, the food minister claimed that out of more than 36,000 ration cards that were examined in Madras city, 3,266 were found to be bogus and were eliminated (Venkatsubramanian 2006: 280). Later on, when the issue price of rice under PDS was artificially pegged at a very low level, the menace of bogus cards assumed menacing proportion. The total number of cards hovered at about 16 million between July 2001 and March 2003, while the number of households in Tamil Nadu, as per the 2001 census, stood only at 14 million; this meant that there were 2 million bogus cards (Venkatsubramanian 2006: 280).

However, the report of the Planning Commission puts the proportion of bogus cards only at 2 per cent. How did Tamil Nadu achieve this? As a first step towards weeding out bogus cards, the government introduced a coupon system according to which each rice cardholder was given a rice coupon book free of cost (Venkatsubramanian 2006: 285). Cardholders could draw rice in the PDS outlet by tendering coupons. However, coupon books were to be issued only to the person whose photo had been affixed in the family card and not to any other person. Each rice cardholder had to personally collect rice at the PDS outlets by producing family cards as well tendering the rice coupon. Another innovation was to convert the cards of those who did not want to purchase commodities from the FPS, but still needed them for identification purposes, into 'honorary' cards. It was further ordered that families with a monthly income of Rs 5,000 and above would be eligible only for 'honorary' cards (Venkatsubramanian 2006: 285).

In Karnataka, for example, the efforts of the Department of Food and Civil Supplies to identify bogus ration cards have yielded the desired results. Karnataka state had 1.75 crore ration cards as against 1.01 crore families (2001 census) (Sastry 2012: 5). Of the 1.75 crore ration cards, there were AAY cards (11.94 lakhs); BPL cards

(99.59 lakhs); APL cards (63.82 lakhs); and temporary cards (58 lakhs) (Sastry 2012: 5). The Department of Food and Civil Supplies undertook the exercise of weeding out bogus cards in association with the NIC. In the exercise which lasted almost a year, 49 lakh bogus cards were weeded out (*The Hindu* 2012e: 7).

The number of ration cards in Karnataka was about 1 crore till 2006 (Sastry 2012: 5). In 2006, the government entrusted the task of distributing digitized ration cards under the biometric system to a private company called the Comat Technologies. Between 2006 and 2010 (when the contract of Comat Technologies was terminated), the company had issued over 58 lakh cards without collecting biometric details and without creating a database (Sastry 2012: 5). As a result, the number of cards shot up over and above the actual number of census families in the state. In order to weed out bogus cards, the department verified the authenticity of ration cards by linking them with revenue register numbers in urban areas and property numbers in rural areas. A detailed list of the number of properties of families and the number of ration cards was prepared at gram panchayat level with the help of Department of Rural Development and Panchayat Raj. The NIC helped the Department of Food and Civil Supplies in identification of bogus cards. A similar exercise was done in urban areas, including Bangalore and other major cities and towns, using the revenue register number details of all the families. Before cancelling bogus ration cards, the department did a thorough verification of all the details by physically visiting the families in whose name the cards were issued (Raghunandan 2012: 5).

After terminating the services of Comat Technologies, the Department of Food and Civil Supplies, in association with the NIC, worked towards creating a computerized database of cardholders in the state (Sastry 2012: 5). Besides helping in the elimination of bogus cards, the computerized database and the newly created system allows an individual to apply for a new ration card online throughout the year. According to B.A. Harish Gowda, the Secretary of the Department of Food and Civil Supplies, who is responsible for bringing about these changes, an applicant has to now provide his biometric information, fingerprints as well as his photograph, along with those of another member of the family, to obtain a ration card (Sastry 2012: 5). According to Harish Gowda, biometric registration has been made mandatory for existing cardholders, holders of temporary cards (issued by Comat Technologies), as well as new applicants (Sastry 2012: 5). The Government of Karnataka did not spend any money on collecting biometric data; instead, it allowed local bodies to collect Rs 20 per applicant in urban areas, and in gram panchayat limits, the biometric details were to be collected by the panchayats after linking the applicants to the property tax register (Sastry 2012: 5).

A survey conducted of the PDS in Andhra Pradesh, Bihar, Chhattisgarh, Himachal Pradesh, Jharkhand, Orissa, Rajasthan, Tamil Nadu, and Uttar Pradesh, in 2011, found:

> Further, since BPL lists were used for sampling purposes, it gave us a chance to investigate the presence of 'ghost' cards on the BPL list. The teams found hardly any bogus name on the BPL lists. Across all states, there were less than 10 names (out of 1,227) on the BPL lists that the survey teams were unable to locate. Nearly all households (93%) possessed only one ration card. A small proportion (6%) of households had two; of these, one-third were joint families. This is significant in the light of claims that bogus and/or duplicate cards are a major source of corruption in the PDS. A possibility remains that bogus cards are floating 'outside' the official BPL lists; this could be verified by checking whether actual PDS allocations (say at the state or district level) exceed what one would expect based on the official BPL lists. (Khera 2011b: 40)

The finding of this survey clearly indicates that the number of ghosts and duplicates has come down drastically. This finding of the survey is corroborated by the annual report of the Department of Food and Civil Supplies, which notes that 208.57 lakh fake ration cards were eliminated across 26 states, as of 2010 (Ramakumar 2011b: 17). In case they do exist, computerization of the database of ration cardholders may be the solution. De-duplication in Chhattisgarh was done by computerizing the database of ration cardholders and distributing new ration cards with holograms, which make each ration card unique. In fact, regular updating of the list of cardholders in Chhattisgarh has allowed the authorities to weed out duplicates from the system (Khera 2011b: 47). If bogus cards are still there 'outside', the obvious thing to do, as the study suggests, is to check whether the PDS allocations are based on the numbers in the PDS list.

The adoption of a very simple mechanism has been found to be useful in identifying bogus cards. In many states, the names of the BPL households are painted outside the FPSs or the panchayat offices (Khera 2011b: 47). This simple transparency safeguard has been able to achieve two things. One, it has helped in identifying ghost and duplicate cardholders. Second, it has helped people to know whether or not they are in the BPL list. Chhattisgarh has done better than most states in this respect. It has painted a sign on the doorframe of each rural house indicating the colour and type of the ration card the household has, associated entitlements, and the BPL census it was based on (Khera 2011b: 47). This simple exercise has helped to tidy the BPL list, create awareness regarding the entitlements, and shame richer households who are in possession of BPL cards.

These experiences have an important lesson. The lesson is that if such simple and inexpensive expedients can work in eliminating bogus cards, there may not be much point in going in for a very expensive and centralized solution that the Aadhaar programme offers for eliminating bogus cards.

Portability of Identification

The UIDAI literature claims that the Aadhaar number can provide PDS beneficiaries with portable entitlements, the assumption being that since Aadhaar is a universal, mobile number that can be verified across retail outlets, beneficiaries would be able to withdraw their entitlements from any ration shop using Aadhaar authentication. According to the UIDAI literature, such choice will give beneficiaries more negotiating power with FPS owners. If the FPS owner refuses to honour beneficiary's entitlement or does not provide the authenticating device to withdraw rations, the beneficiary can go to another FPS to collect benefits. It is also claimed that Aadhaar-based authentication would enable the government to allocate foodgrains to ration shops based on the amount of authentication-linked offtake.

If the Aadhaar number can really enable PDS rations to be drawn from any ration shop, it would be truly beneficial to the migrant poor. Considering that India has about 100–120 million migrants and they are poor, it would mean that most of these migrants would have got the benefit of portable PDS entitlements. However, we need to note that, while the Aadhaar number is mobile, the benefits are not mobile. This is because of operational problems. At present, each FPS has a specified number of local households attached to it. It is allotted grain on the basis of the offtake to these local households and stores grain only for them.

Let us imagine a situation in which the benefits are portable. The owner of the FPS would not be in a position to know how many migrant workers would approach him and demand grain, and for what periods of time. In any case, the FPS owner would not have the stock to provide food and fuel to these migrant workers because the allocations to the PDS outlets are based on the outgo during the previous month. So, matching supplies to an unpredictable and unknowable demand becomes difficult to handle at the level of the FPS. If the portability has to go beyond the state, it becomes even more difficult because, based on the ration card population, each state gets a fixed quantity of foodgrains from the central government and therefore, streamlining supplies to cater to a PDS that allows portability of benefits would be a difficult job, keeping in mind the huge numbers involved in interstate migration. Biraj Patnaik, the Adviser to the Commissioners of Food of the Supreme Court, says: 'India will end up with multiple systems that cannot talk to each other. How can migrants collect their quota of grain anywhere in the country if the systems of different states cannot speak to each other?' (Rajshekhar 2012b: 13).

In other words, the portability of the PDS as proposed by the UIDAI literature is incompatible with the concept of static FPSs (Ramakumar 2011b: 18). Even if the PDS outlets were fully computerized, the nature of circular and seasonal migration would ensure that the system would not be in a position to respond optimally (Ramakumar 2011b: 18).

Authentication in the Supply Chain

According to the UIDAI literature, Aadhaar-based authentication can be used across the supply chain, enabling authorities to track foodgrain as it is exchanged between PDS intermediaries, and this would curb diversions and help identify bottlenecks in delivery. It is also suggested that implementing Aadhaar-based authentication at every exchange point would enable governments to track the movement of food entitlements across the PDS chain, and identify bottlenecks and diversions in real time. According to the UIDAI literature, in the case of centralized procurement, such authentication would begin at the FCI point and cover the state food and civil supply organizations, the district food and civil supply units, FPSs, and the residents.

In the current system as it operates now, the movement of foodgrains is tracked till it leaves the godown for an FPS. Diversion of foodgrains from the PDS takes place mostly in this last stage. So, the problem essentially is one of a functional system of last-mile authentication not being there. The following is a discussion of how this diversion takes place and how it can possibly be checked in a cost-effective manner.

The owner of the FPS maintains a sales register and a monthly stock register, based upon which the rations for the next month are released. However, this monthly squaring of records is operational only in some states like Tamil Nadu, Chhattisgarh, and Himachal Pradesh, and not in other states. That being the case, the FPS owners generally fudge information in these registers. This allows them to divert foodgrains in two ways. First, they do it by cheating the cardholders by giving them less than what is stipulated. For example, the beneficiaries are given only 25 kg out of their entitlement of 35 kg for the family. But the beneficiaries are made to sign for the full quota of 35 kg. The beneficiaries sign under duress because they have no other place to go for subsidized rations. So, the beneficiaries generally accept the lower quantity and sign for the higher quantity. Second, the diversion of PDS foodgrains often takes place en route to the village FPS. The diverted grain is sold illegally in the open market. In the village, the FPS owner pleads his helplessness by saying that he has been given less by the authorities.

Checks and Balances

There are several ways in which such last-mile diversion of foodgrains has been handled. One is by instituting a regime of checks and balances. Tamil Nadu is a case in point (Venkatsubramanian 2006: 274). The monitoring system in Tamil Nadu is especially vigorous. An elaborate system for monitoring and inspection of FPS has been prescribed and what is more important, it is largely followed. A large number of officials are employed by the cooperative department to monitor the FPSs run by cooperatives. In all, some 600 officials are involved in the supervision of FPSs. Targets for inspection of FPSs have been fixed for all the staff. At the district level, there is a deputy registrar exclusively for the PDS. He has to inspect 50 shops per month. Under him are cooperative sub-registrars and senior inspectors of cooperative societies. Together, all cooperative department officers have to inspect 16,925 shops per month.

A similar drill exists for the officers of the Tamil Nadu Civil Supplies Corporation, which also runs FPSs. In addition, district officials, right from the collector to special revenue inspectors, have a monthly target of inspection of FPSs. Each collector has to inspect 10 shops; additional collector, 20 shops; district supply officer, 30 shops; revenue divisional officer, 20 shops; taluka supply officer, 30 shops; and special revenue inspector, 40 shops. During their inspection, they have to verify entries in ration cards for about 20–50 families. They also verify the stock register, and ascertain from members of the public whether the shops are kept open according to schedule (Venkatsubramanian 2006: 274–5).

There is also an elaborate system of reporting and review of the PDS operations in Tamil Nadu. The stock position and the offtake are reported to headquarters on a weekly basis. With such reporting and the increasing use of IT, it is now possible to monitor even the daily stock positions. The movement of stocks from godowns to shops is also effectively monitored. There is a fixed time chart and route chart for tracking the movement of foodgrains. The Members of Legislative Assembly (MLAs) are given access to this information. Following the enactment of the Tamil Nadu Right to Information Act, 1997, the government has issued orders permitting all civil supplies authorities to release information on the flow of food stocks in and out of FPSs to elected representatives and members of the public. The government has also allowed beneficiary registers and information on individual withdrawals to be made available to public. It has also issued a citizens' charter obliging shops to provide information on their timings, prices, stock positions, and grievance redressal processes. Notice boards are placed in all shops to provide such information to consumers. The pilferages and diversion in Tamil Nadu have come down because of this system of checks and balances that is implemented rigorously.

The Tata Economic Consultancy Services, which undertook a study, for the Ministry of Food and Consumer Affairs, Government of India, to ascertain the extent of diversion of PDS commodities, found that the diversion of commodities in Tamil Nadu was of the order of 24 per cent for wheat, 33 per cent for rice, and 28 per cent for sugar, which was among the lowest in the country (Venkatsubramanian 2006: 280). Considering the extremely low price of rice under the PDS in Tamil Nadu, one would have expected a much higher percentage of diversion of rice to the open market (Venkatsubramanian 2006: 280). Clearly, the intense inspection drill of FPSs by the officials and the wide usage of PDS by cardholders have made for the relatively low percentage of rice diversion in the state.

In Tamil Nadu, the food department has put in place a system whereby any ration cardholder can send an SMS to receive instant information regarding the stock of each PDS commodity available in a particular FPS (Khera 2011b: 47). This SMS-based approach to get information on the PDS stock was started in 2009 by the Tamil Nadu government when it began using SMS to receive inputs on stock availability from each FPS across the state. The data thus received was stored in a central server. Once the system was tested, the government started a scheme in which the information about the stock could be shared with the beneficiaries of the PDS. The ration cardholders can now contact the server through an SMS to receive information on the stock availability of the FPS closest to them. Once an SMS is sent to a specified number with the district code and shop code of the particular fair price depot, a message would be received with the details of the stock position of the FPS. This SMS system illustrates the scope for an effective IT-based transparency measure using straightforward and inexpensive technology (Khera 2011b: 47).

In Chhattisgarh, the government provides a service in which mobile phone users can register themselves in order to receive an SMS alert whenever a truck with PDS foodgrain leaves for their village: the SMS also provides details about the truck and the quantity of grain being transported (Khera 2011b: 47). In addition, the fact that grain is delivered to the village in easily identifiable yellow trucks ensures that the FPS owner cannot pretend that he did not get the grain.

These are some of the ways in which the last-mile problem has been addressed. Aadhaar's authenticating biometric information, at the time of purchase, can perform the same function. But compulsory biometric authentication at the last mile would require us to consider cases of old, or disabled, or sick persons who currently rely on neighbours or relatives to bring their rations for them. With biometric authentication, there may not be any scope for relatives buying the rations on behalf of the aged, disabled, or the sick. However, the larger consideration with Aadhaar-based authentication is the cost involved in installing the system. When the last-mile problem can be solved by an intensive system of checks and balances, and through the use of cost-effective and technologically savvy solutions, there may not really be any need for the centralized Aadhaar-based authentication.

The good news is that leakages in the PDS seem to be coming down. This is evident from the findings of the 2011 survey of the PDS that was conducted in Andhra Pradesh, Bihar, Chhattisgarh, Himachal Pradesh, Jharkhand, Orissa, Rajasthan, Tamil Nadu, and Uttar Pradesh (Khera 2011b: 37). The survey found significant improvement in the purchase–entitlement ratio (PER), the PER being the proportion of the full entitlement that is purchased by the BPL households, and the low PER would be due to leakages in the system (Khera 2011b: 40). The study found that the average purchase from the PDS in the past three months ranged from 24 kg and 30.4 kg per month (for BPL and Antyodaya cards respectively). The average entitlement of BPL cardholders (averaged for all states) was between 27.3 and 28.7 kg per month (Khera 2011b: 40). The average PDS purchase in the past three months (24 kg/household per month) was at least 84 per cent of the monthly entitlement (28.7 kg/ household per month) (Khera 2011b: 40). The study also looked at the proportion of households who got their full entitlement normally. Three-quarters of the respondents reported getting their full quota in the nine survey states. On the whole, the survey found a marked improvement in the PER, and this would indicate that leakages are indeed coming down (Khera 2011b: 40).

Enabling Effective Accountability and Monitoring

The UIDAI literature claims that Aadhaar authentication will be a tool for the government to implement high levels of accountability across the system in respect of: (i) accountability in foodgrain movement; (ii) FPS accountability; (iii) beneficiary accountability; and (iv) community participation and monitoring.

In respect of accountability in management of foodgrains, FPS accountability, and beneficiary accountability, we have already noted how it has been done rather successfully in Tamil Nadu and other states. This is also true of beneficiary accountability. Interestingly, these accountabilities have been successfully realized in states where the PDS databases are computerized. There is nothing further to be achieved through Aadhaar authentication in these three areas. In fact, one of the most significant initiatives in the PDS implementation has been the computerization of the records. This has proved to be beneficial in many ways. It has helped in streamlining the chain of distribution ranging from lifting of commodities to distribution at the FPS. It has also helped in the adoption of effective management practices. For example, in Chhattisgarh, the regular updation of the list of cardholders has enabled the system to weed out duplicates. It has helped in the preparation of better records: it has resulted is creation of accurate, consistent, and tamper-proof records. The discipline of strict and accurate record keeping has made corrupt practices very difficult (Khera 2011b: 46–7).

There is one problem, though. In Chhattisgarh and Tamil Nadu, while the details of purchases by each ration cardholder are available in the computerized database, the database is not made public (Khera 2011b: 47). If the members of the public were given access to these databases, it would bring greater transparency to the system. In particular, this would enable community participation in monitoring. Technically, there should not be any problem in granting such access, because such access has already been given in respect of the NREGA MIS. The official NREGA website gives employment information about days of employment, wages earned, etc, in respect of all job cardholders.

In any case, the National Food Security Bill, 2011, which has already been introduced in the Parliament, makes very detailed provisions for ensuring transparency and accountability. Clause 35 provides that all TPDS-related records shall be placed in the public domain and kept open for inspection by the public (PRS Legislative Research 2011: 13). Clause 36 provides for periodic social audits to be conducted on the functioning of FPSs and the TPDS (PRS

Legislative Research 2011: 13). This clause also provides for the findings of the social audits to be publicized and necessary action to be taken on them.

Clause 37 provides for the setting up of vigilance committees for ensuring transparency and proper functioning of the TPDS and accountability of the functionaries in the system (PRS Legislative Research 2011: 13). These vigilance committees are to be set up at the state, district, block, and FPS levels. The functions given to the vigilance committees are: (a) regular supervision of the implementation of all schemes under the Act; (b) informing the district grievance redressal officer, in writing, of any violation of the provisions of the Act; and (c) informing the district grievance redressal officer, in writing, of any malpractice or misappropriation of funds.

Building an MIS

The UIDAI literature claims that if an Aadhaar-based MIS were established across the PDS infrastructure, data would be easily accessible across the supply chain, making it possible for the government to share the information with beneficiaries. Apart from creating new spaces for the civil society to engage and monitor delivery of entitlements, the MIS would make vast amounts of data and information about the PDS available to the government. The government would then be able to build multiple applications to analyse the data and identify problems as well as opportunities. Such application could include tools that can analyse storage and procurement data for addressing bottlenecks, identify weak performers among FPSs, and pinpoint areas where entitlement claims are low. This, in turn, would enable states to make pre-emptive information-led changes and updates to their PDS programme.

As mentioned earlier in this chapter, several state governments have already created successful MISs by using simple and straightforward technologies. The leaders have been Tamil Nadu and Chhattisgarh, but other states are now following in their footstep. The most dramatic breakthrough in MISs for the PDS has come through computerization of records. This has not only provided the governments and the respective food departments with adequate information to manage the system, but has also given the necessary information to the management to streamline the entire supply and distribution chain and introduce effective management practices (Khera 2011b: 45–6).

For example, the Chhattisgarh government has implemented end-to-end computerization of the PDS procurement chain. This has involved the creation of an online registration system for millers of PDS rice, as well as for procurement and movement orders that are issued electronically. The government carries out allocations to the FPSs using the ration card database, and the transmission time for allocations has now been reduced from three weeks to two hours. Continuous monitoring of sales and stock levels at the FPS outlets has ensured in-time stocking of the shops, so that these outlets are in a position to meet the demand from the ration cardholders at all times. As noted earlier, if only the details of the PDS computerized database are made public, it would make a substantial contribution to building a very accountable administration.

That being the case, the installation of an Aadhaar-based MIS within the PDS may not really be necessary. There is also a problem with installing an Aadhaar-based MIS in the PDS. This is because of the fact that it would require process changes across various feeder organizations like the FCI, the state food and civil supply corporations, and the state departments of food and civil supplies. These changes are necessary as the Aadhaar-based MIS requires them to ensure that the system works effectively across PDS procurement, storage, movement, and distribution. Making these changes in these diverse feeder organizations will be a big challenge, apart from the fact that various state governments have already evolved their own systems which have stood the test of time.

Mechanisms for Grievance Redressal

The UIDAI claims that a particularly powerful use of the Aadhaar programme would be in tracking grievances and complaints from PDS beneficiaries. This, the UIDAI claims, would enable: (i) individual recognition; (ii) high visibility; (iii) ensuring impartiality in addressing grievances; and (iv) pre-empting grievances in food delivery.

Many state governments have already put in place functional systems of grievance redressal. Tamil Nadu and Chhattisgarh are the leaders. The system includes providing telephone numbers (help lines) for ration cardholders to call in case of complaints. In Tamil Nadu, the phone numbers of the concerned officers are painted outside each FPS. According to the survey of the PDS done in nine states, the local organizations claimed that the help lines were effective and that the complaints lodged with these help lines led to some effective action.

In any case, the Food Security Bill, 2011 makes very elaborate provisions for grievance redressal. It envisions the setting up of an internal grievance redressal mechanism, including call centres, help lines, and designation of nodal officers in each organization dealing with foodgrain distribution (PRS Legislative Research 2011: 7). It also stipulates a district grievance redressal officer in each district for 'expeditious and effective redressal of grievances of the aggrieved persons in matters relating to distribution of entitled food grains' (PRS Legislative Research 2011: 7). It envisages the creation of requisite staff to be posted at the district level 'to enforce entitlements and investigate and redress grievances' (PRS Legislative Research 2011: 7).

At the state level, the Bill provides for the establishment of a State Food Commission. The State Food Commission will be charged with the responsibility of monitoring and evaluating the implementation of the Act, and looking into violations of entitlements on receipt of complaints or suo motu (PRS Legislative Research 2011: 8). Any complainant who is not satisfied with the orders of the district grievance redressal officer may file an appeal against such an order before the State Food Commission (PRS Legislative Research 2011: 8). The Bill also provides for the establishment of a National Food Commission at the level of central government. The National Food Commission will be charged with the responsibility of monitoring and evaluating the implementation of the Act, inquiring into violations of entitlements, and hearing appeals from the orders of the State Food Commissions (PRS Legislative Research 2011: 8). With such elaborate grievance redressal mechanisms that would be put in place with the coming into force of the National Food Security Act, there may not be any need for the grievance redressal system as proposed by the UIDAI.

In sum, there are only two problems in the PDS that Aadhaar is in a position to address. They are: the last-mile authentication and the elimination of bogus cards. Even in the case of last-mile authentication, it is seen that the other options that some state governments have implemented are cheaper, less disruptive, and more people friendly. In respect of elimination of bogus cards, there is the option of using simple biometric, which does not require access to an integrated database as the Aadhaar programme does. On the whole, the benefits that Aadhaar programme can bring to the PDS are quite modest.

CHAPTER ELEVEN

Aadhaar and the MGNREGS

The UIDAI has a four-page blueprint, indicating how it can help in the implementation of the MGNREGS. The MGNREGS is a scheme to provide legally guaranteed wage employment to the rural poor. The UIDAI blueprint states:

> The NREGS has reached several milestones towards its goal, but suffers from the same challenges like most other public projects—corruption and diversion of funds. Incidents of guaranteed minimum wages being denied to workers have been reported from nearly every state where the programme is currently functional. When implemented and adopted efficiently, the Unique Identification (UID) project possesses the power to eliminate financial exclusion, enhance accessibility, and uplift living standards for the majority poor. This can be achieved when the UID is effectively associated with pro poor welfare projects like the NREGS…The ability of UID to positively establish and authenticate the identity of every individual can overcome many of the challenges faced by targeted benefit programmes. (See 'UID and NREGA' in UIDAI 2010c: 1)

THE CHALLENGES

What are these challenges faced by the MGNREGS? The UIDAI literature lists them as: (i) payment of wages; (ii) theft from beneficiaries; (iii) theft from taxpayers; (iv) ghost beneficiaries; (v) beneficiary misuse; (vi) beneficiary management; (vii) social audit; and (viii) transparency (see 'UID and NREGA' in UIDAI 2010c: 2).

Payment of Wages

According to the UIDAI literature, payment of wages remains one of the major challenges faced by the MGNREGS. Wherever possible, these payments are supposed to be automated through local bank branches or through the post offices. In many areas, the wages continue to be paid in the form of cash. According to UIDAI, Aadhaar can fully replace the need to provide supporting documentation for the standard Know Your Customer (KYC) fields, thereby making opening of a bank account significantly simpler. Arrangements of seamlessly opening a bank account in the name of one of the family members at the time of the job card issue with embedded Aadhaar can also be explored (see 'UID and NREGA' in UIDAI 2010c: 2).

Theft from Beneficiaries

According to the UIDAI literature, one form of corruption in the implementation of MGNREGS is theft from beneficiaries, where officials underpay workers for the work they have done (see 'UID and NREGA' in UIDAI 2010c: 3). The responsibility of determining and authenticating the amount of work done has been given to official supervisors who are prone to siphoning off funds. The system of Aadhaar authentication, when introduced at the worksite, can ensure that there is a match between the hours of work claimed by the worker and the official supervising the site. The ability of Aadhaar to identify the presence of a specific individual also makes it much easier to centrally monitor delinquency among government servants who are authenticating the work and checking whether the allocated work was completed satisfactorily (see 'UID and NREGA' in UIDAI 2010c: 3).

Theft from Taxpayers

According to the UIDAI, there is another form of corruption, which is called 'theft from taxpayers', wherein officials over-report the amount of work done when they send their reports up the hierarchy. This effort can be corroborated against the wages paid to the beneficiaries, thereby establishing the execution of the project. Suspicious activities can be flagged and verified by an appropriate government official (see 'UID and NREGA' in UIDAI 2010c: 3).

Ghost Beneficiaries

The UIDAI literature claims that, if it is made a requirement that a person whose name is there in the job card will have to provide his Aadhaar number before claiming employment, the potential for ghost or fictitious beneficiaries will be eliminated (see 'UID and NREGA' in UIDAI 2010c: 3). A further reinforcement of paying wages only to real workers will happen by way of opening bank accounts with Aadhaar numbers.

Beneficiary Misuse

According to the UIDAI, Aadhaar will ensure that misuse by claiming benefits under multiple job cards is avoided (see 'UID and NREGA' in UIDAI 2010c: 3). The Aadhaar de-duplication process, which will assure a positive identification of every resident in the country, can overcome the challenge of uniquely identifying every worker.

Beneficiary Management

The UIDAI literature claims that the Aadhaar system will provide an excellent platform for managing citizens who relocate or migrate from one place to another and want to seamlessly enjoy benefits of the programme (see 'UID and NREGA' in UIDAI 2010c: 3).

Social Audit

According to the UIDAI, the village-level social audit committee can be selected after authentication with the Aadhaar database. The social audit reports filed by the village-level committees can be authenticated by the biometrics of the committee members and the social audit coordinator (see 'UID and NREGA' in UIDAI 2010c: 3).

Transparency

The UIDAI claims that all these benefits combined with the positive beneficiary identification will ensure that accurate details of benefits are published, providing greater transparency at the individual beneficiary level.

CHANGES TO BE MADE TO MGNREGS
TO MAKE IT AADHAAR FRIENDLY

The UIDAI document also lists out the changes that have to be made to the MGNREGS to make it Aadhaar friendly. The document suggests that, in order to effectively leverage the Aadhar programme, the MGNREGS will have to be modified to incorporate the Aadhaar number into beneficiary interactions (see 'UID and NREGA' in UIDAI 2010c: 1). To accommodate Aadhaar authentication, MGNREGS will need to re-engineer its business processes. The most basic requirement for the change will be in the form of incorporating the Aadhaar method of authentication (see 'UID and NREGA' in UIDAI 2010c: 1). Worksites will have to adhere to norms and procedures specified by the UIDAI for fingerprint capture and verification, and introduce a biometric authentication process at every point (see 'UID and NREGA' in UIDAI 2010c: 1). According to the UIDAI, the key areas which would require changes are:

1. The job cards will need to be updated with the Aadhaar number of all family members. This could be accomplished by issuing a new job card or by collecting and incorporating the Aadhaar numbers into the beneficiary database without reissue of the job cards.
2. The muster rolls should contain a reference to the Aadhaar number of the individual who is earning wages. This can be incorporated at the time of allocation of the workers to the work.
3. The Aadhaar number should be incorporated with the bank/post office account information of a beneficiary to which the wages are being paid. A mechanism to encourage bank/post office to incorporate the Aadhaar into their systems needs to be explored.
4. The transaction authentication against the Aadhaar database should be implemented at different touchpoints starting with the job card. The ideal situation would be the recording of attendance on a hand-held system using biometric authentication. The UIDAI will endeavour to introduce a biometric authentication

for amount withdrawal from the account into which wages are paid (see 'UID and NREGA' in UIDAI 2010c: 1–2).

Aadhaar Enrolment by MGNREGS

According to the UIDAI document, the MGNREGS provides extensive reach and citizen interaction opportunity. The MGNREGS can be used to enrol residents into the Aadhaar programme, with the state machinery acting as registrars (see 'UID and NREGA' in UIDAI 2010c: 4). A resident seeking a job card and not having an Aadhaar number can be enrolled into the Aadhaar system at the point of job card preparation. Necessary arrangements and business model for providing the necessary technology can be put in place. The enrolment into the Aadhaar programme by MGNREGS will provide, to rural citizens, a convenient mode for procuring an Aadhaar number, and also strengthen both programmes. With convenient IT-enabled systems, poor households with changes in the family structure due to death, birth, or marriage, as also relocation, will update changes to their job cards which can be reflected in the Aadhaar database (see 'UID and NREGA' in UIDAI 2010c: 4).

On the whole, the Aadhaar document points out that there are significant synergies between MGNREGS and Aadhaar, which will allow improved implementation of MGNREGS with increased transparency. The Aadhaar programme also benefits by increased enrolment and an opportunity to capture changes to the beneficiary data (see 'UID and NREGA' in UIDAI 2010c: 4).

ANALYSIS OF THE UIDAI CLAIMS

Payment of Wages

The UIDAI claims that the Aadhaar programme will help in the payment of MGNREGS wages in two ways. First, the use of biometrics will ensure that the payments reach only the true beneficiaries. Second, the Aadhaar number can fully replace the need to provide supporting documentation for the standard KYC fields, and thus make it simpler for opening a bank account.

Let us analyse the second claim first. At present, most MGNREGS workers have either an account in the bank or in the post office. This coverage was made possible as a result of a policy initiative that dates back to 2008, which required that all MGNREGS payments should be made through banks or post office accounts (Dey 2011: 124). This was a challenge because the coverage of banks and post offices is inadequate, the ones that exist are understaffed, and post offices in many parts of the country do not maintain computerized records (Khera 2011a: 38). An amendment to Schedule II of the NREGA now makes it mandatory for the state government to ensure that: every beneficiary has a bank or post office account; disbursements are made exclusively through these institutionalized channels; and the beneficiaries receive their wage entitlements within 15 days (*The Economic Times* 2011a: 9). With the universal coverage of MGNREGS workers by banks/post offices, there may not be any need for the Aadhaar number for opening a bank account.

How will Aadhaar help in the actual payment of MGNREGS wages? The UIDAI implemented a transaction pilot in Jharkhand state in December 2011 by using Aadhaar to ensure that MGNREGS payments reach only the true beneficiaries. It will be useful to look at the Jharkhand pilot.

The Jharkhand Pilot

The UIDAI and the Department of Rural Development, Government of Jharkhand, implemented a joint pilot in 12 blocks of the state (*The Economic Times* 2011j: 15). The aim of the pilot was to make sure that wages under the MGNREGS are delivered only to bonafide workers instead of being siphoned off by middlemen. The basis of worker identification is the Aadhaar number, and the idea was to link the worker's NREGA job card, the Aadhaar number, and the bank account number. In all, 174,000 persons in these 12 blocks were expected to benefit from this new process of delivering MGNREGS wages (*The Economic Times* 2011j: 15).

The pilot was to be conducted as follows. When the local administration finalizes the wage payment order, the money will be electronically transferred to the bank accounts of the workers. The workers will have to press a finger on a small fingerprint reader to validate their identity. The device will send the fingerprints to the UIDAI central server in Bangalore for real-time authentication. Once the authentication is confirmed (it takes only 0.2 seconds), the workers can then collect their wages through a common service centre (CSC), which is planned in every panchayat (*The Economic Times* 2011j: 15).

According to the UIDAI and the Department of Rural Development, Government of Jharkhand, the biometric system in Aadhaar would plug leakages. This pilot in Jharkhand, which would be expanded gradually to cover the whole state, was to be the first large-scale test of whether Aadhaar can deliver MGNREGS wages to bonafide workers (*The Economic Times* 2011j: 15).

The UIDAI Solution

The UIDAI claims that, once the local authorities finalize the payment, the Aadhaar-based solution would eliminate all human interface after that. In the pilot, when a payment advice is finalized, an electronic file containing four key details of a worker (Aadhaar number, NREGA job card number, bank account number, and amount due) will be sent to the local lead bank for MGNREGS. The bank will move the money into the worker's account. Likewise, during withdrawals, a worker will go to a CSC and quote his Aadhaar number and give his fingerprints. Once they match with the ones stored in the central UIDAI database, the CSC will make the payment. The UIDAI claims that if the biometric works, no third party can access a worker's bank account and the number of fake workers will also reduce.

The UIDAI was to monitor several parameters to test if its proposition works: what is the time taken for authentication and for a transaction; how many biometrics are rejected and how does the network behave in different ambient conditions; and what is the user experience. The Government of Jharkhand expected that if this transaction pilot succeeds, MGNREGS payments will flow faster through this new paperless process: as against one month that is taken at present, payments will reach the worker's account in one week. The Government of Jharkhand would also assess whether workers can access their bank accounts from multiple locations, and whether the new software integrates into the government MGNREGS software.

The MGNREGS Chain

Before analysing whether the Jharkhand pilot has succeeded in delivering wages to the accounts of the bonafide workers, there is a need to consider whether the proposed Aadhaar-based system of payment of wages is in a position to address the delays/irregularities/ corruption that take place in the payment of MGNREGS wages. For that, the different steps involved in the MGNREGS chain have to be studied. The MGNREGS chain has 10 distinct steps, as detailed next (the brackets show where delays/irregularities/corruption are likely to occur):

1. The worker asks his panchayat for work (the panchayat can ask the worker for bribe to provide work).
2. The panchayat assigns the worker to a project (panchayat can add fake workers to the list).
3. Local supervisor monitors the worker's attendance (the supervisor can tamper with the worker's attendance).
4. Once a week, a panchayat official quantifies work done by the worker(s) and informs the government (panchayat official can approve work done by fake workers, legitimizing them).
5. A government official visits the worksite to cross-check the information (government official can ask for a bribe to approve the project).
6. After the official's approval, the sarpanch of the village panchayat sends the worker's payment advice to the block office (the sarpanch can delay the payment advice till a bribe is paid).
7. The block office clears the worker's payment (the block office can hold back payments till a bribe is paid).
8. The sarpanch writes the worker's cheque and sends it to the bank or post office (the sarpanch can hold back the cheque till a bribe is paid).
9. Bank or post office puts the money into the worker's account.
10. The worker accesses his account (local supervisor collecting payments on behalf of the worker can retain a share—if he has inflated workdays, he can pocket the difference) (*The Economic Times* 2011j: 15).

How exactly would Aadhaar-based payment of wages help with the different steps in this chain? It would only help in respect of step 10, as the local supervisor cannot withdraw cash on behalf of workers any longer. So, in effect, the Aadhaar-based cash transfer system would be in a position to cut down on delays and tackle corruption in respect of only one step of the MGNREGS chain, while it would leave all other steps untouched (*The Economic Times* 2011j: 15).

How does the Aadhaar-based cash transfer of MGNREGS wage payment propose to deliver cash to the worker? In the transaction pilot, this is done through the CSCs (originally established as Pragya Kendras). Under the National e-Governance Plan, the Department of Information Technology is setting up 100,000 CSCs across India, each equipped with computers, a printer, and an Internet connection. The idea is that these centres would offer services in e-governance, education, and health to the villagers (*The Economic Times* 2011k: 15). Jharkhand is taking this concept a step further by equipping these centres with biometric devices and banking software that can link up with multiple banks. It is expected that these centres will offer better reach than banks. As against 1,705 bank branches in the state, Jharkhand has 4,500 panchayats (*The Economic Times* 2011k: 15).

The CSCs are open from 8 a.m. to 8 p.m. They will work online and use biometric authentication for transactions. So, if a worker wants to withdraw money, he will come to the centre and give his fingerprints. The fingerprints will be authenticated real time, using Aadhaar, and the transaction will be approved. Jharkhand is using a public–private partnership model: the central government provides land and infrastructure; and private companies handle software, staffing, training, and operations. Districts are assigned to private companies through a tendering process. Jharkhand has 24 districts. United Telecom Limited (UTL), a Bangalore-based IT company, has been given 15 districts, totaling 2,943 panchayats, and the remaining nine districts are divided between FINO and Zoom Developers. However, the contract of Zoom Developers has been cancelled in 2011 (*The Economic Times* 2011k: 15).

The Government of Jharkhand plans to make all MGNREGS payments through these CSCs. The UTL will have to generate the working capital for such transactions. According to the UTL, it will earn 0.5 per cent as commission from banks: of this, 60–70 per cent will go to the staff of the CSC and the rest will go to UTL (*The Economic Times* 2011k: 15). The services of these CSCs are proposed to be used for making payments for other government schemes, too. As Ajoy Kumar Singh, NREGA Commissioner, Government of Jharkhand, says, 'The centres being Aadhaar-enabled will help provide coverage of all government services (like pensions and Indira Awaas Yojana)' (*The Economic Times* 2011k: 15).

The CSCs in Jharkhand will be in the place of business correspondents (BCs). At present, BCs deliver the last-mile services. The BC company, usually a private one, which wins the contract from the bank to deliver the last-mile services to the village, appoints an agent (BC) to each village. According to government sources, the BC system has two drawbacks. First, the BC system ties the villagers to one BC posted to the village (appointed by the BC company) and to one BC company. In that sense, the BC becomes a power centre in the village. If the villagers can operate their bank accounts from another source, this will reduce the risk of the BC becoming a power centre in the village. Second, the banks and the BC companies delay MGNREGS payments to the beneficiaries for at least a month so that they can earn interest income on the amount. Under the CSC system, it is claimed that the villagers would receive the MGNREGS payments much faster (*The Economic Times* 2011k: 15).

There are drawbacks with the CSC system, too. In Jharkhand, each panchayat has five to 10 villages in its jurisdiction. Since only one CSC is being planned for each panchayat, workers have to travel up to about 10 km to access the CSC. On the other hand, the BC system has one BC in each village, and therefore, has an advantage over the CSC. The other drawback is that Jharkhand's experience with Pragya Kendras, which are now being upgraded into CSCs, has not been particularly encouraging. In response to a question in the Jharkhand Legislative Assembly in August 2011, the IT department of the Government of Jharkhand admitted that many of the 2,817 Pragya Kendras were unable to deliver services (*The Economic Times* 2011k: 15). Ajoy Kumar Singh, the NREGA Commissioner of Jharkhand government, says that these centres face three issues, connectivity, electricity, and adequate infrastructure, and fixing them will take 12–18 months (*The Economic Times* 2011k: 15).

How has the Transaction Pilot Worked on the Ground?

The assessment by the official agencies is complimentary. The NREGA commissioner of Jharkhand government says that 'Against one month now, payments will reach workers' accounts in one week'

(Bhatti *et al.* 2012a: 10). Media reports are also appreciative of the strong gains made by the pilot, and one of them says, 'As the new system ensures payment of wages within a week, the demand for work under the MGNREGS has gone up. Consequently, migration has been checked, families have been reunited and, no less important, some workers have a saving in the bank' (Bhatti *et al.* 2012a: 10). However, an independent evaluation carried out in the field had the following observations to make.

> We headed for the Ratu Block in Ranchi district, the source of most of these [media] reports. It was, at that time (early March), one of the five Blocks where the experiment was launched. On arrival we found that only three gram panchayats (GPs) were involved out of 14 in Ratu Block. The showpiece appeared to be Tigra GP, but it turned out that even there, only one worksite had enjoyed the blessings of Aadhaar-enabled wage payments. In the three GPs together, the system had been implemented in five worksites, employing a total of about 50 workers. We managed to interview 42 of them, with the help of a small team of student volunteers...
>
> [In] Ratu, some aspects of the experiment were a little farcical. For instance, on one occasion, workers from Tigra were asked to collect their wages 10 kilometres away, so that Aadhaar-enabled payments could be done in front of a visiting minister. On a more positive note, the system seemed to work, at least under close supervision. Further, most of the workers had a positive view of it. They appreciated being able to collect their wages closer to their homes, without the hassles of queuing in overcrowded banks or depending on corrupt middlemen to extract their wages from the post office. They did not fully understand the new technology, but nor were they afraid or suspicious of it.
>
> Having said this, there were problems too. Depending on fingerprint recognition, internet connectivity, and the goodwill of the BC created new vulnerabilities. Fingerprint recognition problems alone affected 12 out of 42 respondents. Some workers did not have a UID number, and some had an ID number but no Aadhaar-enabled account. None of them had received bank passbooks making it difficult for them to withdraw their wages from the bank when the Aadhaar system failed. Four respondents were yet to find a way of getting hold of their wages. Otherwise, the payment of wages was reasonably timely, but this had more to do with intensive supervision than with Aadhaar. (Bhatti *et al.* 2012a: 10)

There are several inputs regarding the areas where the use of Aadhaar has been problematic. First, there are fingerprint recognition problems. Second, it is tough on workers if they have to travel quite a few kilometres on foot to collect their payments. Third, the Aadhaar system of real-time online authentication is not likely to work in places where there is little or no mobile phone network (connectivity). Fourth, it has to be ensured that all the workers have bank passbooks; otherwise, it becomes difficult for the workers to get their money from the bank in case there is a failure of the Aadhaar system.

The technical results of the pilot were declared in 2012, and they reveal serious gaps in authentication. The transaction pilot to pay MGNREGS wages in Jharkhand showed only 60 per cent success in the first try and 90 per cent in the third (S. Singh 2012a: 13). According to the UIDAI, the shortfalls in the pilot can be attributed to multiple reasons, the main reasons being: that of breaking of the mobile Internet connection between the fingerprint reader and the central server; the machine operator placing the finger incorrectly on the fingerprint reader; dirty fingerprint reader, dirty finger; and fingerprints not being taken properly during enrolment (S. Singh 2012a: 13). Let us analyse the reasons for the shortfalls. Reasons such as the operator placing the finger incorrectly on the fingerprint reader, the dirty fingerprint reader, dirty finger, and fingerprints not being taken properly can all be remedied with the exercise of due diligence on the part of the workers or with the UIDAI tweaking its processes. But if the reason is that of breaking of the mobile Internet connection between the fingerprint reader and the central server, this is beyond the control of the UIDAI. As a matter of fact, the UIDAI cannot do anything about GPRS connectivity (S. Singh 2012a: 13).

That is why at least three ministries in the central government (Ministry of Rural Development, Ministry of Food and Civil Supplies, and Ministry of Labour) have serious reservations with real-time, biometric authentication as in the case of Aadhaar being used in respect of government schemes (Rajshekhar 2012b: 13). A joint secretary in the Ministry of Rural Development points out that connectivity is unreliable in rural areas, especially in villages below the level of the headquarters of the panchayat (Rajshekhar 2012b: 13). He says: 'I don't see this changing for the next five to ten years.

For this reason, the UIDAI authentication system doesn't meet our requirements' (Rajshekhar 2012b: 13).

In fact, these three ministries prefer offline, smart card-based authentication. That is why the Ministry of Food and Civil Supplies ignored the *Report of the Task Force on an IT Strategy for PDS and an Implementable Solution for the Direct Transfer of Subsidy for Food and Kerosene*, submitted by Nandan Nilekani's Task Force in October 2011 (Rajshekhar 2012b: 13). This report recommended the adoption of real-time, biometric authentication in the PDS. Interestingly, the Ministry of Food and Civil Supplies has framed fresh guidelines for computerization based on a platform developed by the NIC, which uses offline, smart card-based authentication (Rajshekhar 2012b: 13). But, according to the UIDAI, the offline, smart card-based authentication is 'yesterday's technology' as it is not real time (Rajshekhar 2012b: 13). As the UIDAI sources say: 'Mobile connectivity is available across most of the country. For the sake of a small part of the country not being connected already, why would you not roll out an advanced technology across the rest of the country' (Rajshekhar 2012b: 13).

There is no doubt that the biometric route is useful for ensuring that the payments reach only the true beneficiaries. But it is a question of choosing between two biometric options: an offline smart card-based authentication; and real-time authentication as in the case of Aadhaar. The point made by the UIDAI is not particularly valid in the case of MGNREGS because it is mostly in the villages with poor or no mobile connectivity (which the UIDAI euphemistically calls 'a small part of the country') that the implementation of the MGNREGS is so vital because it constitutes the lifeline for the poor.

It is in this context that observations of Nikhil Dey, an activist who has spent a considerable part of his adult life in the villages of Rajasthan working with wage employment programmes, are important. According to Nikhil Dey (2011: 124), it would make more sense to have a localized biometric system rather than linking up with a centralized server as Aadhaar programme proposes to do. A local system can deal with anomalies that a centralized system cannot. From the point of view of MGNREGS, linking it to a central server has no particular merit, while a localized biometric system is certainly beneficial. There is a practical consideration, too.

When biometric does not work, which is not uncommon where work makes fingerprints 'noisy' and cuts and bruises abound, there is a provision for a 'manual override' (Dey 2011: 124). This may create opportunities for tampering with the payments, but that will certainly be a better option than no payment at all. If the payment of MGNREGS wages is linked to the central system without whose recognition the worker would not get paid (as the Aadhaar-enabled payment system proposes), that would leave workers with fingerprint recognition problems in dire straits (Dey 2011: 124). While implementing the MGNREGS, it has generally been the experience that machines, including computers, should be used only in areas where there is a manual backup, or where an alternative exists, because the payment of wages to poor MGNREGS workers cannot be deferred because the technology or devices malfunction (Dey 2011: 124).

Theft from Beneficiaries and Taxpayers

The UIDAI literature claims that Aadhaar can prevent underpayment to MGNREGS workers. According to the UIDAI literature, the system of Aadhaar authentication, when introduced at the worksite, can ensure that there is a match between the hours of work claimed by the worker and the official supervising the site. The ability of Aadhaar to identify the presence of a specific individual also makes it much easier to centrally monitor delinquency among government servants who are authenticating the work and check whether the allocated work was completed satisfactorily. The UIDAI literature also claims that Aadhaar can prevent the theft that takes place when officials over-report the amount of work done. Aadhaar can do this by corroborating the effort against the wages paid to the beneficiaries, thereby enabling flagging of suspicious activity and verification by an appropriate government official.

Presumably, what the UIDAI literature has in mind is the use of biometric checking of attendance with Global Positioning System (GPS) coordinates. We have to consider what would happen in adverse field conditions if biometric is used to check attendance. The use of Aadhaar authentication to check attendance at worksites opens up the possibility of points in time when the machine does not work on-site, not having an alternative available in a remote area, and the whole system being thrown into disarray (Dey 2011: 124). In fact, the suggestion of having biometric checking of attendance with GPS coordinates would only mean that MGNREGS worksites in remote, far-flung regions of the country with poor or no connectivity have to be shut down.

Another claim that the UIDAI literature makes is that Aadhaar can help deal with corruption in the implementation of MGNREGS. Interestingly, even in Jharkhand, where the UIDAI is associated with the implementation of MGNREGS on a pilot basis, the use of Aadhaar for checking corruption is not a part of the agenda. In fact, the Government of Jharkhand is planning to set up a panchayat-level association of MGNREGS workers to talk to the local officials in order to take care of the corruption angle. What is planned is to set up *mazdoor* associations consisting of MGNREGS workers at the panchayat level. Ajoy Kumar Singh, the NREGA Commissioner of the Government of Jharkhand, says, 'This is a forum where workers can talk with local officials about their problems. This should also sizably take care of the corruption we see' (Dey 2011: 124).

In any case, the big corruption story in the implementation of MGNREGS is about material. The usual practice is to use 20 bags of cement and book for 100 bags, or buy cement at Rs 300 a bag and show it in the books as much more. Aadhaar may find it difficult to control this kind of corruption. In some places where the MGNREGS is being implemented, the details, such as the names of all the MGNREGS workers, how many days they have worked, and how much they have earned for doing that work, are painted on the wall of the village panchayat office. The wall also has a summary and details of materials for all the works in the village, making local checks possible. What is needed in MGNREGS is for people themselves to monitor their own works and development expenditure. A top-down solution like Aadhaar may not work in such a context. As Nikhil Dey (2011: 123) suggests, what is needed is not the government watching the people, but people watching every paisa of expenditure.

Ghost Beneficiaries and Beneficiary Misuse

The UIDAI literature claims that, if the worker whose name figures in a job card can provide his Aadhaar identification before claiming employment, the potential for ghost or fictitious beneficiaries would have been eliminated. It also claims that Aadhaar will ensure that misuse by claiming benefits under multiple job cards is avoided. The Aadhaar de-duplication process, which will assure a positive identification of every resident in the country, can provide the solution by its capability of uniquely identifying every MGNREGS worker.

Perhaps, the biometric verification through de-duplication that Aadhaar offers can reduce the number of fake workers, but there is always the possibility of officials at the village level coaxing non-MGNREGS workers to share wages in return for adding their names to the muster rolls. In fact, there is a much simpler solution for eliminating fake workers from the list. This can be done by painting the details of MGNREGS on the village wall, that show the names the MGNREGS workers, how many days they have worked, and how much they have earned for doing that work. The wall in the village is effective in the context of fakes and duplicates. The information on the wall will take care of ghosts and duplicates in the system by leaving it to the vigilance of the villagers to pick up the fake workers (Dey 2011: 123). If the NREGA job card is not filled as required, then the wall acts not only as a fallback for the worker but also as a collective vigilance mechanism. By putting the information on the wall, the information would have been put into the hands of the people who will know how to fight irregularities and corruption at the village level. If people are to act as a collective vigilance mechanism, it can be done only by giving them information, and the important thing is to ensure that the information is localized. The use of the Aadhaar would mean taking the localized information away from the people and putting it in a computer outside the reach of the people, and that may not be the best way to do things in a local setting.

In fact, where the MGNREGS has been particularly successful is in the area of giving job cards very quickly, unlike the ration cards in the PDS. There were very few exclusion errors in the case of job cards. This was because the process was very simple and followed no complicated technology. The villagers lined up, were identified by the sarpanch, and got their job cards, which even had a photograph of the villager. In cases where there were no photographs, the villagers were allowed to work. This was because of the simple fact that in a village scenario, everyone knows the other's name and face. Identification has never been a problem in the village setting.

What the UIDAI literature suggests is that the MGNREGS is to be appropriately modified to incorporate the Aadhaar number into beneficiary interactions. It is suggested that, in order to accommodate Aadhaar authentication, the MGNREGS has to re-engineer its business processes: worksites adhering to norms and procedures specified by the UIDAI for fingerprint capture and verification; and the introduction of a robust authentication process at every point. The re-engineering will mean that the job cards have to be updated with Aadhaar numbers of all family members; the muster rolls should contain a reference to the Aadhaar number of the person who is earning wages; the Aadhaar number is to be incorporated with the bank/post office account information of the person who is being paid wages; and the transaction authentication is to be done against the Aadhaar database at different beneficiary touchpoints, starting with the job card.

Such elaborate re-engineering of the business processes in MGNREGS to make it Aadhaar friendly is not going to be an easy proposition. Let us start with the MGNREGS job card. For the job card to have the Aadhaar number, it will mean that each beneficiary has to be registered with the Aadhaar programme. The biggest problem with the Aadhaar programme is the registration process. If the Aadhaar enrolment does not cover everyone who may seek a job under the MGNREGS, and the Aadhaar is used as a tool for determining entitlements, it will become a tool of exclusion (Dey 2011: 123). The NREGA gives everyone a right to demand work and receive work within 15 days. Making the realization of that right dependent on the whims of a technology that relies on too many external variables and the fancies of its expert structure will, in effect, amount to taking away that right.

Regrettably, it will open the door for manipulations of power (Dey 2011: 124). Because all MGNREGS systems are in the hands of the panchayat and local officers, it has made it difficult for anyone in authority to deny people their right to a job card, without which the guarantee to get work cannot be exercised. When an external technology like that of the Aadhaar is introduced, the solutions to errors and problems are no longer local and the entire system comes into question. The Aadhaar programme has to guarantee 100 per cent coverage, without any exception, before it can be considered for use in the NREGA framework; the fact remains that, even when one eligible person is left out or denied the guarantee to work for not having an Aadhaar number, it will signal the failure of the rights-based NREGA.

The apprehension that the linking of MGNREGS to Aadhaar may cause major disruptions in the implementation of MGNREGS has been a source of worry for many people. In fact, this was the reason that prompted more than 100 individuals from across the world to write a letter urging to keep Aadhaar out of MGNREGS (*The Hindu* 2010d). The signatories to this letter included Nikhil Dey, Aruna Roy, and Shankar Singh (Mazdoor Kisan Shakti Sangathan); Jayati Ghosh (Professor, Centre for Economic Studies and Planning [CESP]/ School of Social Science [SSS], Jawaharlal Nehru University [JNU]); Jean Dreze (Honorary Professor, University of Allahabad); Kamal Mitra Chenoy (Professor, JNU); Reetika Khera (Visitor, Centre for Development Economics); R. Ramakumar (Associate Professor, Tata Institute for Social Sciences); Mallika Sarabhai (Citizens Resource and Action Network Initiative [CRANTI]); and others. The letter said:

> The undersigned demand that the plan to link MGNREGS to Aadhaar be revoked immediately. This is an extremely dangerous move that threatens to cause havoc in MGNREGS's fragile structure.
>
> The Ministry of Rural Development has put out a tender (dated October 11, 2010) worth Rs. 2,162 crore to engage 'service providers' for MGNREGS under a 'public– private partnership' model. The contract includes 'UIDAI compliant enrolment of job card holders under MGNREGS scheme', 'Recording...data in the field such as biometric attendance at the worksite with GPS coordinates...and updation of centralized MIS,' and similar measures.
>
> Clearly, the Ministry intends to link the issue of new job cards to UID enrolment in the States. Job cards issued in 2006 are due to expire in 2011. Job cards are required to claim employment under the MGNREGS. If the issue of new job cards is linked to UID enrolment, there is a danger of creating a jam that would disrupt the programme. The process of job cards renewal, in any case a slow process, will be further slowed down. Many people are likely to be denied their entitlement to 100 days of work as they will be without a job card. Further, in spite of hiring of 'service providers', the entire administrative machinery is likely to be diverted into capturing of

biometrics or supervising 'service providers'. The scale of MGNREGS works is bound to suffer. This would be a gross injustice to NREGA workers, who are already deprived of their basic entitlements.

The proposal of 'biometric attendance at the worksite with GPS coordinates' is completely impractical—many MGNREGS worksites are in remote areas with poor or no connectivity. Does that mean those worksites will close down?

We do welcome the use of technology provided that it enhances transparency, empowers labourers and is cost effective. Such technology has been used with success in Tamil Nadu. For instance, it combines SMS reports on daily attendance with random spot checks to curb the problem of fake muster roll entries. Localized use of biometrics, independent of UID, to speed up payments can be considered. Biometrics and UID are not the same. In Rajasthan, simpler measures have been put in place, such as 'transparency walls' where all job card holders in the Gram Panchayat are listed along with days of work, allowing people to monitor implementation.

There are many problems with the implementation of MGNREGS which need the urgent attention of the Ministry. These include the non-payment of minimum wages, delays in wage payment, insufficient scale of MGNREGS works, discrimination against Dalits and women, and so on.

We therefore demand that neither MGNREGS employment nor wage payments be linked to UID enrolment. Employment of 100 days under MGNREGS is the only universal entitlement that the rural poor enjoy. It should not be jeopardized by the introduction of disruptive technology under pressure from corporate and security lobbies. (*The Hindu* 2010d)

Beneficiary Management

The UIDAI literature claims that Aadhaar will provide an excellent platform for managing citizens who relocate or migrate from one place to another and want to seamlessly enjoy benefits of the programme. But this aspect has already been taken care of by the 'Operational Guidelines' for the implementation of the NREGA. The guidelines provide:

5.1   NREGA Household

5.1.2   All adult members of the household who register may apply for work. To Register, they have to be local residents: 'Local' implies residing within the Gram Panchayat. This includes those that may migrated some time ago but may return.

5.2.7 To allow maximum opportunities to families that may migrate, registration will be open throughout the year at the Gram Panchayat office during working hours. (Ministry of Rural Development 2008: 20–1)

So, the guidelines do provide for allowing maximum opportunities for families that migrate. In any case, the objective of MGNREGS is to provide work to persons from a particular panchayat in that panchayat only. It does not apply to persons who relocate or migrate from one place to another place. We need to appreciate that the idea of MGNREGS is to reduce outward migration from the village.

Transparency

The UIDAI literature claims that positive beneficiary identification through Aadhaar will ensure accurate details of benefits. These details can be published providing greater transparency at the individual beneficiary level. We need to look at this claim in the context of whether the transparency safeguards available in the NREGA are adequate or need to be supplemented by Aadhaar.

The Act itself makes a provision relating to transparency and accountability. Section 23 of the Act reads:

1. The District Programme Coordinator and all implementing agencies in the District shall be responsible for the proper utilization and management of the funds placed at their disposal for the purpose of implementing a Scheme.
2. The state government may prescribe the manner of maintaining proper books and accounts of employment of labourers and the expenditure incurred in connection with the implementation of the provisions of this Act and the Schemes made hereunder.
3. The state government may, by rules, determine the arrangements to be made for the proper execution of schemes and programmes under the schemes and to ensure transparency and accountability at all levels in the implementation of the schemes.
4. All payments of wages in cash and unemployment allowances shall be made directly to the person concerned and in the presence of independent persons of the community on pre-announced dates.

5. If any dispute or complaint arises concerning the implementation of a Scheme by the Gram Panchayat, the matter shall be referred to the Programme Officer.

6. The Programme Officer shall enter every complaint in a complaint register maintained by him and shall dispose of the disputes and complaints within seven days of its receipt and in case it relates to a matter to be resolved by any other authority it shall be forwarded to such authority under intimation to the complainant (Ministry of Law and Justice 2005: 10).

Section 13 of the Schedule I to the Act reads, 'Every scheme shall contain adequate provisions for ensuring transparency and accountability at all levels of implementation'. (Ministry of Law and Justice 2005: 13)

In fact, the NREGA is a unique piece of legislation in the sense that it provides for mechanisms for transparency and accountability. For example, it provides extensive inbuilt transparency safeguards with respect to both documents and processes:

Documents: Job cards recording entitlements (in the custody of workers), written application for employment, Muster Rolls, Measurement Books and Asset Registers

Processes: Acceptance of employment application, issue of dated receipts, time bound work allocation and wage payment, citizen information boards at worksites, vigilance monitoring committees, regular block, district and state level inspections and social audits. (Ministry of Rural Development 2008: 4)

Complete transparency in the process of administration and decision making is ensured by the Act through casting an obligation on the government to suo motu give to people full access to all the relevant information. The Act enjoins that the information about works should be displayed in the local language in the proforma in Annexure B-13 at the worksite and in proforma B-14 at a prominent place in gram panchayat (Ministry of Rural Development 2008: 61).

The village wall is the perfect example of how transparency and accountability can be ensured. Details such as names of all the MGNREGS workers, how many days they have worked, and how much they have earned for doing that work are painted on the wall. The wall also has a summary of details of materials for all works in the village. This is the best safeguard possible to ensure transparency at the level of the individual beneficiary. There is no way that Aadhaar-based authentication can provide stronger transparency and accountability safeguards. These transparency and accountability safeguards have been consciously designed for catering to situations in which the solutions can be kept at the same local level that gives rise to the problems. In contrast, Aadhaar will provide centralized solutions, and that is not what the Act intends.

Clearly, we do not need Aadhaar for better implementation of MGNREGS: it will only clutter up things without being useful. As Nikhil Dey, who has been involved with the implementation of MGNREGS at the village level in Rajasthan for many years now, says:

> To those who are watching the process from close, it seems clear that the NREGA does not need the UID; it is the UID that is trying to piggyback on the NREGA despite its potential to create inefficiency and confusion. Something like the NREGA requires simple, localized systems in the hands of the people. There is nothing what the UID provides that cannot be done as competently and in a more reliable fashion. In the NREGA, where people's hands are callused with work, where worksites cover some of the most extreme climatic conditions, where connectivity is at its most precarious, where dust and heat can ruin any machine and where the UID can make the system completely machine-dependent, it seems clear that the dependency on machine-based technology, which spells potential disaster, should be avoided. (Dey 2011: 124)

As this analysis shows, it is only in respect of payment of wages that Aadhaar can help. The Aadhaar system of real-time, online authentication can ensure that wage payments reach the true beneficiaries. But the fact remains that many villages where MGNREGS is being implemented are in remote, far-flung, and interior areas, with poor or no mobile connectivity. In these areas, the Aadhaar system of real-time, online authentication will not work. What it means is that Aadhaar's applicability in respect of MGNREGS will be limited to worksites which boast of mobile connectivity. Such limited applicability is unacceptable because legally guaranteed wage employment that the NREGA offers is the only universal entitlement that the rural poor enjoy, and any form of dilution will amount to denial of this universal right. So, at their best, the gains from Aadhaar in the implementation of MGNREGS can only be modest.

CHAPTER TWELVE

Aadhaar and Public Health

જ્જી

The UIDAI document that envisions a role for Aadhaar in public health starts with an explanation of how every citizen in India must have a strong incentive or a 'killer application' to go and get an Aadhaar, which is the demand-side pull for the Aadhaar number (see 'UID and Public Health' in UIDAI 2010c: 1). According to the document, the demand-side pull for this needs to be created de novo or fostered on existing platform by the respective ministries (see 'UID and Public Health' in UIDAI 2010c: 1). If the various ministries can conceptualize key applications that leverage existing government entitlement schemes such as the MGNREGS and PDS, it will not only help the ministries to establish mechanisms that generate the demand-side pull, but will also build support from the ministries for the Aadhaar programme even as it gets off the ground (see 'UID and Public Health' in UIDAI 2010c: 1).

The UIDAI document characterizes health and health-related schemes as such killer applications for the Aadhaar programme (see 'UID and Public Health' in UIDAI 2010c: 1). According to the document, after years of neglect, public health in India is witnessing a revolution in terms of:

1. greater commitment towards government financing of public and primary health care;
2. pressure to meet the Millennium Development Goals; and
3. consequent creation of large supply platforms at national levels, such as the National Rural Health Mission and Rashtriya Swasthya

Bima Yojana (RSBY), and complementary state-level initiatives, such as the Rajiv Arogyasri Insurance Scheme in Andhra Pradesh (see 'UID and Public Health' in UIDAI 2010c: 1).

AADHAAR'S ROLE IN PUBLIC HEALTH

According to the document, the major challenges in public health today include:

1. lack of detailed denominator (that is, target population to be covered)–focused services delivery by the government's rural and urban health care systems at district and sub-district levels;
2. poor tracking of health conditions by the International Classification of Diseases (ICD)-10 system; and
3. lack of ability to roll out, at scale, expansion of ambitious national health insurance schemes like the RSBY (see 'UID and Public Health' in UIDAI 2010c: 1).

The UIDAI document also mentions that routine health systems (including vital registration, cause of death identification, disease reporting) that capture and track the morbidity and mortality due to various disease conditions are critical to improving public health outcomes, including the expectancy (see 'UID and Public Health' in UIDAI 2010c: 2). Currently, infrequent national or state surveys are the major mode of capturing data on infectious disease conditions. However, chronic or lifestyle diseases are not captured in any meaningful way even through surveys (see 'UID and Public Health' in UIDAI 2010c: 2). These pose new challenges for an already strained public health system. According to the UIDAI, an integrated routine health system that can capture and track population-level disease conditions, by linking citizen IDs with hospital or other medical facility records generated through facility visits, can: (i) inform the public health system of the prevalence of various routine disease conditions; and (ii) help prepare the health system to respond to unforeseen epidemics (see 'UID and Public Health' in UIDAI 2010c: 2).

The UIDAI document talks about the role that Aadhaar can play in the implementation of RSBY. According to the document, the launch of RSBY by the Ministry of Labour is a great example of a killer application waiting for a platform (see 'UID and Public Health' in UIDAI 2010c: 2). It is intended to eventually provide, in some form or the other, in partnership with states, the country's entire population with insurance coverage. The RSBY does include the provision of a card and supports a putatively large but very simple field registration effort. The UIDAI claims that partnering with this scheme: (i) will provide an additional and fresh, unlikely to be duplicated, source of registrations for Aadhaar; and (ii) more importantly, in conjunction with linkages to a routine health information system, can improve public health in terms of efficiency and outcomes (see 'UID and Public Health' in UIDAI 2010c: 2).

ANALYSIS OF THE UIDAI CLAIMS

The UIDAI document states: 'In health, there is a cumulative historic gap both in terms of demand and supply. The UID could further help catalyze a revolution in India's health outcomes' (see 'UID and Public Health' in UIDAI 2010c: 1). Dr Mohan Rao, Professor in Centre of Social Medicine and Community Health, JNU, understands this statement to mean that Aadhaar can help create a 'demand' for public health care in the country (Rao 2011: 20). If that is what it means, it will be necessary to analyse the present health care scenario in the country in order to ascertain what is the unmet demand and how Aadhaar can generate a demand for public health.

As regards the public health scenario in the country, at present, India is in the midst of an epidemiological and demographic transition with an increasing burden of chronic diseases, decline in mortality and fertility rates, and ageing of the population (Planning Commission 2008b: 61). An estimated 23.1 million people in the country live with human immunodeficiency virus (HIV)/acquired immune deficiency syndrome (AIDS), a communicable disease (Planning Commission 2008b: 61). Malnutrition affects a large proportion of children. An unacceptably high proportion of the population continues to suffer and die from new diseases that are emerging. Non-communicable diseases such as cardiovascular diseases, cancer, blindness, and mental illnesses have imposed the chronic disease burden on the already overstretched health care system of the country (Selvaraj and Karan 2009: 55).

Health Care for the Poor

Health care for the urban and rural poor is analysed separately here because they differ in terms of coverage and quality. Projections of population in urban areas show that growth of slums is expected to surpass the capacity of civic authorities to respond to their health needs. According to 2001 census, 4.26 crore people lived in urban slums spread over 640 towns and cities. The number is growing. Lack of water and sanitation and the high population density in the slums have been responsible for rapid spread of infections. The slum settlements have high incidence of vector-borne diseases, asthma, tuberculosis, malaria, coronary heart diseases, diabetes, et cetera. Poor housing conditions, exposure to heat and cold, air and water pollution, and occupational hazards add to the environmental risks for the poor. The poor in urban areas are vulnerable because they have no backup savings, food stocks, or social support systems to tide over the crisis of illness. Despite the presence of many private and government hospitals in urban areas, a large chunk of the homeless and those living in slums or temporary settlements are left out of the health care system.

In the rural areas of the country, the position is even worse. A quarter of the districts in the country account for 40 per cent of the poor, over half of the malnourished population, and nearly two-thirds of those afflicted by malaria, kala-azar, leprosy, infant and maternal mortality (Planning Commission 2008b: 60–1). Public health care system in rural areas in many states and most regions is in shambles. The existing health infrastructure in the rural areas, by way of sub-centres, primary health centres, and community health centres, is woefully inadequate: the shortfall is estimated to be of the order of 13.16 per cent at the sub-centre level; 18.46 per cent at the primary health centre level; and 40.87 per cent at the community health centre level (Planning Commission 2008b: 64). The shortage at the community health centre level is adversely affecting the secondary health care and linkages. To compound the problem, there are a large number of vacancies in positions of doctors, nurses, and paramedical personnel.

People generally tend to avoid the public health care system if they can. There are a variety of reasons for this: lack of drugs; lack of medical staff; having to pay bribes for services; inconvenient hours; and rude personnel (Rao 2011: 20). Only the poor, especially women, Scheduled Castes (SCs), and Scheduled Tribes (STs), who cannot afford to go to private health care providers, are forced to go to the public health care system. This explains why the utilization of public health facilities for outpatient and inpatient care is so abysmally low. The National Sample Survey Organization (NSSO) data (1986–2004) clearly show a major decline in utilization of public health facilities and a corresponding increase in the utilization of private health care providers in both rural and urban areas (Planning Commission 2008b: 68). With the exception of a few states, there has been very low utilization for outpatient care as well. In 2004, public sector provision of outpatient health care accounted for approximately one-fifth of the total outpatient care, as against over one-fourth (26 per cent) in 1987–8 (Selvaraj and Karan 2009: 56).

With respect to hospitalization care, the share of public health care, which used to cater to around 60 per cent in 1987–8, declined to approximately 40 per cent in 2004 (Selvaraj and Karan 2009: 57). Altogether, currently public sector health care provides care to only 26 per cent of the ailing episodes in India (Selvaraj and Karan 2009: 57). This shift shows people's lack of trust in the public health care system. Critical shortage of health personnel, inadequate incentives, poor working conditions, apathy in posting doctors in rural areas, absenteeism, long wait, inconvenient hospital hours, poor outreach, time of service, insensitivity to local needs, and inadequate planning, management, and monitoring of services/facilities are the main reasons for low utilization of public health facilities (Planning Commission 2008b: 68).

In contrast, the growth of private health sector in India has been impressive in terms of both provisioning and financing. There is great diversity in the composition of private health care providers, which ranges from voluntary, not-for-profit, for-profit, corporate, trusts, stand-alone specialists, diagnostic services to pharmacy shops and a range of highly qualified to unqualified providers, each addressing different market segments. The growth of private hospitals and diagnostic centres was encouraged by the government by offering them tax exemptions and land at concessional rates in return for provision for free treatment for the poor at a certain proportion of outpatients and inpatients. Apart from subsidies, private corporate hospitals receive huge amount of public funds in the form of reimbursements from public sector undertakings, central government, and state governments for treating their employees. Although the growth of private health care sector has been spectacular both in terms of provisioning and financing, the fact remains that the majority of private providers in rural areas are not fully qualified. Moreover, the private provision of health care in rural areas is fraught with problems of quality and lack of basic amenities at health care centres (Selvaraj and Karan 2009: 57). Many small, private providers have poor knowledge base and tend to follow irrational, ineffective, and sometimes even harmful, practices for treating minor ailments. A large proportion of these private providers are not registered, and the few who are registered, are subject to self-regulation under the aegis of their respective State Medical Councils. In practice, however, regulation of these private health professionals is weak and close to non-existent (Planning Commission 2008b: 67).

The cost of health care in the private sector is substantially higher than in the public health care sector. According to NSSO (60th Round), the average expenditure for hospitalized treatment in government hospital was less than half that of private hospital in rural areas and about one-third in urban areas (Planning Commission 2008b: 68). However, the cost of treatment has significantly increased over the years both for inpatients and outpatients. The real cost of hospitalization has risen from less than Rs 1,000 in 1986–7 to approximately Rs 2,000 in 2004 at real prices (Selvaraj and Karan 2009: 58). Similarly, per episode cost of treatment for outpatient has increased in real terms from Rs 33 in 1986–7 to Rs 68 in 2004 (Selvaraj and Karan 2009: 58). The cost of treatment has increased both in private and public health care. However, the increase has been much faster in the former. Per episode hospitalization cost has accelerated by more than 100 per cent in the private sector, while cost of escalation has been much slower in the public sector (Selvaraj and Karan 2009: 58).

It may not be entirely correct to assume that the fast-growing private sector can adequately fill the gaps created by the declining public sector health care system. Apart from the quality of private health care, there remains a serious concern about the affordability of and access to private health care providers (Selvaraj and Karan 2009: 57). This has repercussions for equity and access. As per the NSSO (60th Round), during 2004, 24 per cent of the episodes of ailments among the poor were untreated in rural areas and 22 per cent in urban areas (Planning Commission 2008b: 68). Lack of finances was cited as the reason by 28 per cent of persons with untreated episodes in rural areas and 20 per cent in urban areas (Planning Commission 2008b: 68). Though the proportion of non-treated ailments has remained largely constant over the years, among the reasons for no formal treatment, unavailability of health care services and high costs of treatment have been on the rise in the last decades (Selvaraj and Karan 2009: 57). While inaccessibility of medical facilities has been responsible for untreated ailments in a little over 12 per cent in rural areas, financial reasons account for 28 per cent of persons with untreated ailments (Selvaraj and Karan 2009: 57). This proportion was only 15 per cent in 1986–7, which indicates much better access that the poor had to public health care facilities in rural areas at that time (Selvaraj and Karan 2009: 57).

The rising cost of health care has serious implications for living standards of households. Recent evidence shows that a large proportion of households are required to pay for their medical needs much beyond their paying capacity, particularly when incurring expenditure of catastrophic nature (Selvaraj and Karan 2009: 57). Studies show that 2.4 per cent of the population was pushed below the poverty line due to huge expenditure incurred for hospitalization in 1995–6 (Selvaraj and Karan 2009: 57). During 1999–2000, approximately 32–7 million people in India were pushed below the poverty line due to high out-of-pocket payments for health care (Selvaraj and Karan 2009: 57). In any case, in the wake of escalating health care costs largely led by private health care providers, the impact of both catastrophic events and poverty on the households has been substantial and rising. The numbers are telling: 70 per cent of Indians spend all their income on health care and buying drugs; 47 per cent of rural Indians and 31 per cent of urban Indians finance their health care needs by loans or sale of assets; 30 per cent of people in rural India do not visit hospitals because of high medical expenses; and 37 million people fall below the poverty line because of health care payments (*The Economic Times* 2012a: 15).

This is the present status of health care as available in public and private sectors. Increasingly, people are going to the private sector health care, which is frightfully expensive and threatens to eat them out of their hearth and home eventually. This is only because the public health care system is in shambles and does not offer them the care they need. In fact, it offers nothing more tangible than immunization and family planning. Only those among the poor who cannot afford private health care are forced to go to government health care. There is a huge unmet demand in the public health care system, particularly in supply of quality and comprehensive services (Rao 2011: 20).

The question is: how can Aadhaar help? As this analysis shows, public health care system is in a bad way. It is now characterized by critical shortage of health personnel, inadequate incentives, poor working conditions, absenteeism, long wait, inconvenient hospital hours, poor outreach, and insensitivity to local needs. That is why the utilization of public health care infrastructure for both outpatient and inpatient facilities is abysmally low. The NSSO data clearly show major decline in the utilization of public health care facilities and a corresponding increase in the utilization of private health care facilities. What we are witnessing is a system failure, and no process improvement can remedy the situation. In any case, Aadhaar has nothing to offer to stem the systemic rot. As Dr Mohan Rao (2011: 21) points out, 'the UID is not designed to meet the public health challenges in the country and should not pretend to do so'.

RSBY

The UIDAI document claims that RSBY is a 'killer application' waiting for a platform, and Aadhaar is in a position to provide that platform. As mentioned earlier, according to the UIDAI document, if the Aadhaar is taken as a partner in the RSBY, it will: (i) provide an additional and fresh, unlikely to be duplicated source of registrations for Aadhaar; and (ii) more importantly, in conjunction with linkages to a routine health information system, improve public health in terms of efficiency and outcomes.

How can Aadhaar help in the implementation of RSBY? Answering the question requires a detailed analysis of RSBY. The government launched RSBY in 2008. The RSBY offers a micro-insurance product for BPL families and aims to cover 69 million households throughout the country in five years (Das and Leino 2011: 219). The scheme is designed to provide financial protection for poor households affected by major health shocks and also, to improve health outcomes for them. The RSBY is a demand-side, voucher-like intervention with several features (Das and Leino 2011: 219). Beneficiaries under RSBY are entitled to hospitalization coverage up to Rs 30,000 for most diseases that require hospitalization (Basu 2010: 5). Pre-existing conditions are covered from day one and there is no age limit. Coverage extends to five members of the family, which includes the head of a household, spouse, and up to three dependents. Beneficiaries need to pay only Rs 30 as registration fee, while the government pays the premium to the insurer selected by the state government on the basis of competitive bidding (Basu 2010: 5).

Stakeholders

The Government of India finances 75 per cent of the cost of the scheme (Basu 2010: 5). It lays down the benefit package to be provided and detailed information on the electronic data format for BPL families. The state governments provide 25 per cent of the financing (Basu 2010: 6). They engage in a competitive public bidding process and select a public or private insurance company recognized by the Insurance Regulatory and Development Authority (IRDA) or enabled by a central legislation. The RSBY provides health insurance for the enrolled BPL families up to a maximum number of poor households based on the definition and the figures provided by the Planning Commission. State governments are responsible for the accuracy of their BPL lists. Each state establishes an independent body, the nodal agency, to implement the scheme through insurance companies (Basu 2010: 6).

An electronic list of eligible BPL households is provided to the insurer using a pre-specified data format. The insurance company prepares an enrolment schedule for each village, alongside dates, with the help of district-level officials. The smart card, along with an information pamphlet describing the scheme and the list of hospitals, is provided on the spot to the beneficiary after the registration fee of

Rs 30 has been paid by the beneficiary. This list of enrolled households is maintained centrally and is the basis for financial transfers from the Government of India to state governments. Empanelment of hospitals is done as soon as the insurer gets the contract. The insurer empanels enough hospitals (both public and private) in the district so that beneficiaries do not have to travel very far to get the health care services (Basu 2010: 6).

The empanelled hospitals install necessary hardware and software so that smart card transactions can be processed. After entering the details of the service rendered to the patient, the hospitals send an electronic report to the insurer. The insurer, after going through the information, makes the payment to the hospital within a specified time period which has been agreed upon between the insurer and the hospital. At present, more than 3,200 private hospitals and 1,100 public hospitals across India are RSBY empanelled (Basu 2010: 7).

The transaction process begins when the beneficiary visits the participating hospital. After reaching the hospital, the beneficiary visits the RSBY help desk, where his identity is verified by reference to his photograph and fingerprints stored in his/her smart card. If a diagnosis leads to hospitalization, the beneficiary gets his expenses covered up to Rs 30,000 annually. Any hospital, which is empanelled under RSBY by the insurance company, provides cashless treatment to the beneficiary anywhere in India, choosing from 700 inpatient medical procedures. The outpatient department (OPD) facilities are not covered under this scheme, though OPD consultation is free (Basu 2010: 7).

The operation of RSBY involves three stages: enrolment, hospital transaction, and monitoring (Palacios 2011: 6).

Enrolment

State governments provide an electronic list of eligible BPL households to the insurer in a pre-specified format. The list is posted in each village prior to the enrolment, and the date and location is publicized in advance. Mobile stations are put up in a central place of the village, preferably in the government school. These stations are equipped with hardware required to collect biometric information (fingerprints) of the members of the household and to print smart cards with a photo. The smart card, along with an information pamphlet describing the scheme and the list of hospitals, is printed and provided on the spot to the beneficiary (Palacios 2011: 6).

In addition to the beneficiaries themselves, the representative of the insurance company is required to be present at the time of enrolment. A district-level officer of the concerned state government, who is known as the Key Field Officer (KFO), is also expected to be present, and it is a requirement of RSBY that the FKO must insert his/her centrally issued smart card to verify the legitimacy of the enrolment. After enrolment, the list of households which have been issued smart cards is downloaded from the FKO's card and centralized at the district level and eventually, at the state level. It is only on the basis of this list that premium is paid to the insurance company.

Transaction in Hospitals

The smart card entitles the beneficiary to cashless transaction up to Rs 30,000 per annum. The transaction begins when the beneficiary's smart card is swiped at the hospital. If the diagnosis leads to a procedure, the appropriate prescribed package is selected in the software menu and the procedure is blocked. When the patient leaves the hospital after the procedure, the card is again swiped and the pre-specified cost of the procedure is deducted from the total of Rs 30,000 on the beneficiary's card. The transaction is recorded on the hospital's computer and on the card itself. A receipt is printed and given to the beneficiary. The transport costs are paid by the hospital to the beneficiary in cash (Palacios 2011: 7).

Monitoring

Data on enrolment is downloaded from the FKO cards and aggregated for each district. Insurers separately submit enrolment data in a pre-specified format to the central server of Government of India. A second source of enrolment data is from the FKO cards. The payment of premium is based on this data. Finally, insurers submit data on a rolling basis to the Ministry of Labour and Employment during the enrolment period by Internet. Such data flow enables day-to-day tracking but without the level of detail available from the back-end data submission. In addition to the enrolment data, insurers are also required to submit data on transactions to the Government of India in a pre-specified format on a regular basis.

The transaction data is based on the electronic claims uploaded from each hospital. These data allow state nodal agencies as well as the Ministry of Labour and Employment, Government of India, to monitor utilization patterns and look for anomalies. Over time, the data are used for detailed analysis of the determinants of enrolment and utilization and eventually, for disease mapping and actuarial analysis (Palacios 2011: 7–8). The current system is considered to be temporary and there are plans to replace it with a new Central Information Exchange Service. Among other things, this will allow for inter-insurance clearing to take place efficiently. This will also enable the shift to a direct hospital submission of data to the central server.

Challenges

The RSBY services are now being delivered to the poor by more than 800 hospitals spread across the country (Swarup 2012: 15). It covers 26 million families, providing health insurance to around 100 million poor people, and nearly 3 million people have used these services (Swarup 2012: 15). Independent third-party evaluation reveals a beneficiary satisfaction rating between 70 per cent and 90 per cent (Swarup 2012: 15). There are, however, several challenges that RSBY faces in its implementation. We need to look at these challenges to find out whether Aadhaar can help RSBY in meeting these challenges. The challenges are primarily in the area of enrolment of the poor and hospitalization.

Enrolment of the Poor

At the beginning of the third year of the implementation of RSBY, while one-third of the total number of districts in the country had seen the enrolment of poor in insurance, just about 50 per cent of the poor in the selected districts had been enrolled in RSBY (Narayana 2010: 15–16). The proportion of poor families enrolled in RSBY has varied between 39 per cent in Maharashtra and 81 per cent in Kerala (Narayana 2010: 15–16). States such as Uttar Pradesh, Bihar, and Maharashtra, which have large number of poor households, have reported low enrolment proportions indicating that the bulk of the poor is still not covered by the scheme. One reason for the poor performance in enrolment is that the state governments are either not too keen or do not have the administrative apparatus to get the poor enrolled. The exception is the state of Kerala, which reported 80 per cent coverage, with some districts enrolling almost the entire number of poor households (Narayana 2010: 15–16). In Kerala, it is largely the keenness of the state government and the effort made by gram panchayats which is responsible for this outstanding coverage.

The other reason for poor enrolment is the flawed targeting system that has been used to generate the list of people living below the poverty line. The BPL database of RSBY is based on the BPL list, which was prepared on the basis of a 2002 census. Empirical evidence has revealed large inclusion and exclusion errors (Palacios 2011: 14). Problems with the list in terms of errors and obsolescence have reduced enrolment rates. Errors were caused by several factors, including poor data entry, lost records, and the lack of updates for deaths, births, marriages, and migration (Palacios 2011: 15). Reports from the field suggest that the flaws in the BPL list have led to resentment at the village level, and also reduced enrolment rates significantly (Palacios 2011: 15). If the list does not include a BPL household, or excludes certain members of the household, those people cannot be enrolled in RSBY. For example, in one district, half of the households did not have any dependents listed. This effectively excluded close to half a million individuals who would have otherwise enrolled. On many occasions, enrolment process was disrupted because of such exclusions, and often led to violence. This is a problem over which RSBY does not have any control, but it has certainly affected the process of enrolment.

Seemingly widespread lack of compliance with rules is also a feature of the enrolment process. The requirement of the scheme that smart cards are to be issued at the time of enrolment is often not followed. Instead, cards are printed in a central location and distributed subsequently; sometimes weeks after the enrolment. Surveys in a few districts in Gujurat and Haryana reveal that between one-quarter and one-half of cards had not been distributed on the spot (Narayana 2010: 15–16). On some occasions, intermediaries responsible for distributing the cards demand small payments. It is a fact that it is cheaper for the insurer to have centralized printing and batch distribution but this runs counter to RSBY's process design, which is intended to be user friendly to the beneficiaries.

Hospitalization

Hospitalizations under RSBY in the first three years of the scheme's implementation have been of the order of 1.6 million. The rate of hospitalization is more in districts where the share of private hospitals is larger in the empanelled list. For example, the share of private hospitals is 90 per cent in Kanpur, 87 per cent in Amritsar, 90 per cent in the Dangs, and 100 per cent in Karnal—all high hospitalization districts (Narayana 2010: 17). In Kerala, where 45 per cent of the empanelled hospitals are in the private sector, the rate of hospitalization has varied with the share of hospitals in the private sector (Narayana 2010: 17).

Let us try to understand how the Aadhaar programme can help in the implementation of RSBY in terms of the twin challenges of enrolment and hospitalization. Regarding enrolment, the UIDAI document states that it can provide additional and fresh, unlikely to be duplicated source of registrations for RSBY. Fundamentally, the process of enrolment is almost similar in both RSBY and Aadhaar, the only difference being that in RSBY, insurance companies have an incentive to maximize enrolment since their market-determined premium is paid on the basis of the number of households enrolled. Clearly, Aadhaar is in no position to help here. Regarding the claim of providing a source that is unlikely to be duplicated, the RSBY has adequate safeguards built into the scheme. The RSBY relies on new and extensive electronic data that are introduced in the operation of the biometric smart card. The backbone of the scheme is the electronic list of BPL households that are eligible for enrolment. This list is given by the state government, maintained electronically, and used to verify and permit eligible households to enrol. Whenever a household enrols, the data is sent electronically to a central warehouse. Similarly, whenever a smart card is used at a hospital, data on the place where the card is used, the procedures undertaken, and the costs are electronically recorded and transmitted. Obviously, Aadhaar is no position to offer any help in this respect.

The other part is the flawed targeting system. As noted earlier, the flaw flows from the BPL list; a list that has both exclusion and inclusion errors. As noted in the case of the PDS, the flaws in the BPL list occur when the criteria used for identification of the BPL families are either incorrect or when government criteria are not adhered to. Clearly, misclassification of families in the BPL census has little to do with identity fraud or duplication and, as mentioned earlier, such misclassification of households cannot be controlled with the help of Aadhaar.

Another challenge is the seemingly widespread lack of compliance of the rules of enrolment. This occurred in the initial stages of the implementation of RSBY, and as pointed out earlier, it was because of centralized printing and batch distribution of smart cards. The smart cards had to be printed centrally because, when the scheme was first launched, there was a severe shortage of hardware such as smart card printers and fingerprint scanners (Basu 2010: 11). Now, the smart cards are printed and issued locally.

Regarding the challenge faced with respect to hospitalization, the concern is about the long-run effects of hospital capacity and quality. This concern can only be addressed by developing an adequate system of accreditation and quality ratings of hospitals. Once such a system is in place, it would help the state governments to be more proactive in monitoring capacity and quality, particularly with respect to ensuring that the supply is not expended in undeserved districts. There is nothing much that Aadhaar can do to meet this challenge.

AADHAAR AND HEALTH INFORMATION

The UIDAI document claims that Aadhaar will help in improving public health in terms of efficiency and outcome through its linkages to a routine health information system when it partners with RSBY. In another part of the UIDAI document on public health, it is stated that routine health information systems that capture and track the morbidity and mortality due to various disease conditions are currently based on infrequent national and state surveys, but data about chronic or lifestyle diseases are not captured through these surveys. The document suggests that an integrated routine health system that can capture and track population-level disease conditions by linking citizen IDs with hospital or other medical facility records can inform the public health system of the various routine disease conditions and prepare the health system to respond to unforeseen epidemics.

If disease mapping is what the UIDAI literature has in mind, this is already being done with RSBY data. As noted earlier, it is one of the requirements of the RSBY data monitoring process that the insurers have to submit data on transactions to the Government of India and state nodal agencies in a pre-specified format on a regular basis. This transaction data is based on electronic claims uploaded from each participating hospital. This data is used by the government not only for detailed analysis of determinants of enrolment and utilization but also for disease mapping. So, disease mapping is already on the menu of actions in the RSBY's charter.

Regarding the interest shown by UIDAI in using data from routine health information systems in order to improve public health outcomes, Dr Mohan Rao says:

> The Working Paper (of UIDAI) highlights the fact that we lack good-quality health data or indeed even vital statistics. It is equally true that this should come from integrated routine health systems. But how is the UID to rectify this? People are avoiding the public health system for a variety of reasons: lack of drugs, lack of doctors, having to pay for services, inconvenient hours, rude personnel, and so on. Unless these are attended to, data quality cannot be improved. The UID is no magic bullet.
>
> Thus the UID is not designed to meet public health challenges in the country and should not pretend to do so. On the contrary, given that many diseases continue to bear a stigma in the country, the UID scheme has the unique potential of increasing the stigma by breaching the anonymity of health data collected. If this violates the heart of the medical encounter, namely confidentiality, by making this information potentially available to employers and insurance companies, the scheme bodes further gross violations of health rights. It is this reason above all that persuaded many countries in Europe not to accept such schemes. (Rao 2011: 20–1)

In sum, the Aadhaar programme may not have any contribution to make in respect of public health. It is in no position to create a demand for public health because the public health care system in the country is in shambles and needs systemic reforms. Aadhaar's help may not be needed for enrolling people into RSBY as the process of enrolment is similar in RSBY and Aadhaar, the only difference being that in RSBY, insurance companies have an incentive to maximize enrolment since their market-determined premium is paid on the basis of the number of households enrolled, and therefore, RSBY has perhaps the better enrolment system. Regarding the use of health information to build an integrated routine health system that can capture and track population-level disease conditions by linking citizen IDs with hospital or other medical facility records, the RSBY is already engaged in that activity. On the whole, it is rather difficult to envision a role for the Aadhaar programme in the area of public health care services or in RSBY.

CHAPTER THIRTEEN

Aadhaar and Elementary Education

The UIDAI's document on envisioning a role for Aadhaar in respect of elementary education starts by referring to Section 3(1) of the RTE Act, 2009 (see 'UID and Education' in UIDAI 2010c: 1). Section 3(1) provides:

(1) Every child of the age of six to fourteen years shall have a right to free and compulsory education in a neighbourhood school till completion of elementary education.

(2) For the purpose of sub-section (1), no child shall be liable to pay any kind of fee or charges or expenses which may prevent him or her from pursuing or completing the elementary education. (Ministry of Law and Justice 2009: 3)

According to the UIDAI, the implementation of this provision in the RTE Act would call for an exhaustive survey of all the children in the age group of 6–14 years (see 'UID and Education' in UIDAI 2010c: 1). Providing Aadhaar number to these children will help in locating children who are out of the education system. Once the Aadhaar number is assigned at childhood, it could be used for the entire lifetime, including the stage of education (see 'UID and Education' in UIDAI 2010c: 1). Since the Aadhaar number can be used to track the entire educational career, monitoring of dropouts, which constitutes a significant problem in universalizing elementary education, would become easier (see 'UID and Education' in UIDAI 2010c: 1).

The UIDAI document claims that Aadhaar can also help with implementation problems (see 'UID and Education' in UIDAI

2010c: 1). According to the UIDAI, inflated enrolment at the school level is a serious problem. Inflated enrolment leads to significant leakages in mid-day meal scheme, books, scholarships, provision of uniform and bicycles, etc. More importantly, it gives a distorted picture of achievements of various programmes like the Sarva Shiksha Abhiyan (SSA) (see 'UID and Education' in UIDAI 2010c: 1). The UIDAI literature points out that inflated enrolments take place through enrolment of one child into multiple schools and non-existent children are shown on the rolls. If Aadhaar numbers are given to children, it would remove the problem of multiple enrolments and ghosts. It will also help in implementing uniform teacher–student ratio, which is currently distorted due to inflated enrolment (see 'UID and Education' in UIDAI 2010c: 1).

The UIDAI also claims that Aadhaar would help in putting the children of migrant families in schools in places of their migration (see 'UID and Education' in UIDAI 2010c: 1). The Aadhaar will ensure that there are no problems caused due to migration to students of migrant families anywhere within the country, as one does not have to establish identity at the new location. It will effectively address the issue of children of migrant labour as their children can be admitted at the new place without any other verification. According to the UIDAI, the present strategy of targeting such children at source can be used simultaneously with the strategy of targeting them at destination also.

Another claim of the UIDAI is that provision of Aadhaar at birth would help planners of elementary education systems in terms of planning for schools, teachers, and other logistics (see 'UID and Education' in UIDAI 2010c: 2).

WHAT ARE THE REASONS FOR CHILDREN NOT ENROLLING AND DROPPING OUT?

The UIDAI claims that providing Aadhaar to all the children in the age group of 6–14 years will help to bring the children who are out of school back into the educational system. To analyse the validity of this claim, we need to know why these children are out of school. There are still about 7 million children in the country who are out of school (see 'UID and Education' in UIDAI 2010c: 2). An independent study made by Social and Rural Institute estimates that about 6.9 per cent of the total children in the 6–13 age group are out of school and of them, 2.1 per cent account for dropouts and 4.8 per cent of never-enrolled children, the bulk of whom belong to the poorer segment of rural households (quoted in Planning Commission 2008b: 3). The dropout rate at the elementary level remains high at 50.8 per cent (Planning Commission 2008b: 5). Around 22 per cent of the dropout cases are in Classes 1 and 2 (Planning Commission 2008b: 3). The dropout rates at the primary levels for SCs (34.2 per cent) and STs (42.3 per cent) are substantially higher than the national average of 29 per cent (Planning Commission 2008b: 5). The social gap in dropout rates is particularly acute in respect of girls. The opportunity cost of girl child education is especially high in rural areas, and she is often a 'nowhere' child, neither in the school nor in the labour force but doing domestic work, mostly sibling care.

The Kothari Commission on education argued that the main reason for not enrolling and dropping out was poverty (Education Commission 1966: 269). Subsequently, the National Council of Applied Economic Research (NCAER), in its 1994 study of non-enrolment, dropout, and private expenditure on elementary education, found that economic factors were more important than any other factor in explaining non-enrolment and dropouts in elementary education (NCAER 1994). Tilak (2002), on the basis of his interpretation of data from the 52nd Round of National Sample Survey (NSS), came to the conclusion that more than 50 per cent of non-enrolment was due to economic factors, and a lack of interest in schooling accounted for another 30 per cent.

Figures 13.1 and 13.2 give us insights into the relative importance of various factors responsible for children not enrolling in the elementary stream.

As can be seen from Figures 13.1 and 13.2, the single most important reason for never attending school is that the school costs too much. In fact, contrary to the routine assertion that education is free in government schools, there are several cost considerations that prevent parents from getting their children to school and keeping them there. Tilak (2002) has shown how even the so-called free elementary education is not really free. The 52nd Round of NSS data estimates provide the benchmark for estimating the per capita out-of-

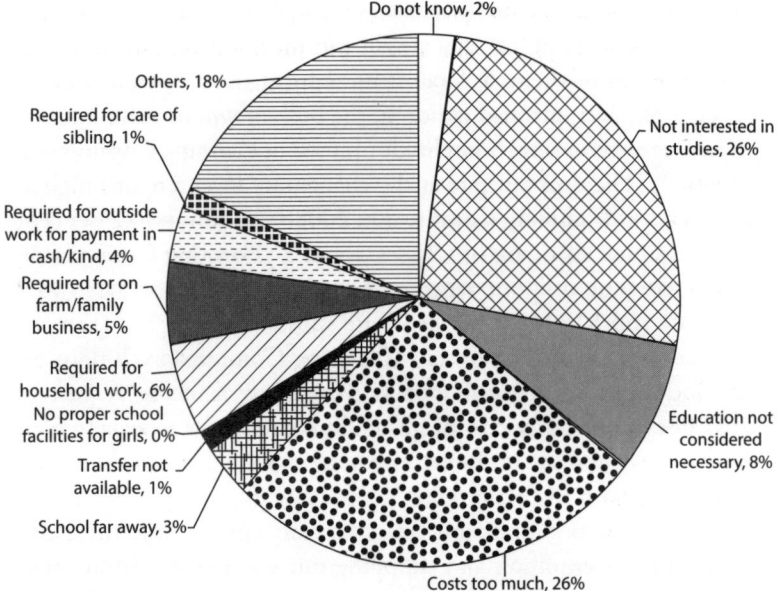

Figure 13.1 Reasons for Never Attending School (Male)

Source: Council for Social Development (2006).

pocket expenditure on elementary education in India. If the numbers of the 52nd Round are adjusted for 2005–6 prices, an average Indian parent spends Rs 701 per annum on primary education and Rs 1,281 per annum on upper primary education of the children out of his/her pocket (Centre for Budget and Governance Accountability 2007: 8).

There are significant variations in out-of-pocket expenditure across states, regions, fractile groups, and type of schools. Though the incidence is different for different fractile groups, it is still harsh on the poorest 20 per cent at Rs 276 for primary schooling and Rs 596 for upper primary schooling, an amount the poor can ill afford. What are the different items in this out-of-pocket expenditure? In the case of a child attending a government school, a large chunk of the out-of-pocket expenditure goes towards books and uniform. If the child attends a private school, the bulk of the out-of-pocket expenditure is for school fees, stationery, uniform, and transport.

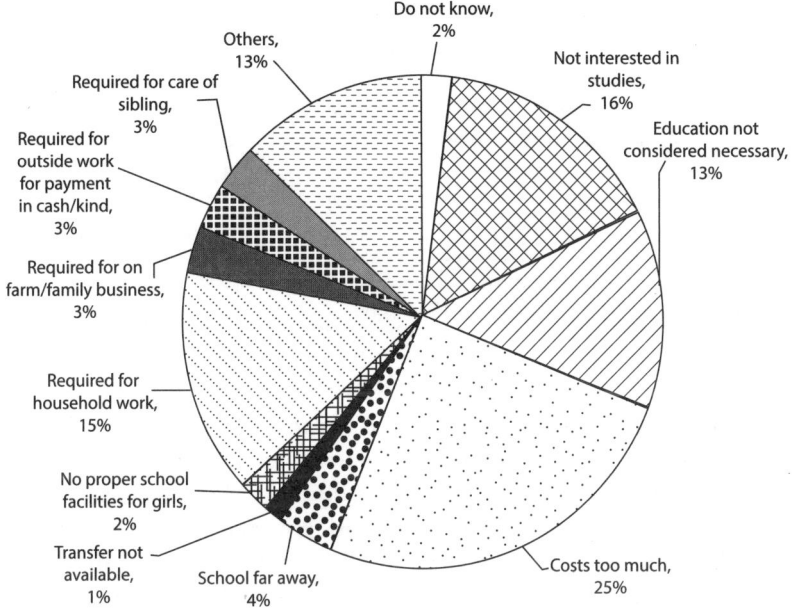

Figure 13.2 Reasons for Never Attending School (Female)

Source: Council for Social Development (2006).

The performance audit of SSA programme conducted by the C&AG in 2006 cited affordability as one of the most important reasons for children not being enrolled in schools. The C&AG report also evaluated the reasons for non-enrolment as in Table 13.1.

As the C&AG report makes it clear, the most important reason for children not getting enrolled is that the parents cannot afford school. This is borne out by observations of Shariff and Ghosh (2000: 1406). According to them, about 58 per cent of the Indian population lives in the lowest-income group (Rs 20,000 or less per annum), and more than half of them have no resources to spend on education at the given price of education. According to them, this is the main reason for non-enrolment. About Rs 2,765 crore are spent towards their children's education due to government's failure to provide free education to children up to 14 years of age.

Table 13.1   Reasons for Non-enrolment

Reasons	Males (%)	Females (%)	Total (%)
Cannot afford school	32.7	39	36.1
Child does not like to go to school	19	15.1	16.9
Too young to go to school	14.3	13.9	14.1
Have to go to work	3.4	3.7	2.9
Other reasons	30.5	28.3	30

Source: Centre for Budget and Governance Accountability (2007).
Note: Based on C&AG Report No.15 of 2006.

The other important reason is that children do not like to go to school. From Figures 13.1 and 13.2, it can be seen that one of the major reasons for never attending school was 'not interested in studies'. Unfortunately, the NSSO, on whose findings this conclusion was reached, does not provide any explanation to help us to decompose the 'not interested in studies' factor. Tilak (2006: 39) argues that this factor, 'not interested in studies', can be attributed to:

1. the poor quality and quantity of physical infrastructure;
2. poor quality of instruction, including the alienness and irrelevance of the curriculum; and
3. economic and other social factors from the side of the family.

Why do children drop out of schools? The C&AG's report on the performance of SSA also cited reasons for non-attendance and evaluated them. The details are provided in Table 13.2.

Table 13.2   Reasons for Non-attendance

Reasons	Males (%)	Females (%)	Total (%)
Do not like to go to school	27.8	20.9	24.4
Cannot afford school	23.8	24.1	23.9
Have to go to work	7.5	5.5	6.5
Not good at studies	3.1	–	3.1
Household chores and related works	3.1	7.4	5.2
Other reasons	34.7	42.1	38.4

Source: Centre for Budget and Governance Accountability (2007).
Note: Based on C&AG Report No.15 of 2006.

The reasons are almost the same as in the case of non-enrolment. Clearly, the phenomenon of children dropping out of school can be seen as a reflection of the inability of the school system to retain children in school until the completion of the given level of education (Tilak 2006: 39).

Access to Schools

Lack of school facilities is a major constraint (Ministry of Education 1985). It is generally accepted that proximity to schools, particularly at the primary and upper primary levels, determines to a very great extent whether the children go to school (Tilak 2006: 40). This is particularly true of children from the poorer sections of the society. But, as the Seventh All-India Educational Survey of 2002 found, only 53 per cent of habitations had a primary school within the habitation and only 18 per cent of habitations had an upper primary school facility (National Council of Educational Research and Training [NCERT] 2005). In fact, the number of primary schools for every one lakh population seems to be going down. In 1990–1, there were 66 primary schools on an average for every one lakh population in the country, and the number has come down to 62.2 in 2000–1 (Tilak 2006: 40).

Irrespective of whether the school is run by government or is aided or privately managed, main users of the primary education system in the country are young children, for whom travelling long distances on a daily basis is a difficult proposition. That is why access to a school that is within walking distance is important. Government/aided primary schools are accessible for 76 per cent of rural and 42 per cent of urban households in the country (Paul et al. 2006: 90). In addition, we also have a good number of primary schools run by private institutions providing primary education. Private primary schools are accessible for 25 per cent of villages and for 25 per cent of urban households (Paul et al. 2006: 90). In both rural and urban areas, ease of access is greater among users of government/aided primary schools.

What does this mean for the poor? There is only a marginal difference between the households of SCs/STs and other communities in respect of ease of access to government primary schools. But there is an interesting insight here. The dependence on government-run and aided primary schools for SC/ST households at 82 per cent is higher than the other communities at 75 per cent (Paul *et al.* 2006: 111).

Provision of Teachers

Provision of teachers is a major constraint. Zero-teacher and single-teacher schools have been a known weakness of the Indian school system. According to the Seventh All-India Educational Survey of 2002, there were 8,000 primary schools without teachers and 1.1 lakh single-teacher schools in the country (NCERT 2005). In addition, in the educationally backward states, there are few women teachers to attract girls to school and retain them there (Planning Commission 2008b: 4). Interestingly, the teacher–student ratio in primary schools has gone up from 24 in 1950–1 to 45 in 2006–7, while the official norm is 1:40.[1] The teacher–student ratio in upper primary schools has gone up from 20 to 35 during the same period, which now corresponds to the official norm of 1:35.[2]

An equally important concern is the quality of teachers. Out of the total number of 22,31,107 primary school teachers in the country, 3,12,355 teachers are untrained.[3] The position for upper primary schools is no better. Out of the total number of 16,57,869 upper primary school teachers in the country, 2,15,523 teachers are untrained.[4] Another concern is the alarming growth in the number of part-time teachers: between 1986 and 1993, the rate of growth per annum in part-time teachers in rural primary schools was 27.8 per cent, while it was as high as 155.3 per cent in government primary schools (Tilak 2006: 41). There were only nine part-time teachers in upper primary schools in 1986, and this number increased by 70 times in seven years (Tilak 2006: 41).

A related concern is the increase in the number of voluntary/contract teachers. Before 1986, this category did not exist. But by 1993, there were as many as 25,000 such teachers in primary schools and another 10,000 teachers in upper primary schools (Tilak 2006: 41). Because of implementation of schemes such as District Primary Education Programme and Education Guarantee Scheme, there has been a virtual explosion in the number of voluntary/contract teachers all across the country going under different names like 'shiksha karmis' in Rajasthan and Madhya Pradesh, 'shiksha mitras' in Uttar Pradesh, and 'vidya sahayaks' in Gujarat. According to the Seventh

All-India Educational Survey of 2002, there were 3.8 lakh part-time and voluntary/contract teachers in various schools in India (NCERT 2005). This has had an adverse impact on the quality of instruction in primary and upper primary schools (Tilak 2006: 41).

Quality of Education

The fact that children drop out of school early reflects the poor quality of education. The average school attendance was about 70 per cent of the enrolment in 2004–5 (Tilak 2006: 42). In states like Uttar Pradesh and Bihar, the average attendance was as low as 57 per cent and 42 per cent respectively (Tilak 2006: 42). One-third of the teachers in Madhya Pradesh, 25 per cent in Bihar, and 20 per cent in Uttar Pradesh did not attend school (Tilak 2006: 42). In addition, repetition rates in such states were also very high, resulting in wastage of human and material resources. Teacher attendance, ability, and motivation appear to be the weakest links of elementary education programmes. Lack of universal pre-schooling and consequent poor vocabulary and poor conceptual development of mind makes even enrolled children less participative in class, even for learning by rote (Tilak 2006: 42).

Financial Provisioning of Elementary Education

The reasons, which keep children out of school, such as access to school, lack of teachers, poor quality and quantity of physical infrastructure, and poor quality of instruction, are all related to the larger issue of financial provisioning of elementary education. Expenditure on elementary education can be broadly categorized under two heads: (i) public expenditure; and (ii) private expenditure. Public expenditure in elementary education is one that is incurred by the government either through its own delivery system or by making transfers to the private sector engaged in the area of elementary education. In India, public expenditure on elementary education is incurred on educational administration, infrastructure, direct transfers to students in the form of benefits or scholarships, and transfer of funds to aided private schools (Centre for Budget and Governance Accountability 2007: 6). Private expenditure is the out-of-pocket expenditure incurred by private education providers as these expenses are eventually recovered in the form of fees from the parents who send their children to private schools.

There are three sources of financing of public elementary education in India: (i) central government; (ii) state government; and (iii) local bodies. Since the government has the responsibility of providing universal elementary education of eight years for every child in the age group of 6–14 years, the responsibility should include full provisioning of resources by the government. This has been unfailingly recognized in the different policy resolutions and recommendations of various committees. The Education Commission (1964–6) recommended that public expenditure on education should be raised to 6 per cent of the national income (Shariff *et al.* 2002: 6). The Government of India accepted this concept in its 1968 policy and fixed a target of 6 per cent of national income to be invested in education from the public exchequer by 1986 (Tilak 2006: 43). The National Policy on Education in 1986 and 1992 also accepted that it should be 6 per cent. Even the National Common Minimum Programme of the UPA-1 government had set a target of raising it to 6 per cent (Planning Commission 2008a: 17). The public expenditure (centre and states) on education is now only around 3.6 per cent of the gross domestic product (GDP). The goal of allocating 6 per cent has not been achieved. It needs to be noted that only less than half the amount of the total educational budget is spent on elementary education (Shariff *et al.* 2002: 6). Public investment in elementary education in India has been grossly inadequate. In fact, elementary education in India has suffered from several decades of underinvestment and as a result, schooling facilities are both quantitatively and qualitatively inadequate, making it difficult to realize the avowed goal of universalization of elementary education.

ANALYSIS OF THE UIDAI CLAIMS RELATED TO EDUCATION

The foregoing analysis makes it clear that the reasons why 7 million children are out of school are systemic in nature and there is nothing that the Aadhaar can do, by way of process improvement, to set things right. The UIDAI document suggests for an exhaustive survey to be conducted of all the children in age group of 6–14 years, and also claims that the Aadhaar number could monitor dropouts. In this respect, the RTE Act and the Rules have made adequate provisions.

For example, Section 9 the RTE Act and Rule 6 provide for the local authority to maintain a record of all children in its jurisdiction through a household survey (Ministry of Law and Justice 2009: 3; also, see Ministry of Human Resource Development 2009: 3–4). Sections 8 and 9 of the Act provide that it shall be the duty of the appropriate government and the local authority (municipality or panchayat) to provide free and compulsory education to every child (Ministry of Law and Justice 2009: 5). The Act also makes it the duty of the appropriate government and the local authority to ensure and monitor admission, attendance, and completion of elementary education by every child. Rule 6 of the 'Model Rules' specifically provides that the local authority shall maintain a record of all children in its jurisdiction, through a household survey, from their birth till they attain 14 years (Ministry of Human Resource Development 2009: 3–4). The rule further provides that the record shall include detail of the class in which the child is studying, and if the education is discontinued in the territorial jurisdiction of the local authority, the reason for such discontinuance. In addition, Section 21 of the Act provides for the constitution of a school management committee, and Rule 13(6) makes it a function of the school management committee to ensure enrolment and continued attendance of all the children from the neighbourhood in the school (Ministry of Law and Justice 2009: 7). The implementation of these provisions of the Act and the Rules will, no doubt, ensure that a survey is made of all the children in the age group of 6–14 years, and that the dropout position is monitored.

Another claim that the UIDAI makes is that, if Aadhaar number is given to children, it will remove problems of multiple enrolment and ghosts, and it will help in implementing uniform teacher–student ratio, which is currently distorted because of inflated enrolment. Admittedly, inflated enrolment has been a problem, but the provisions in the Rules take care of this problem adequately. Rule 6(5) provides for the local authority to ensure that the names of all children enrolled in the schools under its jurisdiction are publicly displayed in each school (Ministry of Human Resource Development 2009: 4). Once this is done, the villagers, who have local knowledge of who is who in the neighbourhood, will ensure that there are no ghosts and multiple enrolments.

The UIDAI also claims that the Aadhaar programme will help in putting the children of migrant families in schools in places of their migration. In fact, provisions in the Act and the Rules make special provisions to take care of the continued education of migrant families. Section 9(k) of the Act provides that every local authority shall ensure admission of children of migrant families (Ministry of Law and Justice 2009: 5). Rule 6 provides for the local authority to maintain a record of all children in its jurisdiction, and Rule 6(4) (f) stipulates that the record maintained by the local authority shall include details of children requiring special facilities/residential facilities on account of migration (Ministry of Human Resource Development 2009: 3–4). Clearly, the enabling provisions in the Act and the Rules will take care of the problems of the children of migrant families to get into the educational stream in places of their migration.

The UIDAI also claims that provision of Aadhaar number at birth will help planners of elementary education systems in terms of planning for schools, teachers, and other logistics. The provisions in the Act and the Rules take care of the planning perspective, too. As far as planning for schools is concerned, Rule 5(2) provides that for the purpose of determining and for establishing neighbourhood schools, the state government/local authority shall undertake a process of school mapping by way of planning for schools, every year (Ministry of Human Resource Development 2009: 3). Regarding planning for teachers and other logistics, Section 22 of the Act enjoins the school management committee to prepare a school development plan, and provides that the school development plan, so prepared, shall be the basis for the plans and grants to be made by the state government or the local authority (Ministry of Law and Justice 2009: 7). Rule 14 takes it further and stipulates that the school development plan shall be a three-year plan comprising three annual sub-plans (Ministry of Human Resource Development 2009: 9). Rule 14 also stipulates that the school development plan shall contain estimates of class-wise enrolments for each year, requirements of additional teachers over a three-year period, physical requirement of additional infrastructure and equipments, and additional financial requirement over the three-year period. That being the case, the process of school mapping and the school development plans, as required under the provisions made in the RTE Act and the Rules thereunder, provide adequate basis for planners of elementary education to plan for schools, teachers, and other logistics.

On the whole, this analysis makes it clear that there is very little that Aadhaar can do in the area of elementary education. The RTE Act of 2009, which declares that every child of the age of 6–14 years shall have a right to free and compulsory education, has a number of enabling provisions, the proper implementation of which can make the realization of this right possible.

NOTES

1. See Ministry of Human Resource Development, available at http://www.education.nic.in/secedu-sec_stats.asy, accessed 26 April 2011.

2. Ministry of Human Resource Development, available at http://www.education.nic.in/secedu-sec_stats.asy, accessed 26 April 2011.

3. Ministry of Human Resource Development, available at http://www.education.nic.in/secedu-sec_stats.asy, accessed 26 April 2011.

4. Ministry of Human Resource Development, available at http://www.education.nic.in/secedu-sec_stats.asy, accessed 26 April 2011.

CHAPTER FOURTEEN

Aadhaar-based Financial Inclusion for the Poor

The UIDAI document on financial inclusion for the poor opens with the statement that Aadhaar can play a critical role in giving the poor access to formal financial mechanisms by helping them to authenticate their identity to financial institutions (UIDAI 2010d: 1). This, in turn, can significantly improve the effectiveness of existing financial inclusion strategies, and address the last-mile challenges that the poor now face in accessing financial services. According to the UIDAI document, all financial services eventually involve a financial institution making payment to the customer or vice versa. This poses the challenge of creating a payment system that can handle a large number of small-value transactions. According to the UIDAI, the Aadhaar approach to financial inclusion focuses on the creation of such a micropayments platform, addressing the last-mile problems, streamlining the delivery of government benefits, and providing access to finance to those who have so far been excluded (UIDAI 2010d: 1).

ACCESS TO FINANCE

According to the UIDAI document, India has made substantial progress in broadening financial inclusion in recent years (UIDAI 2010d: 2). The growth of BCs has expanded banking services in rural India. Liberalized branch expansion and automated teller machine (ATM) policies have encouraged rural banking, and new business models such as mobile banking are rapidly emerging. The notion of reduced Know Your Customer (KYC) norms for no-frills accounts (accounts where bank balances do not exceed Rs 50,000 and credit does not go above Rs 1,00,000 a year) makes it easier for the unbanked poor now to get a bank account. Despite these efforts, large segments of the population outside the urban, non-poor population remain financially excluded. Large variations still exist across states in bank account penetration (UIDAI 2010d: 3). According to the UIDAI, there are the following challenges for financial inclusion of the poor.

KYC

Even with reduced KYC norms, banks must corroborate the identity and address of a person before he/she gets a bank account. Prospective customers applying for a no-frills account must provide identity documentation or letters from local authorities verifying their identity and residence. These requirements make it difficult for the poor to get a bank account. This challenge is further accentuated for the migrant poor, who, due to their mobility and transitory work, are less likely to have either relevant identity documentation or acceptable substitutes (UIDAI 2010d: 3).

High Costs

Despite the network of 82,000 bank branches of commercial banks across the country, India's banks cater to only 5 per cent of the villages. The cost of this financial distance is paid by the poor. A visit to the bank for the poor often means substantial travel and expense, and the loss of a day's wages. The poor find such costs especially untenable given their preference for micro-transactions (UIDAI 2010d: 3).

Limited Accessibility

The challenges that the poor face as beneficiaries of government schemes and programmes are common across much of rural India. The lack of a common shared payments infrastructure across government schemes and programmes means that beneficiaries have little choice in where their accounts reside and as a result, they have to collect different payments—National Rural Employment Guarantee Act (NREGA) and Janani Suraksha Yojana benefits, SSA salaries and pensions—from different agencies. The distance that the beneficiaries are required to travel to various agencies for their money incurs opportunity costs as well as travel costs. The costly processes of cash management, cumbersome identity verification processes, and high transaction volumes create inefficiencies across the system and a web of delayed payments and long waiting times for the ultimate beneficiaries. The information asymmetry between the bank and the beneficiaries on when the payments have arrived also gives rise to middlemen, who pass on this information to the beneficiaries for a price. The net cost that beneficiaries have to incur in order to access their payments across government schemes and programmes is estimated to be in excess of Rs 6,000 crore. These constraints prevent the poor from using banking services regularly. If persons move away from their village, their ability to access their money becomes even more challenging. Benefit payments that the poor receive are often tied to their location. This affects the poor in a variety of situations: when they migrate for jobs to the city and then return to the village; when they move to the village or town where their son/daughter lives; or when pregnant women move to their parents' home for delivery (UIDAI 2010d: 3–4).

Storing Savings Safely

The lack of access to banking services, for the poor, also makes the safety of their savings a challenge. Due to the limited safety of savings stored at home, the poor resort to other means to ensure the safety of their money, including converting it into investments in gold or livestock, or lending it to friends and family. The lack of access to institutional services for savings means that the poor pay a premium to private agents such as moneylenders to store their cash securely and ensure safety of their money (UIDAI 2010d: 4–5).

Challenges for Banks

Banks in India face special challenges in fulfilling the goals of greater financial accessibility and affordability for the poor. In much of rural India, unbanked regions are those that are sparsely populated, which lack basic infrastructure, and where large number of small transactions is common. As a result, banks face high costs of customer acquisition, high potential transaction costs of micropayments, and large expenditures on infrastructure and IT (UIDAI 2010d: 5).

A TIPPING POINT FOR FINANCIAL INCLUSION

According to the UIDAI literature, the Ministry of Finance, banks, non-bank financial institutions, and regulators have done a lot to achieve financial inclusion, and a tipping point for financial inclusion has now been reached due to the recent alignment of various policy as well as market factors because of the following developments (UIDAI 2010d: 6).

Conducive Policy Environment

The regulator has expanded the list of entities that can act as Business Correspondents (BCs). This list, among others, includes kirana shops, petrol pumps, self-help groups, etc. Thus, banks, either by themselves or along with retail partners such as fast-moving consumer goods (FMCG) firms, microfinance institutions (MFIs), and telcos, can appoint kirana shops, self-help groups, and other similar entities as BCs. The regulator prescribes outsourcing guidelines, which ensure that there is no conflict of interest when certain banking activities are outsourced (UIDAI 2010d: 6).

The finance minister, in the 2010 budget speech, indicated converting several subsidies into direct cash benefits. The government has created two kinds of funds for financial inclusion, which can be instrumental in scaling-up financial efforts in the country. Various benefits programmes may even be able to bear part of the capital and operation costs, if an effective micropayments system can be put in place. Thus, the last mile, which is expensive to reach given the country's large size and geographical diversity, can be serviced effectively (UIDAI 2010d: 6).

Conducive Technology Environment

The National Payments Corporation of India (NPCI) has been set up to manage the national payments infrastructure. It will deploy an interoperable modern payment, clearing, and settlement infrastructure that can handle large volumes of transactions at very low cost. This, combined with the increasing ubiquity of mobile communications, can make branchless banking a reality. The regulator prescribes guidelines for mobile banking that ensure protection of customer data and customer interest. As a result, crucial parts of the technology infrastructure for micropayments are already falling into place (UIDAI 2010d: 6).

Scalable Model with Aadhaar-enabled Micropayments

The final piece of the micropayments solution is the Aadhaar number. The banks can leverage the Aadhaar enrolment process and infrastructure to acquire customers and open Aadhaar-enabled bank accounts. Thus, banks do not have to bear the cost of biometric devices, or pay for enrolment agencies to travel from village to village, acquiring customers. The KYR verification performed by Aadhaar will match the KYC verification done by banks. When Aadhaar KYR is accepted as KYC for no-frills bank accounts, banks will save on KYC costs. Lastly, since a person's Aadhaar will be tagged to every transaction, the regulator achieves full traceability and accountability. Thus, no trade-off is necessary between inclusion and security (UIDAI 2010d: 7).

On the whole, the Aadhaar-based micropayments model is similar to the familiar online PoS/ATM world that banks are already comfortable with. Using similar ideas and infrastructure would dramatically bring down operational costs and risks. The real-time online authentication offered by UADAI also provides secure identification of branchless banking customers to banks at low cost. The current policy and technology environments, combined with the benefits of using the Aadhaar infrastructure as an overlay on the existing banking infrastructure, can usher in an era of ubiquitous branchless banking (UIDAI 2010d: 7).

Aadhaar-enabled Micropayments

A stable and secure channel for the delivery of micropayments is central to successful, widespread financial access. The UIDAI's claim is that an Aadhaar-enabled bank account linked to an Aadhaar number can provide this channel. Customers can access their Aadhaar-enabled bank account through a BC operating a microATM device. The microATM is the device that will be used by BCs to deliver basic banking services at the last mile. For the purpose, there needs to be interoperability among the different systems adopted by different banks. Today, with the ATM network, customers of any bank can withdraw funds from any other bank. Similarly, it is proposed that customers banking through a BC should be able to access their Aadhaar-enabled bank account at any bank, and operate it. Another important aspect is that payments into Aadhaar-enabled bank account will depend on having online connectivity, and this connectivity can be in the form of a mobile, fixed line, or Internet connectivity. The UIDAI hopes that the recent initiatives of the Department of Telecommunications to connect every Common Service Centre (CSC) and gram panchayat with a high-speed fibre optics network over the next few years would make Internet access ubiquitous, making micropayments to the poor feasible across the country. The UIDAI envisages the microATM as the first step towards providing an online, interoperable, low-cost payments platform to the poor.

In terms of the claim made by the UIDAI, an Aadhaar-enabled bank account would provide the following four basic features for financial inclusion of the poor:

1. It will provide a convenient store of cash for savings, with a facility for making electronic deposits and withdrawals in micro-accounts.
2. It will be a convenient way to make payments.
3. It will work as a fast channel for sending and receiving remittances.
4. It will allow balance queries and provide a history of transactions (UIDAI 2010d: 8).

Transactions on the Aadhaar-based bank account will function essentially as a prepaid system, similar to that used by mobile operators. This will enable local BCs to offer basic banking services at low risk to the bank. The customers are already familiar with this model and comfortable with paying for talktime, an electronic good. The BC starts out by depositing a certain amount with a banking institution. The 'prepaid balance' paid up by the BC to the bank changes with every transaction that the BC makes. It decreases when a customer makes a deposit transaction, when some part of it is transferred to the customer's account, and increases when a customer withdraws money. When the customer is making a deposit, he pays physical cash to the BC who subsequently makes an electronic transfer from the BC's account to the customer account. When making a withdrawal, the electronic transfer is made from the customer account to the BC's account, and the BC hands out physical cash to the customer. This transfer from physical cash to its electronic equivalent has precedence across India (including villages) in the purchase of mobile prepaid cards. The bulk of mobile subscribers have prepaid subscriptions, and each time a customer purchases talktime for his phone in the form of Rs 10 or Rs 15 prepaid cards, he is exchanging physical cash for electronic cash in the form of talktime. The primary advantage of this approach is that even as it runs electronic transactions at the account level, thus bringing down the costs of cash management for banks, it also supports physical cash transactions at the local level, which is an important component of rural banking (UIDAI 2010d: 8). This approach, the UIDAI claims, will substantially reduce risk to the bank, since the BC has already paid up the cash transacted at the local level. The banking institution is consequently protected from fraudulent actions of the BC (UIDAI 2010d: 9).

ADDRESSING CHALLENGES FOR CUSTOMERS

The UIDAI literature claims that the Aadhaar-enabled micropayments will address challenges for customers in three ways: (i) identity verification; (ii) access to finance; and (iii) using the bank account (UIDAI 2010d: 9). In respect of identity verification, residents will be able to verify their identity to banking institutions easily, in real time and at low cost, using Aadhaar ID, which will be available even in rural areas through telecom networks. With regard to access to finance, remote verification of identity will enable local agencies to act as BCs (UIDAI 2010d: 9). This will solve the last-mile problem for the rural poor in financial access, while simultaneously giving residents choice and mobility: they will have choice among local service providers and can operate their bank account anywhere through any BC. In respect of the use of bank account, with Aadhaar-enabled bank accounts, government can deliver EBTs to the resident's account. This, in turn, will encourage the poor to get bank accounts for themselves so that they can get the EBTs and remittances. Having bank facilities at the doorstep will encourage more transactions on the account, rather than withdrawing the full amount, as is observed in many cases today (UIDAI 2010d: 9).

ADDRESSING CHALLENGES FOR BANKS

Traditionally, banks provide a variety of free services to their customers. The bank bears the cost of customer acquisition, the cost of account maintenance, and the cost of all transactions. This is possible because the bank enjoys the float in the customer's deposit account, which covers the cost of these services. No-frills accounts, however, offer very little float to the bank. Thus, a scalable model for financial inclusion must be built on a low-cost infrastructure, with a transparent per transaction pricing model. Banks will need to address the following major challenges to achieve large-scale financial inclusion (UIDAI 2010d: 10–11).

Customer Acquisition Costs

According to the UIDAI, banks bear an estimated cost of Rs 100 for customer acquisition for a no-frills account. The cost of account maintenance is estimated at Rs 100 every year. Aligning KYC requirements of no-frills bank accounts with Aadhaar KYR standards and authentication can ensure that anyone with an Aadhaar number is eligible for an Aadhaar-enabled bank account. Customer acquisition costs can come down substantially by leveraging the Aadhaar enrolment and saving the costs of biometric devices and labour. Additionally, Aadhaar authentication will ensure that only the eligible beneficiary can operate the Aadhaar-enabled bank account. This simplifies and strengthens the security of transactions, both for the banks and the customers.

Fixed Costs of IT

The existing banking infrastructure is not suited for no-frills banking. For example, core banking systems at banks today, which are required for electronic transactions, provide for accounts with a whole range of features, and have formidable fixed and marginal costs for no-frills accounts. Given the diversity of core banking platforms and IT capabilities of banks, adding hundreds of millions of no-frills accounts to existing core banking systems may not be feasible. A fresh look at hosting no-frills accounts on new platforms that either the banks implement or outsource may be necessary to achieve the desired transaction costs. The costs can be brought down by hosting no-frills accounts on the bank's existing core banking systems, or on a separate dedicated system. Alternatively, banks may outsource the hosting to a low-cost depository.

Transaction Costs

Transaction costs are also high: it costs a bank roughly Rs 40 for each teller transaction and Rs 10 for each ATM transaction. Passbook updates take time, and increase the cost of labour per transaction. Technology can be used to bring down the cost of transactions. For example, mobile, phone, and Internet banking are much cheaper than traditional channels. Further, costs will fall substantially with volumes as fixed costs get shared over a large number of transactions, as has been observed in mobile telephony. A technology infrastructure that enables a transaction of Rs 10 for a cost of, say, 10 paise can help build a high-volume, low-cost model, which is beneficial for all stakeholders.

ROLE OF TECHNOLOGY

According to the UIDAI, technology is a central part of the micropayments structure and essential to a cost-effective solution. Any technology solution that is deployed for micropayments must have the following features:

1. *Interoperability among banks*: Today, with the ATM network, customers of any bank can withdraw funds from any other bank. Similarly, customers banking through a BC must be able to access their Aadhaar-enabled bank account at any bank, and operate it.
2. *Cost-effective BC network*: It must be profitable to create and maintain a BC network for banks. Thus, the devices deployed and the networks created must be cost effective.

3. *Leveraging existing systems*: Banks have made a significant investment in payment network. The NPCI has been set up to run a pan-India payments, clearing, and settlement network. To the extent possible, existing technology can be used to minimize time to market and bring down the costs.
4. *Connectivity*: Aadhaar-enabled micropayments depend on online connectivity which could be through mobile, fixed line, or Internet connections. One can expect substantial expansion in online connectivity with the implementation of the proposed initiative of the Department of Telecommunications to connect all gram panchayats with high-speed fibre optic network (UIDAI 2010d: 12).

Keeping these goals in mind, UIDAI has proposed the following technology solutions.

MicroATM Standardization

The microATM is a device that will be used by a multitude of BCs to deliver basic banking services at the last mile. The costs of failing to standardize a device like the microATM are high, as large sections of the Indian society will continue to be left out of the country's financial system. The telecom industry is widely regarded for relentlessly driving down costs and bringing coverage to large parts of the Indian population. Similar success is possible in the payments industry. The microATM is a first step towards providing an online, interoperable, low-cost payments platform to everyone in the country. The microATM device design and system architecture are influenced by the design of debit/credit card processing on PoS terminals, combined with authentication services that the UIDAI will provide. The microATM is deployed by banks either directly or through service providers. The microATM standards are broad based, standard based, and generic. They are based on bank-led model for financial inclusion, where the Aadhaar infrastructure is an overlay on the existing infrastructure. The basic transaction types that the microATM will support are:

1. deposits;
2. withdrawals;

3. funds transfer; and
4. balance enquiry and mini-statement (UIDAI 2010d: 12–13).

The objectives of these specifications are to:

1. bring down transaction costs;
2. ensure interoperability;
3. ensure security and transparency of transactions;
4. bring down the cost by being compatible with existing systems;
5. provide a uniform customer experience; and
6. reduce agent training needs (UIDAI 2010d: 13).

An Aadhaar-enabled Interoperable Payments Switch

Choice and mobility is the key to the success of Aadhaar-enabled micropayments. A customer should thus be able to go any BC with a microATM device and access his account, much the same way as an ATM. It should not matter if the BC is appointed by his own bank or by a different bank. Thus, a payment switch that makes the model interoperable is essential (UIDAI 2010d: 14).

The NPCI has been formed to switch all the retail payments and fund transfer transactions in India to a central infrastructure. The NPCI has defined business lines to process inter-bank transactions for ATM, PoS, 24x7 remittance, and also set up an Automatic Clearance House (ACH). The NPCI will also offer Aadhaar authentication on its switches, and has defined message formats for interoperability (UIDAI 2010d: 14).

The architecture that will route all inter-bank payment messages is similar to what already exists for ATM and PoS switching, and is used by several banks. Most transactions in villages are expected to be ON-US transactions, where both the customer and the BC are from the same bank. In urban areas, and when customers travel, the inter-bank OFF-US transactions make it possible for them to access their bank accounts through any BC with a microATM. Aadhaar-enabled micropayments will only require minor modifications to carry a biometric payload in the messages and the ability to authenticate from a central location. The rest of the banking infrastructure remains unmodified (UIDAI 2010d: 14).

Aadhaar-enabled Deposit of Government Benefits

A critical part of the Aadhaar-enabled micropayments infrastructure is the direct deposit of government benefits into the accounts of the beneficiaries. A government department should be able to disburse benefits by simply generating a list that contains the Aadhaar in one column and the amount in another column. At a certain level, this is no different from the payroll of a firm, where on a given day, money is transferred directly from a firm's account to its employees' accounts. However, what makes this process challenging is the scale and complexity. Government benefit programmes are typically funded by the central government, but implemented by state governments. Different state and local governments park their funds in different banks. The beneficiaries, for reasons of convenience and access, have their accounts spread across a number of banks. Two critical pieces of infrastructure are required to implement Aadhaar-enabled disbursement of government benefits:

1. Government departments must have IT systems that maintain a list of beneficiaries by Aadhaar numbers, and also track any programme-specific information required for disbursing the benefit. At the time of disbursement, a list of Aadhaars and amounts are generated and sent to the bank servicing the concerned government department.
2. A nationwide payments infrastructure can then distribute payments into beneficiary's accounts using their Aadhaar numbers (UIDAI 2010d: 15).

The first piece of infrastructure, where the government generates the payment instruction, needs to be in place in various government departments. The second piece of infrastructure, which is the actual payment, can be handled by an Aadhaar-aware ACH that is being put in place at the NPCI (UIDAI 2010d: 15).

Bridging the Last Mile with Mobile Connectivity

Several local groups and agencies working as BCs will put the process of financial inclusion into high gear across the country. Further gains are possible by letting customers access their Aadhaar-enabled bank accounts through mobile phones owned by them or the BC. Mobile phones are fast becoming a ubiquitous phenomenon across the country, including in rural India, and can offer people far away from the closest branch of the banking institution affordable access to financial services. They can serve as simple, secure, and reliable links for transactions: their utility can range from basic information alerts to more advanced cashless person-to-person transactions. The advantages of such infrastructure are significant in the following ways:

1. Mobile phones can instantly notify customers of cash transfers from the customer account to the BC's account, and vice versa, via SMS. If the customer does not own a mobile phone, he/she can make an interactive voice response system (IVRS) call through any available phone to check if the transaction has been made. Governments can also make use of the mobile SMS platform or IVRS to inform beneficiaries whenever money has been credited into their accounts.
2. A voice-activated system can be used to let the customers control every transaction and be aware of each step in the transaction process. An interactive voice menu activated either by the mobile phone's handset keys or by the customer's voice can provide users simplified access to informed banking.
3. A mobile phone will allow customers to place a complaint against any BC who they think has tampered with the transaction or short-changed them, and the transaction can be put on hold.
4. The Aadhaar-based mobile transaction will offer real-time online verification and authentication.
5. By combining the ubiquity of mobile phones with high-volume, low-cost payments network, it will be possible to reach a stage of effortless person-to-person cashless transactions (UIDAI 2010d: 15–16).

ANALYSIS OF THE UIDAI CLAIMS

Any solution for financial inclusion of the poor needs to be analysed as to whether it meets the requirements of:

1. providing proof of identification and proof of address;
2. enabling access;

3. enabling payments; and
4. providing hassle-free transactions (*The Economic Times* 2011c: 13).

Does the financial inclusion solution proposed by the Aadhaar programme meet these requirements?

PROOF OF IDENTIFICATION AND PROOF OF ADDRESS

In banking operations, opening of a bank account requires the applicant to provide proof of identification and address. The UIDAI claims that the Aadhaar number will help the poor in meeting these two requirements. According to the UIDAI, the strong identification that Aadhaar offers, combined with its KYR standards, can remove the need for individual KYC required by banks for opening a no-frills account. Aadhaar can thus serve as sufficient proof of identification and address, akin to the SSN in the US.

The claim that Aadhaar should suffice as proof of identity and address was partly validated when, in June 2011, oil marketing companies, such as the Indian Oil Corporation, Bharat Petroleum Corporation, and Hindustan Petroleum Corporation, decided to accept Aadhaar as proof of identity and proof of address while accepting booking for LPG cooking gas connection. However, the RBI, India's banking regulator, issued instructions in 2011 to the effect that, while Aadhaar can be accepted as a proof of identification, a separate proof of address was required to open a bank account (*The Times of India* 2011b: 23). In a circular to banks, issued on 28 September 2011, the RBI stated, 'It is reiterated that while opening accounts based on Aadhaar also, banks must satisfy themselves about the current address of the customer by obtaining required proof of the same as per extant instructions' (*The Times of India* 2011b: 23).

Now, with this RBI directive that the Aadhaar number will not suffice for providing proof of address, it meets the KYC norms of banks only halfway. This, unfortunately, would have the effect of subverting the goal of Aadhaar-based financial inclusion for the poor. According to bankers, while it is possible for the poor to produce proof of identity in the form of a voter ID card, it is the proof of address that is really a challenging task in view of the fact there are many among the poor who own neither a landline telephone nor any home ownership documents. Although there is high mobile penetration in India now, most of these phones are prepaid and therefore, the customers do not have the bills that could have sufficed as proof of address. However, this does not seem to be an unsurmountable constraint, because the RBI can be prevailed upon to accept Aadhaar as a proof of address.

Access

In terms of access, the spread of banking institutions in rural areas, where most of the poor live, becomes important. It is estimated that 480 million people in India do not have access to banking services, and almost all of them live in India's 630,000 villages (Rajshekhar 2012a: 13). It is an irony that, 60 years after independence, India continues to be appallingly underbanked. Average population handled by a bank branch is as high as 14,000 (Gupta 2012: 11). This becomes a big challenge, considering the additional baggage that rural India carries in terms of vast differences in topography, population, and a big bucket of regional differences every few 100 km (Gupta 2012: 11).

It is true that in post-independent India, a slew of development schemes were initiated to address structural poverty by directing both subsidy-based schemes as well as credit into specific chunks of population and neglected sectors of the economy, and these schemes were weighted in favour of the poor (Gupta 2012: 11). Though these schemes were in operation for several decades till the 1990s, they had very little impact in enabling financial inclusion of the poor. In fact, the first index of financial inclusion, prepared by the Indian Council of Research on International Economic Relations (ICRIER) to determine the extent of the reach of banking services in 100 countries, placed India at the 50th spot, which was way below the ranking of countries like Kenya and Morocco (*The Times of India* 2012a: 21).

Taking serious note of the sluggish growth in expansion of banking services in rural areas and its visibly negative impact on financial inclusion for the poor, the RBI set time-bound targets in 2009. The targets stipulated that 72,800 villages in the country with a population of above 2,000 should have banking access by March

2012, and 348,000 villages with a population of above 1,000 should be covered before 2013 (Rajshekhar 2012a: 13). To realize these targets, the banking sector identified 74,414 villages with population over 2,000 for provision of banking facilities and 74,199 of these have been covered till March 2012 (Gupta 2012: 11). Total banking outlets as per the June 2012 update have reached 1,47,534, which is almost twice of what it was a year ago (Gupta 2012: 11). The number of no-frills accounts has shot up to 103 million and some 23.34 million-odd Kissan Credit Cards have been issued for the year ending March 2012 (Gupta 2012: 11). The numbers are certainly impressive. This kind of growth in the number of villages covered and bank accounts opened had not been witnessed in India before. Usha Thorat, the former Deputy Governor of the RBI, says, 'What could not be done in the last fifty years has been done in the last six' (Rajshekhar 2012a: 13). While the banks opened brick-and-mortar branches in 25 per cent of these villages, BCs were placed in the remaining places (Rajshekhar 2012a: 13).

In May 2012, Government of India decided to deepen financial inclusion even further with a view to accommodating a wider swathe of the population in the banking net (Ray 2012: 10). In a circular issued on 18 May 2012, the Ministry of Finance directed all State Level Bankers Committees (SLBCs) to draw up action plans and identify villages by the end of June 2012, and instructed banks to ensure that the implementation of the action plans was completed by March 2013 (Ray 2012: 10). Banks were told to reach out to villages with a population of 1,600 and above (as per the 2001 census) through bank branches or BCs, while the earlier direction of the RBI was to extend banking services to places with a population over 2,000. According to the Ministry of Finance, villages with 1,600 or more people, as per the 2001 census, would have crossed the 2,000 population mark with a decade having passed after the 2001 census.

What this directive of the Ministry of Finance means is that banks in 16 states would have to follow the new instructions, while the ministry had earlier set a benchmark of 1,000 people and above in Jammu & Kashmir, Himachal Pradesh, Uttarakhand, and eight north-eastern states, including Sikkim. Banks in Chhattisgarh and union territories were now asked to reach out to villages with 1,000 inhabitants by September 2012. In addition, the RBI has advised all banks to set up low-cost outlets, or ultra small branches, to act as a bridge between bank branches and BCs (Ray 2012: 10). These low-cost branches are expected to provide support for eight to 10 BC units and have a minimum infrastructure like passbook printer, cash retention facility, and terminals equipped with modern banking technology.

While the number of villages covered and bank accounts opened between March 2010 and May 2011, and the subsequent plans drawn up, look impressive on paper, the ground reality is different with respect to the financial inclusion actually achieved for the poor. Three independent studies conducted by Microsave, Centre for Microfinance Research, and Skoch, in three different parts of the country, show that 80–90 per cent of these accounts are inactive (Rajshekhar 2012a: 13). The poor hardly use these accounts, and banks, citing a poor business case, are not particularly enthusiastic in promoting these accounts. The study by Skoch found that only 11 per cent of the 25.1 million no-frills accounts opened between April 2007 and May 2009 were active, which was confirmed by the findings of a study by Microsave. According to the numbers available in June 2011, 20 per cent of the no-frills accounts had not been used for 0–6 months, 19 per cent had not been used for six months to one year, and 59 per cent had not been used for more than one year, while two per cent had not been used at all.

Why is the situation so bleak? Most of these accounts are either no-frills accounts or EBT accounts. Earlier, banks used to stipulate that a bank account must have a certain minimum balance, and this was a constraint for the poor to operate their bank accounts. That is why, in 2005, the RBI asked banks to open no-frills accounts, which do not stipulate a minimum balance requirement. The no-frills accounts allow an account holder to make deposits and withdrawals. They even offer an overdraft facility, a savings product like a recurring deposit, and a Kissan Credit Card. The EBT accounts are opened to enable transfer of welfare payments like the MGNREGS wages and the pensions directly to the bank accounts of the beneficiaries. The EBT accounts are a kind of no-frills account where account holders can make only withdrawals.

The problem with the no-frills accounts is that they are not financially viable. A study of no-frills accounts in Cuddalore district in Tamil Nadu, conducted by S. Thyagarajan and Jayaram Venkatesan

(2008), found that no-frills accounts are expensive to create and operate, largely due to the fact that the process is labour intensive for the banks. Since most no-frills accounts have very little balance, banks cannot recoup the account through float. The study, however, brought out the interesting insight that no-frills accounts, which stay active, have steadily increasing balances as time progresses.

The banks have their own method of calculating what makes a banking account viable. It costs the banks Rs 200 to open an account and every transaction at a branch costs the bank at least Rs 20. So, the average account balance needs to be Rs 2,000–Rs 3,000 for the account to be viable, and the average account balance in no-frills accounts is much less. As a manager in State Bank of India (SBI) says, 'For our no-frills accounts to be viable, the average balance should be Rs 2,000–3,000. Right now, it is Rs. 67' (Rajshekhar 2012a: 13). Banks hope to make money on no-frills accounts by lending out what is deposited in them, but as it happens, not enough money resides or flows through them, and the banks cannot make any money on these no-frills accounts. That is why banks are averse to bear the financial burden caused by no-frills accounts. They have tried to get over this problem by outsourcing the no-frills accounts to BC companies. This relieves the banks from setting up branches in rural areas, which are also not particularly profitable.

However, D. Subbarao, former Governor of the RBI, thinks that the banks are eschewing low-value customers and small transactions because of their mindset and their failure to see opportunity at the bottom of the pyramid (*The Times of India* 2012a: 21). As he says: 'Unless banks are convinced that reaching out to the common man is just not a forced regulatory imperative but a potential business opportunity, the numbers will remain without life. The Reserve Bank looks forward to competition among banks to develop business models for such small, low staff and low cost branches' (*The Times of India* 2012a: 21). According to Subbarao, bank branches should focus on financial inclusion and not leave the job for BCs. He is of the view that there is a strong case for a much larger effort on innovating a cost-effective village branch model. He says:

> By and large banks have outsourced the 'last mile' to intermediaries such as microfinance institutions and self-help groups. This is a model that has worked, and one that we should pursue, and refine.

Nevertheless, the question is, 'Is there a business case for banks to do some of the last mile themselves? Can banks rely entirely on outsourcing? Isn't there a valuable experience to be gained by banks by dirtying their hands more and reoccupying the last mile?'

The general impression I got is that frontline bank managers treat no-frills accounts as a nuisance and low-income households as an intrusion to their time and their business. This is disappointing to say the least. Banks should look upon financial inclusion not as an obligation but as an opportunity to build fortune at the bottom of the pyramid. I am also conscious that the bulk of our effort so far has been from the supply side—opening branches, appointing BCs and opening accounts that remain largely inoperative. If this is all that happens, the entire effort is both futile and wasteful. We need to supplement the supply side effort by a demand side effort—by reaching out to people left behind, inspiring their trust and confidence in the banking system and supporting them in improving the quality of their lives. (*The Times of India* 2012a: 21)

Branchless Banking

The governor, RBI, may have his reservations, but branchless banking has emerged as an alternative to brick-and-mortar bank branches as a means of reaching out to unbanked areas. Such branchless banking, in which banks are permitted to engage agents, was made possible due to changes made by the RBI in the regulatory framework for provision of financial and banking services. An important step in this direction was taken when the RBI (2006a) issued guidelines, in January 2006, for engagement of BCs by banks. Since then, the regulatory framework for the BC model has gradually been honed to ensure that consumer protection is not compromised while facilitating enhanced outreach of banking services.[1] These relaxations in the regulatory framework have come about because of rapid changes in technology—both in terms of core banking solutions (CBS) as well as relatively low-cost biometric hand-held devices—for ensuring authenticity and preventing fraud. In fact, the entire financial inclusion hemisphere, today, is ruled by technology. Technology is the key driver not only because of the cost and outreach parameters but also for the fact that it has become increasingly difficult for a simple brick-and-mortar bank branch to provide the entire gamut of services on the traditional platform (Gupta 2012: 11). Another reason is that the products required by the poor, like micro-pension, micro-insurance, remittances, as well as EBTs, are now essentially designed to work on technology (Gupta 2012: 11).

Business Correspondents

The BCs are retail agents engaged by banks for providing banking services at locations other than a bank branch/ATM (RBI 2010a: 1). Banks are required to take full responsibility for all acts of omission and commission by BCs whom they engage (RBI 2010a: 1). That being the case, it is necessary for the banks to exercise due diligence and install additional safeguards so that agency risk can be minimized. Basically, BCs enable a bank to expand its outreach and offer limited range of banking services at a low cost. The BCs, thus, are an integral part of the business strategy for achieving greater financial inclusion. The regulatory framework, evolved by the RBI, permits BCs to perform a variety of activities, which include:

1. identification of borrowers;
2. collection and preliminary processing of loan applications, including verification of primary information/data;
3. creating awareness about savings and other products, and education and advice on managing money and debt counselling;
4. processing and submission of applications to banks;
5. promoting, nurturing, and monitoring of self-help groups/joint liability groups/credit groups/others;
6. post-sanction monitoring;
7. follow-up for recovery;
8. disbursal of small-value credit;
9. recovery of principal/collection of interest;
10. collection of small-value deposits;
11. sale of micro-insurance/mutual fund products/pension products/ other third-party products; and
12. receipt and delivery of small-value remittances/other payment instruments (RBI 2010b: 2).

On the whole, the activities undertaken by BCs are fully within the normal course of the bank's banking business, but conducted through them at places other than the bank premises and ATMs.

Eligible Individuals/Entities

The banks are permitted to engage the following individuals/entities as BCs:

1. Individuals such as retired bank employees, retired teachers, retired government employees and ex-servicemen, individual owners of kirana/medical/FPSs, individual public call office operators, agents of small savings schemes of Government of India/insurance companies, individuals who own petrol pumps, authorized functionaries of well-run self-help groups which are linked to banks, and any other individuals, including those operating CSCs.
2. The NGOs/MFIs set up under societies/trust acts and Section 25 companies.
3. Cooperative societies registered under Mutually Aided Cooperative Societies Acts of states/Multi-state Cooperative Societies Act.
4. Post offices.
5. Companies registered under the Indian Companies Act, 1956, with large and widespread retail outlets, excluding non-banking financial companies (NBFCs) (RBI 2010b: 1–2).

Distance Criterion

Every BC is required to be attached to and under the oversight of a specific brick-and-mortar bank branch designated as the base branch. This is necessary in order to ensure that adequate supervision is exercised over the operations and activities of BCs by banks. This is also required by the guidelines issued by the RBI in April 2008, which stipulate that the distance between the place of business of a BC and the base branch should not exceed 15 km in rural, semi-urban, and urban areas, and 5 km in metropolitan centres. However, the guidelines also provide the waiver that, in case there is a need to relax the distance criterion, the District Consultative Committee/ SLBC could consider and approve relaxation on merits in respect of underbanked areas, etc (RBI 2010b: 2). Subsequently, the maximum distance criterion in respect of rural, semi-urban, and urban areas was raised from 15 km to 30 km (RBI 2010a: 1).

Transactions through the BC

The engagement of intermediaries such as BCs involves significant reputational, legal, and operational risks, and therefore, banks which appoint BCs are generally sensitive to these risks. In fact, banks adopt technology-based solutions for managing these risks, besides increasing the outreach in a cost-effective manner. The transactions are normally through ICT devices (hand-held device/mobile phone) that are seamlessly integrated to the CBS of the bank. The transactions are counted on a real-time basis and the customers receive immediate verification of the transaction through visuals (screen based) or other means (debit or credit slip) (RBI 2010b: 2).

Performance of the BC model

T.K. Arun (2012: 11) of *The Economic Times* says, 'Making the brick and mortar model banking inclusive through use of business correspondent has been a failure.' In fact, although various categories of entities and individuals are permitted by the RBI to act as BCs, only a few banks have engaged them: out of 50 private and public sector banks, only 27 banks have reported engaging BCs (RBI 2010a: 2). Most of these banks have engaged Section 25 companies/trusts/societies as BCs (RBI 2010a: 2). Almost all the Section 25 companies engaged by banks have been floated by the technology service providers who provide smart cards or biometric solutions for account openings, etc (RBI 2010a: 2). FINO, a technology company working together with its non-profit partner, Fintech Foundation, which acts as BC network manager, has opened about 10 million accounts on behalf of 14 banks, post offices, and government agencies (RBI 2010a: 2). A Little World (ALW) and its non-profit partner, Zero Mass Foundation, have opened about 4 million accounts as BCs for 20 banks (RBI 2010a: 2). Eko is a similar technology-focused company, with Eko Aspire Foundation, a parallel non-profit organization, operating as BC for SBI (RBI 2010a: 2). Similarly, Integra Micro Systems has also provided technology solution under the BC model to a few banks (RBI 2010a: 2). But the numbers are limited. While many banks have accepted the adoption of the BC model in principle, only a few of them have scaled it up beyond the pilot stage (RBI 2010a: 2).

Transfer of Government Welfare Benefits

Banks also use BCs to transfer government welfare benefits to beneficiaries. However, the financial margin provided for transferring these benefits to the beneficiaries is rather low. When the state government takes the help of banks to make transfers of welfare benefits to beneficiaries through BCs, it pays a flat fee to the banks. However, the general complaint of BC companies is that the banks do not pay them enough. The banks, in turn, say that the government does not pay them enough. According to Usha Thorat, the former Deputy Governor of the RBI, 'There is great reluctance inside the government to pay, saying there is a float the banks enjoy' (Rajshekhar 2012a: 13). Usually, the state governments pay two per cent of the transfer amount to the banks (Rajshekhar 2012a: 13). The banks say, 'We're not breaking even with this. The BC takes 1.75%. We are left with just 0.25%, out of which we also have to pay for the smart card. It is for states to give banks some margin. Most states are not willing to pass us any margin' (Rajshekhar 2012a: 13). Manish Khera, the CEO of FINO, a BC company, says, 'There is no scientific basis for the 1.75%' (Rajshekhar 2012a: 13).

The BC model is under strain because the margin is low. To compound the problem, more and more private companies are entering the fray. With so many players coming in, competition among BC companies has become fierce and they submit low bids in order to win contracts. In the process, several BC companies, which have won contracts with low bids, fail to deliver. In most cases, these companies try to cut their costs by deploying fewer agents and terminals. As a former executive of a BC company complains, 'They give their agents such large territories that they travel to each village infrequently' (Rajshekhar 2012a: 13). This makes the villagers nervous and leads to a situation in which the villagers, unsure of when the agent would come next, are forced to keep as little money in their no-frills accounts as possible (Rajshekhar 2012a: 13).

Inadequate margins combined with the absence of well-defined service standards have had an adverse impact on the delivery of welfare benefits to beneficiaries in rural areas through BCs. One example is the payment of MGNREGS wages. An amendment to Schedule II of the NREGA now makes it mandatory for the state governments to ensure that the beneficiaries receive their wage entitlements within 15 days (*The Economic Times* 2011a: 9). In Andhra Pradesh, beneficiaries did not get their wages within 15 days when wages were being paid through BCs. Reddy Subramaniam, Principal Secretary, Rural Development Department, Government of Andhra Pradesh, says, 'Banks and Business Correspondents were delaying payments in order to earn interest income [from the float]' (Rajshekhar 2012a: 13). That is why the central government and the state government instructed the banks and BCs to pay wages within the period stipulated by the NREGA. To reinforce their point, the instructions defined payment as full withdrawal by the account holder.

The banks as well as BC companies have serious reservations about these instructions. As a bank manager says, 'First, states told us that we could not charge for payments as money would stay in the accounts, and we could earn interest. Now, they want the entire cash withdrawn. This is not banking for me. I gain when he keeps the money in my account...' (Rajshekhar 2012a: 13). The BC companies have also reacted sharply to these instructions. Manish Khera, CEO of FINO, says, 'Pensions now have to be paid in the first four days of the month. This means that we need to hire people to meet peak demand' (Rajshekhar 2012a: 13). He is of the view that BC companies cannot survive on the existing charge of 1.75 per cent of the disbursed amount. According to Manish Khera, if FINO was maintaining a working capital of Rs 5,000 with an agent, it will now mean keeping 2–3 lakh rupees in the beginning of every month (Rajshekhar 2012a: 13). Khera points out, 'My risk goes up. As does my cost to deliver. I could send Rs. 5,000 on a motorcycle. One guy could go and service five or six BCs. But now, I will need a van' (Rajshekhar 2012a: 13). Khera estimates that, as the service standards expected of the BCs are on the rise, the break-even margin would be of the order of five per cent. The banks also voice similar concerns. They say, 'We are saving states a lot of money by reducing corruption. For NREGA, the Centre gives states six per cent as administrative cost. Why can't they give us more from this?' (Rajshekhar 2012a: 13).

It so happens that the motivation of each of the stakeholder involved in the process is different. As far as banks are concerned, they strive to please the RBI by complying with the order of the regulator to extend banking to unbanked areas, but, in reality, they are not particularly interested in these transactions. They also want to keep their costs down. That is why they prefer BCs to bank branches. In addition, instead of hiring BCs who work with their branch staff, they prefer to outsource the BC operations to companies like FINO. For the BC companies, the motivation is to make profit in spite of the low margin.

The banks now assess bids from BC companies on two parameters: (i) the cost of opening accounts; and (ii) the cost of servicing them. The BC companies ask for more money for opening of accounts and less money for servicing them. As Manish Khera says, 'And then, they open accounts with low quality infrastructure. Practically everyone is doing this. With banks awarding contracts to the lowest bidder, there is no check on quality' (Rajshekhar 2012a: 13).

The matter is compounded by the fact that there is substantial attrition in the rank of BCs. As Anurag Yadav, Additional Commissioner, NREGA, Government of Uttar Pradesh, says: 'The attrition rate is 70–80 per cent, even 100 per cent. When an agent leaves, a village loses access to banking till a new agent is found. Their income is too low. If he is running an existing business, he will not have the time to run around for these small transactions' (Rajshekhar 2012a: 13). The attrition rate among BCs being so high, those who see other advantages in becoming BCs are interested in taking up these assignments. About 75 per cent of the BCs in Punjab are either the sarpanches themselves or their kith and kin. This can subvert the implementation of MGNREGS. The system of payments of wages to MGNREGS workers through banks was started in order to ensure that sarpanches, who allotted work, did not handle payments too. This was for the reason that if they handled payments, they would fake muster rolls. This safeguard will not work once the sarpanch or his kin is the BC for the bank handling MGNREGS payments.

Has the institution of BCs succeeded in delivering welfare payments to beneficiaries in rural India? The experience has not been particularly rewarding. Andhra Pradesh, which experimented with the system of BCs along with other modes of payment, came to the conclusion that post offices are more efficient and easier to monitor than BCs. Jharkhand has a BC system, with an agent posted to almost every village (*The Economic Times* 2011k: 15). At present, BCs in Jharkhand are entrusted with the responsibility of delivering MGNREGS payments to the beneficiaries by the banks. The general complaint is that banks and BCs delay MGNREGS payments for a month or more to earn interest on the money that should be paid to workers (*The Economic Times* 2011k: 15). In Jharkhand, another complaint is that the BC system has tied the villagers to a BC of a particular company. This has made the BC a power centre in the village. If the villagers are allowed to access their bank account from another source, this would reduce the risk of the BC becoming a power centre in the village (*The Economic Times* 2011k: 15).

Haryana was one of the first states to experiment with delivery of government benefits through the BC system, starting with social sector pensions in 2011 (Rajshekhar 2012a: 13). But, after widespread complaints of payment delays and absent BCs, the state reverted to payments through village sarpanches in six months. Chastened by the Haryana experience, the SBI, India's largest bank, is seriously considering about its participation in such schemes (Rajshekhar 2012a: 13). A senior manager of the SBI says, 'After Haryana, we have not bid for any state government contracts [on electronic transfer of welfare benefits]' (Rajshekhar 2012a: 13).

In Haryana, welfare benefits amounting to 130 crore rupees are paid every month to 21 lakh beneficiaries, consisting of senior citizens, widows, destitute, and disabled (Khemka 2012: 12). For the purpose, more than two million bank accounts have been created in the Department of Social Justice and Empowerment (Khemka 2012: 12). The success of the programme depends on the timely payment of the benefits without leakages. To catalyse quicker implementation, the state started crediting financial benefits electronically under various social security schemes directly into the bank accounts under the EBT scheme handled by BCs (Khemka 2012: 12). The EBTs go directly into bank accounts ensuring benefits reach the intended targets without time lag, minimizing chances of misappropriation. In Haryana, the EBT scheme operates in 20 out of the 21 districts in the state, with 1.9 million accounts in active use (Khemka 2012: 12).

Why did things go wrong in Haryana? Ashok Khemka, Director General, Social Justice and Empowerment, Government of Haryana, blames a 20–5 per cent error in identification using biometrics and severely inadequate infrastructure of BCs (Rajshekhar 2012a: 13). The minutes of a state-level review (December 2011) chaired by the chief minister record that the implementation by bank-appointed BCs 'is not satisfactory'; is 'tantamount to denial of banking service to senior citizens, destitute and disabled beneficiaries and their right to enjoy the benefit of timely remittance' (Rajshekhar 2012a: 13). The minutes also record that 'the schedule of visits of the BC is uncertain causing inconvenience'; BC's visits are infrequent—'in some villages, there has been no visit at all in the last 6 months' (Rajshekhar 2012a: 13). Other problems include 'manual payments', 'not carrying out biometrics based de-duplication', and 'non-supply of transaction data for monitoring' (Rajshekhar 2012a: 13). In addition, 18 of the 20 districts had far fewer terminals than agreed upon, with the shortfall ranging from 73.9 per cent to 99.9 per cent (Rajshekhar 2012a: 13). S.S. Ghungre, General Manager of the Union Bank's financial inclusion department agrees and says, 'There were not enough terminals' (Rajshekhar 2012a: 13). The other side of the picture is provided by Manish Khera of FINO, the BC company operating in Mewat. He says that Government of Haryana changed terms midway: it halved the number of customers per agent in January 2011 and in the middle of that year, asked BCs to make payments in four days (Rajshekhar 2012a: 13).

Clearly, the infrastructure was grossly inadequate. The problems, as was pointed out, are the infrequent visit of the BC to the village, lack of biometric-based de-duplication, and lack of terminals. What we need under the circumstances is that there must be at least one BC in each village so that the villagers do not have to wait for the BC's visit to the village. It also establishes the need for the BC in the village to be equipped with a microATM, which can be shared by multiple banks. But the most serious problem seems to be that the margin is low and that is why the institution of BCs is not financially viable.

PAYMENTS

Things looked up in April 2010 when the government accepted a comprehensive mobile banking framework recommended by the Inter-Ministerial Group on Delivery of Basic Financial Services Using Mobile Phones, which specifically targeted the unbanked poor.[2] The report recommended the creation of mobile-linked no-frills accounts by the banks. Mobile users could deposit and draw cash instantly from these accounts through BCs. The report described an electronic payments architecture consisting of a central low-cost accounts repository, a mobile number and Aadhaar-based account mapper, an interoperable payments switch, and the usage of biometric microATMs and mobile phones at the last mile.[3] In terms of this report of the Inter-Ministerial Group, the users of the account and the BC only needed to have their mobile phones to make cash deposits and withdraw money. The account holders could also transfer money to each other electronically by specifying their mobile numbers. The government also could transfer welfare payments to these accounts. The overall logic of this kind of delivery of basic financial services was that it would reduce transaction costs for the poor significantly (Krishnan 2011: 14).

The Inter-Ministerial Group also recommended that multiple banks should share the same BC in a village for deposits and withdrawals.[4] The system that the Inter-Ministerial Group proposed is very much like the general collaborative environment that has evolved around the mobile phone business, in which competing mobile operators share the front-end outlets of airtime vendors (Krishnan 2011: 14). The system is also like the ATM network of the banks, in which the customer of any bank can withdraw funds from any other bank (Krishnan 2011: 14). In fact, as the Inter-Ministerial Group envisioned it, the poor in rural India, banking through the BC in their village, should be able to access their bank account at any bank, and should be able to operate it (Krishnan 2011: 14).

However, the problem was that the regulatory framework laid down by the RBI did not allow the services of a BC of a particular bank to be shared by multiple banks. In fact, the circular of the RBI on BC model, dated 28 September 2010, stated: 'While a Business Correspondent can be a Business Correspondent for more than one bank, at the point of customer interface, a retail outlet or a sub-agent of the Banking Correspondent shall represent and provide banking services of one bank' (RBI 2010b: 2). That is why the Inter-Ministerial Group had recommended that multiple banks should share the same BC in a village for deposits and withdrawals, and had urged the RBI to relax its stipulation. The RBI, in its circular dated 2 March 2012, has now instructed:

> In this connection, it has been decided to permit interoperability at the retail outlets or sub-agents of Business Correspondents (i.e. at the point of customer interface), provided the technology available with the bank, which has appointed the Business Correspondent, supports interoperability, subject to the following conditions:

a) The transactions and authentications at such retail outlets or sub-agents of Business Correspondents are carried out on-line;

b) The transactions are carried out on Core Banking Solution (CBS) platforms; and

c) The banks follow the standard operating procedures to be advised by the Indian Banks Association (IBA). However, the Business Correspondent or its retail outlet or sub-agent at the point of customer interface would continue to represent the bank, which has appointed the Business Correspondent. (RBI 2012: 1)

The Inter-Ministerial Group had also urged the RBI to relax its stipulation that the BC or his sub-agent should be within a 30 km distance of a branch of the sponsoring bank, in cases where there is no bank branch within a 30 km distance. We need to appreciate that this stipulation of the RBI is, by no means, absolute. The RBI had stipulated:

> The distance between the place of business of a retail outlet/sub-agent of Business Correspondent and the base branch should ordinarily not exceed 30 kms in rural, semi-urban and urban areas and 5 kms in metropolitan centres. In case there is a need to relax the distance criterion, the District Consultative Committee (DCC)/State level Bankers Committee (SLBC) could approve relaxation on merits in respect of under-banked areas etc. (RBI 2010b: 2)

So, there is an enabling provision to grant relaxation of the stipulation in cases where there is no bank branch within a 30 km distance. The more important question is: is such tethering of the branchless model's inherent flexibility to a physical branch a constraint? This has to be considered against the background that such tethering is necessary with a view to ensuring that the banks have to exercise adequate supervision over the operations and activities of the retail outlets/sub-agents of the BCs. That is why every retail outlet/sub-agent of the BC is required to be attached to, and under the oversight of, a specific bank branch designated as the base branch.

TRANSACTIONS

There is a great deal of similarity between the system used by mobile operators and the nature of the transaction as contemplated to be made on the Aadhaar-based bank account. The bulk of mobile subscribers have prepaid subscriptions and each time a customer purchases talktime for his phone in the form of Rs 10 or Rs 15 prepaid cards, he is exchanging physical cash for electronic cash in the form of talktime. Similarly, the BC deposits a certain amount with a bank. Every transaction made by the BC would change the pre-paid balance paid by the BC to the bank. For example, it would increase when a customer withdraws money. On the other hand, it would decrease when a customer makes a deposit transaction, in which a part is transferred to the account of the customer. When a deposit is made by the customer, it would mean that the customer is paying physical cash to the BC who, in turn, would make an electronic transfer to the account of the customer from the account of the BC. This approach has some positive advantages: the electronic transfer lowers the costs of cash management for banks, and it also enables physical cash transaction at the rural and local level (this is an important objective of rural banking). This also enables the local BC to offer basic banking services at low risk to the bank.

In the scheme of financial inclusion of the poor, the essential thing is to enable them to open bank accounts and to give them access to their accounts. The idea is to do this through BCs. But the poor can access their accounts only in locations where their bank's BC has a presence. When transactions are not updated real time between the BC and the server of the BC's company, villagers can bank only with the agent. This has ramifications at the field level. As noted earlier, agents of the BC companies are given such large territories that they travel to each village infrequently, and villagers, unsure when the agent would come next, withdraw all their money right away.

Telecom and Other Companies

The Inter-Ministerial Group on Delivery of Basic Financial Services Using Mobile Phones had suggested that the RBI should permit corporate entities to step in and establish BC networks. The idea was to leverage the large number of distribution outlets established by telecom companies, FMCG companies, and so on, as cash-in and cash-out points. Telecom companies have already offered to convert mobile money into cash to facilitate the Aadhaar-enabled payments infrastructure. It is true that telecom companies can certainly help bridge the last mile not only through communication but also by becoming BCs and appointing sub-agents on the ground (Krishnan 2011: 14). Telecom companies, with their high mobile phone penetration, have made out a case that they are in a position to handle payments by using their millions of sale/recharge points to convert mobile money into cash. In fact, Bharti Airtel wants the government to send cash on people's mobile phones, which they can then withdraw at a mobile recharge point.

In addition, prepaid card companies like ITZ Cash are also making out a case to handle welfare payments. Even retailers of companies with a big rural presence are eager to double up as BCs to handle these payments. For example, the SBI is talking to Hindustan Unilever, among others, to take up this work. These companies are interested in the proposition because they do not have retailers for their products in poorer and smaller villages, and the new arrangement will help them to sell their products to the poor in these villages.

With telecom and other corporates willing to come in, the financial inclusion strategy could become a reality for the poor. As T.K. Arun (2012: 11) of *The Economic Times* says: 'To achieve banking inclusion, India needs to harness the technology of mobile phones and the business and the business savvy of making big money from millions of small transactions that underlies mobile telephony in India.' In fact, when the BC model was introduced in 2006, the entities permitted by the RBI to act as BCs included, amongst others, Section 25 companies (RBI 2010a: 1). However, it was subsequently clarified in April 2008 that banks can engage such companies as BCs provided the companies are stand-alone entities or Section 25 companies in which NBFCs, banks, telecom companies, and other corporate entities or their holding companies do not have holdings in excess of 10 per cent (RBI 2010a: 1). Subsequently, as announced in the annual policy statement of the RBI for the year 2010–11, a discussion paper on engagement of 'for-profit' companies as BCs was placed on the website of the RBI, indicating the suggestions received from several quarters (RBI 2010b: 1).

The discussion paper noted that the suggestion from some quarters was to allow banks to use corporates, including telecom companies, as BCs. According to the RBI, the BC model may evolve into two distinct patterns (RBI 2010a: 2). One is that the banks could enter into separate agreements with corporates for using their retail networks, with specific responsibilities and functions to be performed by the corporates for a fee, while the retail outlet is directly appointed as agent of the bank (RBI 2010a: 2). The other pattern is that the banks could make the corporates as BC with no direct privity of contract between the retail outlet and the bank (RBI 2010a: 2). In the second model, the retail outlet becomes a sub-agent of the corporate BC (RBI 2010a: 2). Under both models, banks have to be responsible for all acts of the retail agent as it is the point of contact for the customer where banking transactions take place (RBI 2010a: 2).

The discussion paper assessed the pros and cons of appointing corporates as BCs. They were:

1. Pros

    i. Corporates with large and widespread retail network bring in large resources, higher organizational strength, and financial backing needed for a large network of BCs, besides providing financial security to the bank.
    ii. Corporates as BCs would be more suitable to render banking services in accordance with the bank's internal policies and standards than individual and other small entities.
    iii. Over the years, these companies have developed efficient systems of monitoring and control over the retail outlets/ franchises, including cash management, which could be used to advantage. These outlets are already dealing with the local population and are familiar with them.
    iv. The shopkeepers and other retail agents of the large corporate may be more comfortable dealing with the company that they are already used to and familiar with, rather than with the bank.
    v. Failure of large companies as BCs would mean a reputation risk to the company and endanger its substantive business. As such, the companies could be relied upon to ensure that their agents do not jeopardize their reputation.
    vi. A corporate is likely to continue as BC for a longer period than individuals, thus ensuring continuity of services.

2. Cons

i. Banking and financial services are essentially 'pull' products that are 'sought out' and like postal services, have to be accessible at affordable cost. Banking and financial services should not be 'pushed' towards at the customer, unlike other goods sold by retail agents. Companies may, in the interest of revenue maximization, use their resources and wide distribution network to push banking and financial products unmindful of whether they are suitable or appropriate to such persons. In other words, there are concerns of mis-selling of banking and other products, especially amongst uninformed and illiterate consumers.

ii. A retail agent of a corporate may tend to provide banking services only to those customers who patronize the corporate's products as that would enhance his earnings: this represents a conflict of interest.

iii. Corporate BCs could misuse customer-related information for their own commercial interests. Unfair coercive practices by corporate agents for marketing financial products/recovery of loans, etc, would lead to reputation risks for the banks which have appointed them, besides affecting the confidence of the public in the banking system.

iv. In case the corporate shrinks its business requiring it to discontinue its retail, it may become difficult for banks to find immediate replacement/substitution of the BC, thereby affecting continuity of services (RBI 2010a: 2–3).

Taking into consideration the pros and cons, the RBI stated, in its circular instructions dated 28 September 2010: 'It has been decided to permit banks to engage companies registered under the Indian Companies Act, 1956, excluding NBFCs, as BCs in addition to the individuals/entities permitted earlier, subject to compliance with the guidelines' (RBI 2010b: 1). This decision of the RBI is heartening as far as India's poor are concerned. The RBI is perfectly aware of the fact that, if these companies are appointed as BCs, they will use customer-related information for their own commercial interests, and yet it decided to permit banks to engage these companies as BCs. This is, indeed, cheering news for India's poor. It means that not only the financial inclusion strategy for them would have been complete but also that these companies would use customer-related information for their own commercial interests and armed with that information, sell their products and services to the poor.

On the whole, all the elements for financial inclusion of the poor seem to be in place. As noted earlier, achieving the objective of financial inclusion for the poor requires a combination of organizational innovation, technology application, and financial viability. The solution offered by UIDAI in the form of Aadhaar-enabled bank account offers this combination. As the UIDAI literature makes it clear, the poor in a village can access their Aadhaar-enabled bank account through a BC operating a microATM device. For the purpose, there needs to be interoperability among the different systems adopted by different banks. That is how customers banking through a BC would be able to access their Aadhaar-enabled bank account at any bank, and operate it. Another important aspect is that payment into Aadhaar-enabled bank account depends on having online connectivity, and this connectivity can be in the form of a mobile, fixed line, or Internet connectivity. The UIDAI envisages the microATM as the first step towards providing the online, interoperable, low-cost payments platform to the poor.

The institution of BC is the organizational key to the scheme of financial inclusion for the poor because it provides the important last-mile connectivity in the chain. For the BC model to succeed, two things must happen. First, there must be at least one retail outlet or a sub-agent of the BC company in each village, which should be shared by multiple banks. Second, this financial inclusion initiative will be sustainable only if it is commercially viable for all the stakeholders—banks themselves and the entities they use as BCs to increase penetration and provide financial inclusion for the poor. A critical requirement for financial inclusion to be a viable proposition would be the direct deposit of government welfare payments and financial benefits into the accounts of the beneficiaries. This will be discussed in greater detail in the next chapter.

Notes

1. For a history of the changes made, see RBI (2010a).

2. See the *Report of the Inter-Ministerial Group on Delivery of Basic Financial Services Using Mobile Phones*, available at http://www.gov.in/sites/upload_files/dit/files/ReportoftheInterMinisterialGroup.pdf.

3. *Report of the Inter-Ministerial Group on Delivery of Basic Financial Services Using Mobile Phones*, available at http://www.gov.in/sites/upload_files/dit/files/ReportoftheInterMinisterialGroup.pdf.

4. *Report of the Inter-Ministerial Group on Delivery of Basic Financial Services Using Mobile Phones*, available at http://www.gov.in/sites/upload_files/dit/files/ReportoftheInterMinisterialGroup.pdf.

CHAPTER FIFTEEN

Aadhaar and India's Poor

The villagers of Tembhli, with whom this narrative was started, have not found any particular use for their Aadhaar cards. Ranjana Sadashiv Sonawane, who made headlines when she received the first-ever Aadhaar number from Prime Minister Manmohan Singh and Congress President Sonia Gandhi, is, today, a disillusioned woman. Her dream of getting a concrete house, regular employment, toilet facility, and free medical treatment—all the benefits that would have brought some cheer to her wretched life—lies shattered. So disgusted is she with the turn of events that she has now dumped her unique Aadhaar card under a pile of discarded clothes in a metal box that the Bhils keep for storing away their not-so-frequently used stuff (Swamy 2011: 1).

The disenchanted villagers of Tembhli are now left with the feeling that the administration had been economical with the truth while explaining what the Aadhaar card could fetch for them. The administration had promised that the Aadhaar number would get them concrete houses, employment for the unemployed, free bus passes, and overall prosperity for the entire village. Then Sahada Tehsildar, Yuvraj Rajput, had, in fact, drawn up a list of villagers who would get concrete houses, and also chosen around 40 of them to be given seed capital for self-employment. The self-employment proposal had on its agenda generous grants for buying cycle rickshaws and setting up flour mills and eateries (Swamy 2011: 2). The proposal of the tehsildar has been gathering dust in the secretariat in Mumbai. 'It is pending with the Mantralaya,' Rajput now says, 'I sent it six months back. The proposal has nothing to do with the UID' (Swamy 2011: 2). But, the villagers of

Tembhli cannot quite understand why the promises made so liberally to them have not come true, although they were the first ones in the country to get those coveted Aadhaar numbers.

Ranjana Sonawane throws up her hands in despair and laments, 'I showed the card in the hospital and was told that it will be useful for big operations. We still live in a kuccha hut and no toilet has been made in our street. Moreover, I still toil in others' farms. We have not benefited at all from the card' (Swamy 2011: 4). But nothing had prepared Ranjana Sonawane for the trauma that was waiting for her during her trip to her mother's house. She showed her Aadhaar card to the conductor of bus and asked for a concession in her bus fare. The conductor told her, rather rudely she thought: '*Iss pe government ka sikka nahin hai. Akha desh ko fayda nahin hoga. Rakh do peti mein isko* (It does not have government's stamp. It won't benefit the entire country. Dump it in the box)' (Swamy 2011: 4).

Bansi Gora Chendul, a neighbour of Sonawane, says: 'We were told that card would solve all our problems. We would get pucca houses. There is no gain from it' (Swamy 2011: 6). Chendul beats his hairy chest and points out that the village *patwari* had noted down his name for the grant of Rs 30,000 for purchasing a bullock cart on the production of his Aadhaar card (Swamy 2011: 6). But the promised help did not materialize. Like Ranjana Sonawane, he too has dumped his Aadhaar card in the tin box meant for storing junk, and brings it out only to show it to the visiting journalists.

However, Subhas Narsingh Sonawane, a member of the last village panchayat in Tembhli, counts grant of pension to 45 villagers, goats to another 10, and bullock carts to 15 others as benefits from Aadhaar (Swamy 2011: 6). Promod Bhamre, the present Tehsildar of Sahada, disagrees, 'Aadhaar has nothing to do with all these. It only helps one to establish identity' (Swamy 2011: 7). The Aadhaar card has not been linked to the PDS in Tembhli and the villagers still get their rations on the basis of the yellow ration card (Swamy 2011: 7). Small wonder, then, that the villagers think the Aadhaar programme has been a huge disappointment. 'They said the card would end all our woes. No such thing has happened. We are where we were,' say Vanibai and Fhulsingh Tarsingh Thakre, holding their Aadhaar cards above their heads for everyone to see (Swamy 2011: 7).

As the analysis in the last few chapters has shown, the gains that the Aadhaar programme would bring to the poor in the implementation of PDS, MGNREGS, public health and RBSY, and elementary education are only modest. The analysis also shows that Aadhaar-enabled bank account does provide the necessary combination of organizational innovation and technology application for financial inclusion of the poor. But, for the scheme of financial inclusion to be viable and sustainable, there should be direct cash transfer of subsidies into the accounts of beneficiaries.

Interestingly, Nandan Nilekani, the chief programmer of the Aadhaar programme, makes a very persuasive case for direct cash transfers of subsidies. He says:

> What we need to do for rural India and agriculture is, first and foremost, carry out the 'great unwind' of subsidies and move to a direct benefit system. Right now, subsidies on food, fertilizer, fuel and power are mounting by the day. 'In 2007', Chidambaram tells me, 'we spent more than ten trillion rupees on subsidies alone.' …We ought to pause for a moment and consider what Rs 10 trillion could do for the welfare in India if put to effective use, rather than being lost to 'leakage' or given to the wrong people. A government willing to transform these pay-outs into direct benefits—cash payments, vouchers, and lifeline subsidies—would see an impact that would be the Indian equivalent of the New Deal. It would create massive new wealth and opportunity for the middle and working class, and would give the party or coalition that implements an endurance in politics that India has not seen since 1977…
>
>   The shift to direct benefits would be a fundamental change… It [the government] ought to acknowledge this fact when it comes to spending money on its citizens as well: the move from indirect subsidies to direct benefits accepts that our voters are not undifferentiated 'masses' with a single demand, such as cheaper rice or kerosene. Rather, we are individual citizens who have unique needs, and the government has to cater to personal choice by giving people direct cash benefits to do what they choose with it. Such an approach also allows us to target welfare to make them more effective providing direct payments, for example, to the women in poor families, who are more dependable when it comes to spending money on education, health and food. (Nilekani 2008: 308–10)

Nilekani's point is rather simple. We should move from indirect subsidies to direct benefits, and the government should cater to personal choice by giving people cash to do what they choose with it. Interestingly, after Nandan Nilekani made this suggestion, cash transfers became the rage in policy circles (Dreze 2011: 11). A Planning Commission document argued that cash transfers required 'a biometric identification system', now made possible by the 'initiation of a Unique Identification System (UID) for the entire population' (Dreze 2011: 11). The same document went on to recommend a string of mega cash transfers to replace the PDS (Dreze 2011: 11).

Nilekani's suggestion of direct cash transfer also found support in other influential quarters. For example, *The Economic Times* wrote in an editorial:

> *Welfare Muddle: The shift to cash transfers won't happen in a day, but we need to do it*
>
> Every year, India spends a vast amount of money on worthy causes, designed to benefit its poor and elderly. These include subsidies on food, fertilizers and fuel; cash handouts through NREGS, the Awas Yojanas and the rural health mission and social services like mid-day meals and education schemes. The money spent, more than 3,00,000 crore rupees, is substantial, but much of it finds its way into the pockets of administrators at various levels of governments, middlemen and traders. The system of subsidies is crumbling, resulting in losses from storage, waste, theft and in the case of oil subsidies, funding a pan-India mafia...Direct transfers of cash were supposed to plug many of these leaks...What cash transfers do is to obviate distortions such as dual pricing of kerosene and cooking gas, paving the way for adulteration of diesel and a black market, or spoilage and pilferage of grain in government stocks. The shift to cash transfers will need a lot of work, but that's inevitable when there's no silver bullet to get the job done. (*The Economic Times* 2011d: 12)

The official endorsement of Nilekani's suggestion came in the speech of the finance minister when he presented the budget for 2011–12 on 28 February 2011. The finance minister said:

> The Government provides subsidies, notably on fuel and food grains, to enable the common man to have access to these basic necessities at affordable prices. A significant proportion of subsidized fuel does not reach the targeted beneficiaries and there is large scale diversion

of subsidized kerosene oil. A recent tragic event has highlighted this practice. We have deliberated for long the modalities of implementing such subsidies. The debate now has to make way for decision. To ensure greater efficiency, cost effectiveness and better delivery for both kerosene and fertilizers, the Government will move towards direct transfer of cash subsidy to people living below the poverty line in a phased manner.[1]

The finance minister's budget speech also made a mention of the establishment of a task force headed by Nandan Nilekani. The speech stated, 'A task force headed by Shri Nandan Nilekani has been set up to work out the modalities for the proposed system of direct transfer of subsidy for kerosene, LPG and fertilizers. The interim report of the task force is expected by June 2011. The system will be in place by March 2012.'[2]

An Outline of the Interim and Final Reports of the Task Force

The task force was set up on 14 February 2011, 'in order to evolve a suitable mechanism for direct subsidies to individuals/families who are entitled to kerosene, LPG and fertiliser, and to evolve a model of direct transfer of subsidies on these items by re-engineering existing systems, processes and procedures in the implementation process'.[3] The task force was also mandated to suggest a common framework to be adopted to provide direct subsidies in cash or otherwise for other government welfare schemes (Ministry of Finance 2011b: 61).

The task force, in its interim report submitted in June 2011, proposed a subsidy framework that would enable direct subsidy transfer to the beneficiary in respect of government welfare schemes. The interim report pointed out that the framework 'can be an effective strategy to channel subsidies to beneficiaries, especially in multiple price markets with pervasive incentive distortions, and it is desirable to provide choice to beneficiaries' (Ministry of Finance 2011b: 10). It also recommended that the solution architecture for direct transfer of subsidies should consist of a core subsidy management system (CSMS). It suggested that a real-time nature of direct subsidy transfer was essential for its success, and would require the following:

1. Ministry of Finance should fund the subsidies in advance to the implementing ministries so that funds are available for real-time transfers.
2. Ministry of Finance, in consultation with implementing ministries, should amend the General Financial Rules (GFR) that allows for a fully electronic subsidy transfer process.
3. The implementing ministries should devise processes and systems for a fully electronic subsidy transfer process (Ministry of Finance 2011b: 17).

The interim report suggested that Aadhaar would offer several benefits for the implementation of the new framework of subsidy delivery. First, the Aadhaar infrastructure will guarantee that one person can only have one Aadhaar number, and this can be utilized to verify identity across public schemes and programmes (Ministry of Finance 2011b: 22). The Aadhar number would help in the implementation of subsidy programmes by eliminating the twin errors of inclusion and exclusion in identifying beneficiaries. The assurance of uniqueness through biometric information in the Aadhaar programme would deal with inclusion errors by eliminating duplicate, fake, and ghost beneficiaries. The availability of a universal identity number would help in addressing errors of exclusion, by enabling the poor to easily establish their identity to welfare agencies. The Aadhaar number would also help to confirm the eligibility of beneficiaries for subsidies/ entitlements in some cases. It could, for example, help verify the age of pension beneficiaries, since the demographic information includes the date of birth. In the longer term, it would help BPL families fulfil certain criteria for eligibility for inclusion in the BPL list, such as not owning an Aadhaar-linked PAN card or Aadhaar-linked LPG connection (Ministry of Finance 2011b: 22).

Second, the Aadhaar programme will enable real-time authentication of identity at the time of subsidy delivery. The Aadhaar number will make possible online, 'anytime, anywhere, anyhow' verification of an individual's identity (Ministry of Finance 2011b: 22). An authenticating agency can provide the resident's Aadhaar number and biometric/demographic information to the central Aadhaar database, which would verify the information in a few seconds. Such real-time authentication of identity would:

1. Enable beneficiaries to confirm that the subsidy has reached them and not been diverted.
2. Allow individuals to access benefits when they have moved out of their home village or town, since Aadhaar makes it possible to verify identity anywhere in the country. Any service provider providing a particular subsidy would be able to easily verify if the person is who he says he is. To enable this, subsidy providers could implement a cloud-based application within their infrastructure, which would standardize their processes as well as share beneficiary information seamlessly across service delivery points.
3. Enable the beneficiary to access information about his entitlements and status.
4. Help government to identify leakages as the subsidy moves from the intermediary agency to the intended beneficiary.
5. Help government to enforce accountability in supply chain management (Ministry of Finance 2011b: 22–3).

Third, Aadhaar will enable delivery of welfare benefits and subsidies through direct cash transfer into Aadhaar-enabled bank account using the Aadhaar payments bridge (Ministry of Finance 2011b: 23).

Fourth, this will give the poor greater choice and agency in utilizing their entitlements. The Aadhaar number, when coupled with the total financial inclusion initiative (which aims to give every resident in the country a bank account), would help strengthen the direct delivery of such benefits to individuals. An Aadhaar-enabled bank account for every individual would enable governments and public agencies to transfer cash benefits electronically and directly into the individual's Aadhaar-linked bank account. The individual would then be able to access their money once they undergo Aadhaar authentication, either through local bank-appointed merchants or BCs. Aadhaar authentication can be one-time exercise for KYC, or connecting to the subsidy account, but transactional authentication (if not using Aadhaar biometric) could be done by the application itself (Ministry of Finance 2011b: 23).

The interim report proposed a general solution framework for direct transfer of subsidies as in the following:

1. A subsidy, by its very nature, introduces two or more prices for the same good, and creates incentives for pilferage and diversion.

As a result, the poor suffer the most. Ensuring that goods move in the supply chain at market prices can minimize the incentives for diversion.

2. Where possible, it is best to empower beneficiaries and give them the choice to receive subsidies in the form of subsidized goods and services, or as cash, based on their own preferences. Further, beneficiaries should also be offered choice to exercise their preference at any participating location, rather than restricting the service delivery point to a specific location.

3. Creation of a CSMS for the purpose of maintaining bookkeeping information on entitlements and subsidies for all beneficiaries will provide increased transparency in the movement of goods, level of stocks, prediction and aggregation of demand, and identification of beneficiaries. It will be in a position to use analytics to detect fraud and diversion.

4. Just as a real-time transfer of funds takes place when people top up their mobile talktime, the government, through the SMS, will transfer the cash components of subsidies directly and in real time to the bank accounts of beneficiaries. Beneficiaries may then access these funds through various banking channels such as bank branches, ATMs, BCs, Internet, and mobile banking. Achieving full financial inclusion is crucial for direct transfer of subsidies.

5. As the subsidy management systems assume same configuration under CSMS, integration of all subsidies and entitlements under one umbrella is also achievable.

6. The transition to direct transfer of subsidies will lead to best practices in modern retail being incorporated in public provisioning, and also to increased competition and efficiency in the manufacturing, distribution, and retailing. The use of technology makes it possible to strengthen and automate checks and balances, which will encourage participants to benefit from compliance, while simultaneously making pilferage difficult (Ministry of Finance 2011b: 1–2).

The task force submitted its final report in October 2011 (Ministry of Finance 2011c). In addition to reiterating the idea of a common framework for direct cash payment for all government welfare schemes, as was suggested in the interim report, the final report recommended an IT strategy for the PDS as well as an implementable solution for direct transfer of subsidy for food and kerosene. With respect to the PDS, the final report suggested the following reforms:

1. A solution that is incentive compatible for all the stakeholders, so that they benefit by participating in the system, rather than trying to benefit through subverting the system. For example, the commission rates for the FPS owners should be set in a manner that ensures that they can earn adequate returns on their investment.
2. Strengthening the public provision of the state with appropriate use of technology, to bring it on par with best practices in the field. Strategic control needs to be retained within the government at all times.
3. A token-agnostic technology solution that can accept physical coupons, and even facilitate direct cash transfers, where different states may choose from different solutions based on their own requirements.
4. Providing beneficiaries with maximum choices:
   i. choice of location;
   ii. choice of the mix of commodities;
   iii. choice to purchase commodities in convenient quantities, and in any number of instalments; and
   iv. choice to purchase commodities or receive a direct cash transfer of subsidies.
5. Aadhaar can be used to simplify a number of processes:
   i. simplification of ration card registration so that beneficiaries can apply for a ration card conveniently;
   ii. cleaning up the beneficiary database;
   iii. use of Aadhaar authentication as appropriate; and
   iv. use of Aadhaar payments bridge and Aadhaar-enabled payments system to channel subsidy funds for approved commodities to Aadhaar-enabled bank accounts (Ministry of Finance 2011c: 1–2).

One thing that stands out in the recommendations of the task force is its language of choice. The report says that the solution it offers would provide beneficiaries maximum choice, whether the choice is in terms of location, or in the mix of commodities in terms of quantities and instalments, or choice in terms of purchasing the commodities or not, or the ultimate choice in terms of receiving a direct transfer of subsidies for approved commodities. The technology solution that the report offers is also replete with choices: it provides for a token-agnostic technology solution that can accept physical coupons, smart cards, electronic coupons, or direct cash transfers. The menu of choices is unambiguously laid out and the poor are now free to choose.

In September 2011, the government expanded the terms of reference of the task force (*Deccan Herald* 2011e: 7). The task force was now asked to work out and recommend a definition of Aadhaar-enabled unified payment structure. It was mandated to devise a suitable architecture for e-banking through interoperable BCs and examine the alignment of current standards for devices that will be deployed by them. It was also asked to suggest an architecture that can align the recommendations of the Inter-Ministerial Group on a framework for delivery of basic financial services using mobile phones with Aadhaar-enabled payments infrastructure (*Deccan Herald* 2011e: 7).

The task force submitted its report to the finance minister on 23 February 2012 on the Aadhaar-enabled unified payment infrastructure (*The New Indian Express* 2012b: 15). It suggested a blueprint for single platform electronic payments gateway to facilitate transfer of subsidies and payments for various government schemes and programmes (Kurup 2012a: 7). This solution, to be linked to and enabled by Aadhaar, provides for a standard platform for various government departments and institutions so that they can make payments in an automated manner. According to the blueprint suggested by the task force, an interoperable network of BCs will be the key to address the objective of financial inclusion of the poor (Kurup 2012a: 7). The network will use the combined infrastructure of banks and Indian post offices across 2.25 lakh gram panchayats in the country (Kurup 2012a: 7). Widely perceived as a precursor to introduction of cash transfers of subsidies, this payment gateway is to be implemented by the NPCI, an organization that is promoted by leading Indian banks (Kurup 2012a: 7).

While recommending direct cash payment of subsidy through electronic payments into Aadhaar-enabled accounts, the task force suggested setting up of a network of 10 lakh microATMs to facilitate banking and financial services in rural areas across the country (*The New Indian Express* 2012b: 15). These microATMs were the ones developed by the UIDAI and were to be tried out in the pilot scheme taken up in rural Jharkhand jointly by the UIDAI and Government of Jharkhand for disbursement of MGNREGS wages (Kurup 2012a: 7). The task force also recommended that, for the establishment of the network of microATMs, a last-mile transaction fee of 3.14 per cent, with a cap of Rs 20 per transaction, should be paid by the government to banks for all the payments made by the government (*The New Indian Express* 2012b: 15). The task force also suggested that the government should hire 10 lakh BCs to facilitate banking and financial services in rural areas that lack banking services (*Deccan Herald* 2012c: 13). According to the task force report, these BCs would be in a position to ensure that the benefits of the social sector schemes reach the targeted beneficiaries in about 6 lakh villages (*Deccan Herald* 2012c: 13). The 10 lakh microATMs are to be operated by these BCs to make payments to beneficiaries in 2.25 lakh gram panchayats spread across 6 lakh villages, besides serving the urban poor (*Deccan Herald* 2012c: 13). In order to set up the BC network, banks can utilize the funds that they would get from the government by way of last-mile transaction fee of 3.14 per cent (*Deccan Herald* 2012c: 13).

The task force recommended that the process of transferring funds from the Ministry of Finance to various departments, both for direct transfer of subsidies and electronic benefit of transfers, should be automated. It envisaged that the government department would send an encrypted file containing the Aadhaar number and the payment amount to the accredited bank. An interoperable Aadhaar payments bridge would send the information to the NPCI, which will interface with the accredited banks. Each Aadhaar number will be mapped to the beneficiary's account at the back end of the system (*Deccan Herald* 2012c: 13).

As noted in Chapter 14, the institution of BC, as it functions now, is not a viable proposition. That being the case, the recommendation of the task force that a last-mile transaction fee of 3.14 per cent should be paid by the government to banks for all government payments is a step in the right direction. The task force has also recommended that the banks can utilize this money for setting up the BC network as well as the network of microATMs. In the previous chapter, it was also noted that, at present, BCs have been given such large territories that they can travel to each village only infrequently, with the result that the villagers, unsure of when the BC would come next, withdraw all their money right away. The recommendation of the task force that there should be 10 lakh BCs to cover 6 lakh villages (which would mean at least one BC for each village in the country) will take care of this constraint.

While presenting the budget proposals for 2012–13 on 16 March 2012, the finance minister stated that the recommendations of the task force headed by Nandan Nilekani on IT strategy for direct transfer of subsidy have been accepted.[4] 'It will be our endeavour,' the finance minister said in his budget speech, 'to scale up and roll out these Aadhaar-enabled payments for various government schemes in at least 50 selected districts within the next six months'.[5]

LAUNCH OF AADHAAR-ENABLED DIRECT CASH TRANSFER PROGRAMME

On 20 October 2012, Prime Minister Manmohan Singh and the UPA chairperson, Sonia Gandhi, launched the Aadhaar-enabled direct cash transfer programme at a public function in the small town of Dudu near Jaipur (*The Hindu* 2012c: 14). Speaking at the function, the prime minister said that the Aadhaar programme would facilitate the transfer of cash benefits directly to the account of beneficiaries (*The Hindu* 2012c: 14). He declared: 'It will ensure the extension of benefits to the deserving people and do away with the role of middlemen…Our government wants to make maximum use of technology, especially IT, on a large scale to reduce dishonesty and improve transparency and accountability in the system' (*The Hindu* 2012c: 14).

Moving swiftly on the announcement he made in Dudu in Rajasthan, the prime minister constituted a high-powered National Committee on Direct Cash Transfers on 25 October 2012 (*The Hindu* 2012d: 12). The Committee is expected to facilitate the introduction of direct cash transfers to the poor eligible for government's many welfare programmes. The prime minister will chair the National Committee himself. Its other members will be 11 cabinet ministers, two ministers of state with independent charge, the deputy chairman of the Planning Commission, the chairman of the UIDAI, and the cabinet secretary (*The Hindu* 2012d: 12). The principal secretary to the prime minister will be the convenor. An official press release on the subject said:

> Leveraging the investments made in the Aadhaar project and with the objective of enhancing efficiency, transparency and accountability, the Committee has been mandated to provide an overarching vision and direction, as well as to determine broad policy objectives and strategies. To enable cash transfers, it will also suggest the extent and scope of such transfers for selected cash transfers for selected government programmes, and coordinate the activities of the Ministries and agencies involved in the project to ensure its timely and speedy rollout across the country. Finally, the Committee will review the progress of implementation and provide guidance for mid-course corrections. (*The Hindu* 2012d: 12)

The Committee will be assisted by an executive committee, chaired by the principal secretary to the prime minister, and its members will be the secretaries of the ministries concerned, and the Director General, UIDAI, will be the convenor (*The Hindu* 2012d: 12). Three mission mode committees—on technology, financial inclusion and implementation—will help design and implement the cash transfer system. The Technology Committee will deal with the technology, payment architecture, and IT issues; the Financial Inclusion Committee will focus on ensuring universal access to banking and complete financial inclusion; and the Implementation Committee on Electronic Transfer of Benefits, at the ministry level, will work out the details of cash transfers for each department (*The Hindu* 2012d: 12).

This scheme of direct cash transfer to the poor through Aadhaar-based payouts, which the government is going to implement, has been hailed as marking a new era in banking and budgetary transfers (*The Economic Times* 2012h: 12). *The Economic Times* called it 'a revolution', and said in its leading editorial:

> When the Prime Minister launched a new, unique identity-based service delivery mechanism in Rajasthan on Saturday, it marked the

beginning of nothing less than a revolution in financial inclusion and administration of welfare payments and subsidies...Aadhaar-linked delivery brings about three big changes. One, it creates the physical and technological infrastructure needed to facilitate mass electronic banking. It can help realise the full potential of mobile banking and create swipe machines to facilitate a cashless system of payments throughout India. The point is, in an underbanked country like ours, many of the poor still do not have bank account. Aadhaar being recognised as sufficient know-your-customer data will facilitate opening of accounts...Two, it transforms subsidy, reducing leakage and allowing restructuring of subsidy to leave product pricing to a competitive market while the government transfers cash subsidy directly to the intended beneficiary. Three, it can totally eliminate leakage and delay in distribution of welfare payments and scholarships. (*The Economic Times* 2012h: 12)

SIZE OF THE CASH TRANSFER

What is the size of the welfare pie that would finally be given to the poor in cash? The annual welfare benefits are estimated at Rs 300,000 crore (*The Economic Times* 2011c: 13). According to the report on Aadhaar-enabled unified payment infrastructure, the combined volume of EBT, direct transfer of subsidy, and other last-mile government payments in 2011–12 was approximately Rs 3,00,000 crore, and what is more, this is expected to increase manifold in future (Saini 2012: 13). The subsidies that major schemes provide annually are: rural development programmes, including MGNREGS (Rs 74,143 crore), food (Rs 60,570 crore), fertilizers (Rs 50,000 crore), LPG and Kerosene (Rs 3,050 crore), pensions (Rs 54,000 crore), Indira Awaas Yojana (Rs 10,000 crore), mid-day meals (Rs 10,380 crore), and SSA (Rs 7,100 crore) (*The Economic Times* 2011c: 13). In addition, it is estimated that the subsidy implications of the National Food Security Bill, which has already been introduced in the Lok Sabha in December 2011, will be of the order of Rs 95,000 crore, thereby marking an increase of about Rs 21,000 crore over the present food subsidy (*The Economic Times* 2011l). Moreover, the National Food Security Bill entitles every pregnant woman and lactating mother to meals free of cost during pregnancy and six months after childbirth (*The Economic*

Times 2011l). The Bill also provides for cash benefits of Rs 1,000 per month to meet increased food requirements of pregnant women for the first six months of pregnancy. At Rs 1,000 per month and covering 225 crore women, a subsidy expenditure of nearly 15,000 crore rupees has been estimated (*The Economic Times* 2011l). Taking all these into account, the size of the welfare pie can be estimated to be of the order of Rs 3,68,573 crore annually.

In fact, the government planned to implement the cash transfer scheme with effect from 1 January 2013 on a nationwide scale (*The Economic Times* 2012i: 1). The scheme aimed to put a total of Rs 3.2 lakh crores per year in the bank accounts of 10 crore poor families (*The Economic Times* 2012i: 1). The scheme was to be implemented in three phases: the first phase, starting from 1 January 2013, was to be implemented in 51 districts in 15 states and three union teritorries; the second phase of implementation was to start from 1 April 2013 and was to cover all districts in 18 states; and the third and final stage of implementation, which was to start from 1 April 2014, was to cover all districts in all states and union teritorries (*The Economic Times* 2012i: 1). The per family/per year cash transfer amount would be Rs 32,000, almost three times the average annual earnings of a BPL family (*The Economic Times* 2012i: 1).

IMPACT OF THE CASH TRANSFER SCHEME

So, we have the good news that cash amounting to Rs 32,000 per year is going to be deposited directly into the bank accounts of 10 crore poor household in India. This comes as a windfall for India's poor. Thanks to Nandan Nilekani's Aadhaar, the poor in India would have got two huge benefits: (i) they will now have the right to an acknowledged existence on the basis of their UID number; and (ii) through the UID number, there will be a platform that would deliver their welfare money into their pockets right at their doorstep.

Now, the poor families in India will have much more cash at their disposal. According to officials in the Prime Minister's Office, the 'big difference' in this welfare reform will be a 'huge spending impact on the economy' (*The Economic Times* 2012i: 1). The fact that India's rural poor would have so much of money at their disposal has aroused, in the corporate world, a great deal of interest in the poor as consumers for the market. The corporates do not normally evince much interest in the poor, because nothing much is known about the poor as consumers of products and services. Some data is available about the consumer profiles of the urban poor who live in slums, earn up to 10,000 rupees a month, and account for 10 per cent of the urban income: the size of this urban poor market is estimated at Rs 30,000 crore (*The Economic Times* 2011h: 15). In fact, now companies like PepsiCo, Nestle, the Future Group, Godrej, Abbott Truecare, and Dabur have drawn up impressive corporate strategies to target the urban poor, and the strategies are beginning to fructify (*The Economic Times* 2011h: 15). It is only recently that a few corporates have evinced interest in the rural poor as consumers for the market. Interestingly, some of these corporate entities that spent money in building consumer profiles in rural areas have struck it rich. Airtel, the telecom company, is a case in point. In 2005, Airtel hired Mart to study the rural market for mobile usage, with the idea of finding five potential consumers in each village (*The New Sunday Express* 2011: 11). Five years later, rural India had 200 million connections (*The New Sunday Express* 2011: 11). Take the case of Bansbeegha, a village 25 km from Patna, which rarely gets electricity and does not have motorable roads in a 5 km radius. It has 80 per cent mobile penetration now, and also an Airtel service centre (*The New Sunday Express* 2011: 11).

The FMCG companies are also planning to move into the rural areas in a big way. It is estimated that the amount of rural FMCG sales would reach $100 billion by 2025 (*The Economic Times* 2012b: 15). The reasons why the FMCG companies consider rural areas as productive terrains now are: (i) government-supported schemes like MGNREGS and increased Minimum Support Price (MSP) have allowed the consumer pattern of India's rural population to turn increasingly aspirational; and (ii) FMCG companies have upped their capital investment plans in rural areas, helped by tax incentives propagated by various state governments (*The Economic Times* 2012b: 15).

Interestingly, it is the poor in rural areas or the bottom of the pyramid (BoP) as they are called now, that these companies are targeting. There is even a philosophical angle to it. As a captain of the consumer goods industry points out:

What many people might miss in today's environment is that it is enterprise that has been responsible for a large amount of progress we have seen over the years. It is business that has helped deliver a range of products and services that are affordable, that help improve lives and are distributed to the remotest corners as part of a system that runs relentlessly because it runs profitably. Equally, what many of us miss is that it is possible to do well while doing good, and that there are innumerable opportunities to shine in a business while serving society. Serving the Bottom of the Pyramid (BoP) can be as much a profitable opportunity as it is an opportunity to improve the lives of those on the margin. The BoP market can provide the new focus to firms because:

a) It is here that we have a large unmet need.
b) High volumes can be sustained here.
c) Growth is as rapid as the consumer base is widened.
d) BoP demands adjustments that force companies to innovate. (Paranjpe 2012: 15)

What are these BoP demands and how will the companies innovate? Rama Bijapurkar (2012: 15), the independent market strategy consultant, has the answer. Bijapurkar points out that there should be a new mindset to open new markets. In the first place, 'the poor' should be renamed as 'modest-income' consumers (MIC) because that would 'remind us that these are regular customers, who do have a little money apiece to spend. The task of making the markets work for them is to enable their money to stretch and to buy them the things that they need' (Bijapurkar 2012: 15). She outlines two ways to achieve this:

1. Remove additional middlemen, 'who thrive in MIC areas, where because the total demand is too low for viability, regular company distribution channels stay away, middlemen also provide the service of breaking economically viable large packs and selling smaller parts, but at a higher price per gram e.g. biscuits or edible oil' (Bijapurkar 2012: 15). According to her, removing the middleman, yet offering the same quality and price as for other customers, is the challenge to make markets work better for MIC.
2. Facilitate the MIC's consumption pattern. This should be, typically, a small quantity, consumed infrequently though regularly. As she

says, 'The celebrated shampoo sachet does this, Sachet-ization applies to durables too e.g. laundromats, custom hiring of tractors, and more generally, pay-as-you-use models' (Bijapurkar 2012: 15).

According to Bijapurkar (2012: 15), implementing such businesses requires a multi-player ecosystem, built and managed by an ethical company, willing to apply the same standards of quality to MICs as it does to high-income consumers, investment in capex, and the stomach to play a low-price–low-margin–large-volume game. Only large volumes will impact many MICs and create enough value for good companies, but it is a long haul requiring patient capital and long-horizon thinking. The toughest challenge, however, is to design appropriate price–performance–margin-right products/services that are win-win for MICs and for companies. This would require appropriate performance, and appropriateness is about designing features that add value to customers. As she says:

> They (MICs) have complex needs, all of which makes it very hard to serve them very profitably, with a low price tag. The interpretation of 'financial inclusion' by banks to mean opening bank accounts is woefully inappropriate for complex MIC needs (when you have less money you need to juggle more), and is also not profitable for banks, the way their current business system works. To make financial work for the MIC, understanding of consumer needs has to be the starting point… (Bijapurkar 2012: 15)

Perhaps, Hindustan Unilever is the ethical company that would meet Rama Bijapurkar's specifications. More than 40 per cent of Unilever's products are consumed in the fast-growing markets of rural India (*The Economic Times* 2012g: 7). The company has been a pioneer in developing rural markets through affordable brands and unparalleled distribution reach. Unilever's network directly reaches nearly 1.3 lakh villages (*The Economic Times* 2012g: 7). In fact, Unilever is already talking with SBI to work as a BC company in order to bring financial inclusion to rural India. Shakti ammas of Unilever act as banking agents and provide basic financial services in villages where bank branches do not exist (*The Economic Times* 2012g: 7). The Unilever has taken up pilots in Karnataka and Maharashtra, and plans to scale them up across the country once these two pilots meet their action standards (*The Economic Times* 2012g: 7).

Rural India and the poor it inhabits constitute an integral part of Unilever's business model. As Harish Manani, the Chairman of Hindustan Unilever, told the company's annual general meeting (AGM) held on 23 July 2012:

The population of rural India is about 12% of the world's population, which makes it bigger than the size of Europe. If the 800 million people living in rural India can be provided with the skills to be fully productive, this will unleash yet another force to create the emerging rural middle class that can transform India into fastest growing economy in the world. It is not an impossible vision of rural India matching rural China in 10 years time. This could potentially create an incremental GDP of USD1.8 trillion, the size of the current Indian economy. The impact will be transformational not only for India but for the global economy...

Lack of access to capital is one of the most serious deterrents to development in rural India. Access to formal banking would not only eliminate unbearable debt for the poor but also bring capital investments into rural...Along with the government, the banks and corporates can play a synergistic role in realizing the plan. Companies like the HUL have a wider distribution network than any government agency. After all, our products reach almost every village in the country. And leveraging this high quality last-mile can bring financial inclusion to every Indian.

For HUL, rural India is an integral part of its business model to deliver consistent and sustainable growth...Rural India is a powerhouse waiting to emerge. This is an incredible opportunity of potentially adding USD1.8 trillion to our economy, equal to the current GDP of India! We need to build a new generation of leaders and entrepreneurs from our villages who will help power the future of our nation. In order to realize this vision, we need inclusive growth...We need a broad based strategy to provide rural India access to markets and technology, financial inclusion and human capital development. (*The Economic Times* 2012g: 7)

For Unilever, the rural India is the emerging powerhouse. So, Unilever talks of providing rural poor access to market and technology, and financial inclusion, as well as building a new generation of leaders and entrepreneurs from India's villages. For Rama Bijapurkar, understanding of consumer needs is the starting point for making the financial work for the MICs (the poor). This is where dataveillance that the Aadhaar programme enables is going to be useful. It would facilitate the mapping of the need and consumption patterns of India's poor, by providing the link to Aadhaar's integrated pan-India database. With such dataveillance, it will now be possible to profile the poor as consumers for the market, and understand what their needs are.

BIG DATA

It is in this context that one begins to understand why Indian corporates are now waking up to the value of 'big data' (the term is used in technology vernacular to refer to data sets that are large and tough to manage) (Kurup 2012b: 8). Driven by the all-pervasive use of mobile networks and cloud storage, data are getting bigger and bigger, so much so that the term 'big data' has come to be known as one that has no prescribed upper limit. As storage capacity, computing power, and parallel processing capabilities expand, it is being realized that these huge amounts of data can be crunched to create insights or meaningful information (Kurup 2012b: 8). The growing interest of Indian corporates in 'big data' has obviously to do with the fact that huge amounts of data can be crunched to create meaningful information, making it possible for them to see what can best serve their business interests.

What makes it particularly attractive for the companies is that the process of crunching of data, which used to take hours and even days, can now be done in real time (Kurup 2012b: 8). Earlier, taking this data and analysing it required a two or three week cycle, but now most of this is possible in real time, and the benefits of that are immense. As a result, the focus has shifted to analytics and query interface, and technology-wise, companies are now concentrating on finding ways to make analytics and query interface as simple as possible. In fact, Google provides analytics as a service. As Rahul Kulkarni, Senior Product Manager at Google India explains, 'What we attempt to deliver is analytics interfaces that are so simple that a marketing officer can use it to pose ad-hoc queries to the data set, and be able to extract information that can be used meaningfully' (quoted in Kurup 2012b: 8). Venu Reddy of International Data Corporation says, 'There's a good deal of growth, especially when businesses come to see the importance of seeing pattern or habits within the data when analysed' (*Deccan Herald* 2012f: 13).

So, the 'big data' in the integrated pan-India Aadhaar database (the Aadhaar programme has been aptly described as the world's largest data management project; Jayashankar and Ramnath 2010: 1) can be distilled and analysed by corporates, armed as they are now with the necessary analytics and query interface, in order to develop a more thorough and insightful understanding of the need and consumption patterns of India's poor. With this knowledge, these companies would provide the poor with access to the market, and in the process, build a new generation of leaders and entrepreneurs from India's villages. This would be a win-win situation for both the corporates and the poor. This would enable the corporates to serve the poor and improve their lives, and also create profitable opportunities for themselves. Now that companies with large and widespread retail network qualify to be appointed as BCs, they would use the customer-related information from the Aadhaar database to share appropriate products and services with the poor. On the whole, it is certainly a huge bonanza for India's poor, and the Aadhaar programme would have made it possible.

FREEDOM OF CHOICE FOR THE POOR

In any case, Aadhaar-enabled direct cash transfer of subsidies to the poor would have given them the freedom of choice. We can appreciate the freedom of choice it brings to India's poor only when we contrast this with the prevailing subsidy regime. The prevailing regime is designed with the objective of delivering specific products and services to pre-defined categories of citizens. The PDS is a case in point. The PDS is intended to deliver food and kerosene to eligible beneficiaries. The consumers of PDS have to purchase their subsidized products from the designated FPS. In many of these cases, both the product eligible for subsidy and the location of its purchase is pre-defined. To that extent, the choice of the poor is restricted, both in terms of the product to be purchased and the location of the purchase. In fact, we can go to the extent of saying that the prevailing subsidy regime gives the poor no choice at all.

It is a pity that the idea of the proposed cash transfer in the PDS has invited opposition despite the fact that it empowers the poor with choice and freedom. For example, the Government of Delhi has plans of providing 2 lakh vulnerable families with 600 rupees in cash transfers every month instead of rations, and a total of Rs 144 crore has already been allocated for the project to be implemented in 920 *jhuggi-jhonpri* clusters across the state (Nayar 2012: 40–1). A pilot was carried out for the purpose in Raghubir Nagar in west Delhi in 2011, in which female heads of 100 families were provided with Rs 1,000 each in their bank accounts, with the freedom to buy what they liked (Nayar 2012: 40–1). In 2012, another pilot on the same lines, in jhuggi-jhonpri clusters of Jahangirpuri, was stalled by protests against the government plans to 'empower' people by giving the subsidy amount in cash transfers directly into the bank accounts of the poor (Nayar 2012: 40–1). As Sharoon, one of the protesters from the slum settlement of Jahangirpuri who has 13 members in the family to feed, says: 'In our house, the money could end up being used for something else, given the many demands. I'd prefer to get rations' (Nayar 2012: 40–1).

M.S. Swaminathan, the eminent agricultural scientist and an MP, is of the view that direct cash transfers can trigger corruption and the money to buy food may not reach the target group (*Deccan Herald* 2012e: 12). In addition, he says that, if the government stopped procurement of foodgrains from farmers at a remunerative price starting with the MSP, and storing them to ensure availability of food, India's agriculture production will be hit as farmers will have no incentive to grow food crops and may even go for a crop holiday (*Deccan Herald* 2012e: 12).

Professor Swaminathan obviously does not take into consideration the fact that direct cash transfers can do great things for India's poor. The poor will have the money now to buy products and services that will enable them to define who they are. They would thus be in a position to establish a particular identity for themselves through consumption. Importantly, the poor will now be free to choose products and services. Arvind Panagariya (2012: 20), Professor of Economics at Columbia University, puts this point in focus when he says:

> Critics often deride cash transfers on the ground that the beneficiary might not spend them on the goods and services for which they are intended and may even shell them on alcohol and gambling. But

this same fate can also meet in-kind transfers as currently practiced. Subsidised foodgrain received through public distribution system can be sold for cash in the open market and the cash used to buy alcohol. Subsidised services are not subject to similar conversion but they too free up the other income of the beneficiary, allowing him to indulge into his favourite consumption. Transfers to individuals are just as fungible as foreign aid to governments.

An editorial in *The Times of India* gets it right when it points out:

> A switchover from product subsidies to direct cash has other important implications. At the political level it would help deal with the widely circulated canard that reforms are anti-poor. Direct cash transfers would, on the contrary, empower the poor and allow them the freedom to spend the benefits according to their choice. This is a fundamental shift from the current system of patronage where the government exercises complete control and imposes its choices with scant regard to quality or availability. Entitlement to regular cash payment brings in other benefits too. It can boost credit-worthiness of the beneficiaries allowing them greater access to formal credit including from banks. (*The Times of India* 2012b: 10)

Taha Mehmood (2011: 5) has also the same view. He says:

> For a moment let us imagine the state pays 5,000 rupees as subsidy to an under-privileged farmer to buy fertilizer. What is the guarantee that when he has that money he is going to spend it on buying fertilizer? Can he not use that money to buy something else, like a mobile phone, may be watch a film or have a bottle of nice whiskey for a change?

What Arvind Panagariya, the editorial in *The Times of India*, and Taha Mehmood have to say goes on to confirm that the Aadhaar programme would have given the poor the freedom to choose. Arvind Panagariya points out that the cash transfer would make the poor beneficiary the king, with the provider playing to his tune. As he says:

> They [cash transfers and vouchers] empower the beneficiary rather than the provider. Today, the beneficiary is at the mercy of the public distribution shop. Even under NREGS, he must play to the tune of this or that official. Just calling something 'guarantee' or 'right' does not turn it into one. But cash transfers and vouchers make

the beneficiary truly the king with the provider, whether private or public, playing to his tune. (Panagariya 2012: 20)

This is also the point that Nandan Nilekani (2008: 310) makes in his book, *Imagining India*, when he says, 'we are individual citizens to have unique needs, and the government has to cater to personal choice by giving people direct cash benefits to do what they choose to do with it'. So, the point is very clear: the poor would not merely be free to choose, but that they would also be obliged to be free in the sense of enacting their lives in terms of choice. It is a freedom for them to realize their potential and their dreams through reshaping the ways they conduct their lives by becoming sovereign consumers; sovereign consumers not only to pursue individual self-fulfilment and freedom through choice but also to exercise enterprising conduct by making responsible decisions in consumption and lifestyle.

In Chapter 1, it was proposed that by using the governmentality approach, the following questions can be answered: who is to be governed?; why should they be governed?; how should they be governed?; and to what ends should they be governed? Now that an empirical analysis of the Aadhaar programme has been done, the answers to these questions can be provided.

Who is to be Governed?

As this analysis of the UIDAI literature—consisting of interviews, working papers, brochures, manuals, strategy papers, discussion papers, and training modules—and the statements of UIDAI's programmers and pronouncements of political authorities shows, it is India's poor who are to be governed through the Aadhaar programme. Though the Aadhaar programme is officially stated to be for all residents, it is primarily addressed to India's poor. As Nandan Nilekani takes the trouble to point out, the genesis of the Aadhaar programme lay in the fact that most of India's poor do not have any identity, and this has become a form of exclusion (*Tehelka* 2010: 26). According to him, increasingly more and more benefits— either public or private—depend on proving who you are (*Tehelka* 2010: 26). So, identity becomes a form of divide, and it is basically to bridge this divide that the Aadhaar programme is designed (*Tehelka* 2010: 26).

The fact that the Aadhaar programme is primarily addressed to India's poor comes across in several ways. The UIDAI literature and the interviews of Aadhaar programmers make it abundantly clear that the Aadhaar programme is specifically intended to provide unique identities to the poor who do not have any recognized identity given by the state and are, therefore, bereft of any form of acknowledged existence. As the literature and interviews tell us, the inability to prove identity is one of the biggest barriers preventing India's poor from accessing benefits which are meant for them. They point out how the Aadhaar number would transform the delivery of social welfare programmes by making them more inclusive of the poor who are now cut off from such benefits due to lack of identification.

The pro-poor approach of the Aadhaar programme comes across very clearly from the UIDAI literature as well as interviews given by the UIDAI programmers. With respect to enrolment, the UIDAI literature envisions full enrolment of all Indian residents, but with a special focus on enrolling India's poor. According to the UIDAI literature, the registrars that the UIDAI seeks to partner with— NREGA, RSBY, and PDS—are expected to bring the poor into the Aadhaar system. While the UIDAI plans to target registrars that have large networks among the poor and rural communities in India, it has also evolved multiple approaches to reach specific, frequently marginalized groups. The UIDAI's strategy entails special measures to reach the urban poor, which, according to the UIDAI, is one of the most ignored and disadvantaged section of India's population as it consists of migrant workers with temporary or seasonal jobs. As Nandan Nilekani, the chief programmer, said in an interview:

> The domestic movement within India is slated to escalate due to development and climate change that would drive migration. Due to lack of identity proof, 100 million people are unable to avail of public schemes. It is here that the unique identification number will make a difference as it will be the 'number of life' for them. (*The Economic Times on Sunday* 2010: 4)

The UIDAI literature makes it clear that the Aadhaar authentication is designed to improve service delivery to the poor in areas of public distribution of food and fuel and provision of wage employment, elementary education, and health care. According to the UIDAI, the

Aadhaar programme is envisioned to play a critical role in providing access to the poor to formal financial mechanisms, by helping them to easily authenticate their identity to financial institutions. This, in turn, is expected to improve the effectiveness of existing financial inclusion strategies, and address challenges that India's poor now face in accessing financial services. The UIDAI literature emphasizes the point that the Aadhaar approach to financial inclusion for the poor will focus on the creation of a micropayments platform by addressing the last-mile problem, streamlining the delivery of government benefits, and providing access to finance for those who have so far been excluded from such services. According to the UIDAI literature, Aadhaar-enabled financial inclusion is specifically intended to give the poor the resources to migrate for better jobs, invest in entrepreneurship, and insure themselves against bad times and economic shocks.

While it is true that programmatically, the Aadhaar programme is universal in its coverage and applicable to all residents of India, its special focus is on the poor. It is as Nandan Nilekani says: 'The UID would be given to all Indians irrespective of their financial or residential status. However, the main aim of issuing these numbers is to ensure better service delivery to those who have been excluded from public schemes, be it related to finance or food' (*The Economic Times on Sunday* 2010: 4). Nilekani has always maintained that the main purpose of the Aadhaar project is to empower the vast numbers of excluded Indians (*The Dayafter* 2010: 33). As he says: 'For the poor, this is a huge benefit because they have no identities, no birth certificates, degree certificates, driver's licenses, passports or even addresses' (*The Dayafter* 2010: 33).

Clearly, it is the India's poor who are intended to be governed through the Aadhaar programme.

WHY SHOULD THEY BE GOVERNED?

The present policy of the government is to provide wage employment, social security, elementary education, health, food security, and housing to the poor through the implementation of various welfare schemes. Such public provisioning for the poor is now achieved by means of state planning and interventions in the economy. The conception, concretization, and implementation of the schemes are done through a bureaucratically staffed apparatus, which delivers these welfare schemes to the poor, mainly in kind. The political rationality for these welfare measures is based on the assumption that it is the duty of state to provide for the poor in kind, and the ills of the social and economic life that plague the poor should be addressed by the government. In place of this political rationality, the government now seeks to create a new political rationality, which reasons that such public provisioning by the government in kind has a damaging effect on the poor by producing a culture of dependency based on expectations that government must do what, in reality, can be done by the poor themselves. The thrust of the reasoning is that the poor need to be governed in a manner that gives them financial agency, choice, and freedom from the culture of dependency.

What the government seeks to do now, through the instrumentality of the Aadhaar programme, is to link a massive reduction in government welfare services in kind to a call for the poor to become enterprising and autonomous individuals. Through the Aadhaar programme, the government plans to make the poor free; a process that asks the poor not only to be free to choose but also be obliged to be free in the sense of living their lives in terms of choice and freedom. The government wants that India's poor must act upon themselves as both free and responsible. It can then begin to govern the poor, not through the bureaucratic apparatuses, but through the structuring of the possible field of action in which the poor govern themselves, so that the government can govern them through their freedom. The tactics and techniques of the government aim at transforming the poor, who now solely depend on welfare services in kind and have to be governed as such, into individuals with freedom through choice of consumption and lifestyle.

HOW SHOULD THEY BE GOVERNED?

The new political rationality calls for a reorganization of government welfare programmes for governing the personal life of the poor. In terms of the new rationality, the poor need to become entrepreneurial individuals, endowed with freedom, autonomy, and responsibility. A sphere of freedom is to be established, in which the poor, as autonomous agents, would make their own decisions, pursue their preferences, and seek to maximize the quality of their lives. Thus, creation of freedom for the poor becomes the key to the process of governing them. The poor will now be required to conduct themselves responsibly in terms of their freedom. Freedom, as choice, autonomy, and self-responsibility, and the obligation to maximize life as an enterprise, is the strategy that underpins the new political rationality of the government to govern the poor. In the name of freedom, the government will divest itself of its welfare obligations to the poor and devolve them to the poor themselves.

Some commentators have pointed out that the Aadhaar programme would bring about a fundamental reduction in the role of the state and leave us with a retreating state. As S. Ramakumar (2010: 12) says:

> The second dimension of the UID project is the following: it would qualitatively restructure the role of the state in the social sector...The UIDAI claims that UID would help the government shift from a number of indirect benefits into direct benefits. In reality, such a shift would represent the opposite: a transformation in the role of the state from a direct provider to an indirect provider. For the UIDAI, the UID is a tool of empowerment. In reality, the UID would be an alibi for the state to leave the citizen unmarked in the market for social services. Nowhere is the illustration more telling than in the case of PDS. Let me state the argument upfront. The UID project is a larger effort to dismantle the PDS in India. The aim is to ensure a back-door entry of food stamps in the place of PDS and later graduate it to a cash transfer scheme, thereby completing the state's withdrawal from the sphere of food procurement and distribution.

It would make more sense, however, to see this apparent retreat of the state as the way in which the government actually seeks to extend itself. Such an extension has two dimensions. First, the state in India, through the instrumentality of the Aadhaar project, seeks to enhance its ability to direct populations, or significant parts of them, to behave in desired ways (Rao 2013: 72). The Aadhaar project is, in fact, based on the premise that the state can and must guide the behaviour of its citizens to reach development goals, and since the majority of the development schemes and programmes are addressed to the poor, the premise is that the state can and must guide the behaviour of the poor. As the analysis shows, the Aadhaar project subscribes to the vision of a state in control, which has succeeded in persuading the poor to follow state directions and thus fulfil national targets (Rao 2013: 72). It is against this backdrop that we need to view the clarion call of the Aadhaar project to India's poor, who live mostly in the informal economy, to enter the institutions and regime of the formal economy, and the Aadhaar project makes it abundantly clear that this is an essential precondition for the poor to prosper and flourish. Second, such an extension consists of replacing the direct governance of the poor by the state with a form of government at a distance. As noted earlier, this process would enable the government to govern the poor, neither through the bureaucratic apparatuses nor through the exercise of legal authority, but through the possible field of action in which the poor govern themselves so that the government can govern them through their freedom. This would have been achieved by having recourse to a range of techniques that enables the state to devolve its obligations towards the poor to the poor themselves by acting through the instrumentality of UIDAI, an organization of expertise, which functions autonomously of the government.

The analysis of the Aadhaar programme has shown how the government has allowed the UIDAI to function as a fully autonomous organization even though it is a direct-line government department as an attached office of the Planning Commission. In fact, as noted earlier, the UIDAI is so different from a run-of-the-mill government department that the common impression created is that it is a 'private' organization, and that the Aadhaar programme is a private project (*The Hindu* 2012a: 1). Or, as *The Economic Times* (2012d: 13) describes it in more nuanced terms, the UIDAI is 'the state entity with a private sector soul'. From the dyed-in-the-wool governmental perspective, this may appear to be subversive of government discipline and ethos, but it certainly has the merit of making the UIDAI acceptable to the people because they, then, begin to see it as independent and autonomous of the government, and therefore, far removed from the murky vote-seeking machinations of political authorities and self-interested behaviour of predatory bureaucrats.

People's acceptance of the UIDAI is, in essence, linked to the expertise it embodies. As the analysis shows, the poor accept the UIDAI as an organization of experts that can do good things for them.

They find the pro-poor Aadhaar discourse appealing and persuasive. They see the UIDAI as a body of expertise which is capable of doing beneficial things for them based on its technical knowledge. They believe that the Aadhaar programme would give them an identity, which they never had; an identity through which they would become visible. They think that the Aadhaar programme can be relied upon to plug leakages in public service delivery and make it work for them. They also applaud the virtues of expertise that makes all these good and beneficial things possible. Expertise is the key component in this process. The Aadhaar programme is seen as a triumph of expertise that can deliver socially relevant outcomes. The expertise it offers is viewed as embodying objectivity and skill; a potent but neutral force that can be harnessed to do good things for the poor.

It makes sense to view the Aadhaar programme and the solutions it offers as a kind of double alliance. On the one hand, the experts in the UIDAI, who act autonomously of the government, have allied with the government, identifying the shortcomings of the public service delivery system that plague the poor, characterizing the shortcomings as problems, translating the problems into the vocabulary of management and technology, and offering pro-poor knowledge-based solutions. On the other hand, they have allied with the poor, characterizing their trials and tribulations as a problem for which they have a technology solution, and claiming to free them from their hardship through the use of their expertise. This double alliance does an important thing: it allows vital links to be established between the political objectives of the government and the minutiae of the poor's daily existence. By offering solutions that are acceptable to both the government and the poor, the Aadhaar programme not only gives the poor choice and freedom but also provides legitimacy to the political government.

When it comes to the Aadhaar programme providing legitimacy to the political government, it is a fact that the then government (UPA-II) hoped to reap political dividend from the Aadhaar programme (Deshpande 2012: 8). As Deshpande (2012: 8) comments:

> In a significant moment for UPA-II's plans to make cash transfers a reform motif and a pro-poor vote hook, Prime Minister Manmohan Singh and Congress chief Sonia Gandhi will hand out Aadhaar number 21 crore in the Rajasthan village of Dudu on Saturday. Situated some

60-odd km from Jaipur, Dudu will be the stage for the launch of a scheme integrating benefits like rural employment guarantee, pensions and state scholarships for the socially disadvantaged that the government hopes will earn it goodwill ahead of the 2014 parliamentary election...

Bolstered by cash transfer pilot projects for public distribution system, fertilizer and cooking gas showing positive results, the government is hoping to press ahead with a phased rollout that will see Aadhaar's unique identity numbers playing a key role in linking beneficiaries and bank accounts...Political gains that the UPA is eyeing factor in transferring cash to bank accounts of crores of beneficiaries, which an estimate suggests can add up to around 10% of the population even if a full rollout is not possible by the time the polls are due.

The idea that the Aadhaar-linked cash transfer would legitimize the then political government and bring it political dividend found support in influential quarters. *The Times of India* (2012c: 14) wrote in its leading editorial:

The UPA's been credited for promoting schemes like the NREG or RTE that are need-based, and hence secular in approach. It must now work to counter populist propaganda that pitches systemic reform as anti-people, moving towards social security coverage—as in developed nations—that makes people less and less dependent on bureaucracy. Aadhaar-linked electronic cash transfer is likely to go down well with common people, and even prove an electoral winner. That's because it'll empower the needy in two crucial ways. It'll give them a notion of entitlement based on individual identity. Equally important, it'll give them choice and a sense of financial agency.

Two days before the prime minister made the announcement of the cash transfer scheme and its rollout timetable, *The Economic Times* carried an article on its front page on 24 November 2012, entitled 'Day After, UPA Declares Elections with Cash Transfers'. The article said:

Monday will see UPA-II playing what it hopes will be its biggest election card—nationwide cash transfer scheme that aims to put a total of Rs 3.2 lakh crore per year in the bank accounts of 10 crore poor families, starting January next year...Massive in administrative scope and political ambition, the rollout is expected to be completed

by April 2014, just in time for the scheduled general elections...
Congress strategists are looking at cash transfers as the 'NREG of
UPA-II', a senior leader said. (*The Economic Times* 2012i: 1)

In addition to providing legitimacy to the political government,
the UIDAI is expected to help the government in one other respect.
It will enable the government to govern the poor from a distance in
the name of their freedom without being responsible for them. By
using the Aadhaar programme to accomplish the shift from public
provisioning in kind to cash transfers, the government provides
choices to the poor, and in the process, empowers the poor to recognize
and act upon themselves as both free and responsible. But what it
also means is that the government will no longer be responsible for
the poor: it is the poor who will have to assume responsibility for
their activities and possible failures arising from them. This strategy
of making the poor 'free' and 'responsible' would, in effect, mean
transferring the responsibility for social risks such as illness, illiteracy,
unemployment, and poverty to the poor themselves.

To What Ends should They be Governed?

The political project of the government is to create another rationality
of government, in the name of freedom, through a range of tactics
and techniques that enables the state to divest itself of its obligations
and devolve them to the poor. The government wants, in the name
of freedom, a particular capability to be installed in the poor so that
they can conduct themselves in a manner that is in alignment with
objectives of the political project of the government. Instead of being
dependent on the government, the poor must maximize their life
as a kind of enterprise form: they should become 'entrepreneurs
of themselves', and it is as such they need to be bonded into the
society through the choices they make, the risks that they take, and
the responsibilities for themselves which they are now required to
assume.

Through the instrumentality of the Aadhaar programme, the
government seeks to create a political subject that is less a social citizen
with entitlements deriving from membership of the society, and more
as an individual whose citizenship is active. This active citizenship is
to be manifested not in the receipt of government welfare in kind,

but in the energetic pursuit of personal fulfilment by the exercise of freedom of choice and consumption. Citizenship will no longer be exercised in a relationship to the state, but in a relationship with the market. Governance is to be vested in the entrepreneurial activities of producers and suppliers of goods and services, and the operation of the market aligning the activities of producers and suppliers with the choices of consumers seeking to maximize their lifestyles and quality of life. It is consumption through the market that will shape the identities of the poor. As far as the government is concerned, it needs to act as an enterprise whose task is to universalize competition and invent market-shaped actions for the poor.

In Chapter 4, it was noted that there is a distinct possibility of the Aadhaar programme enabling dataveillance. It was also noted that the convergence of information in the Aadhaar database would facilitate profiling of the poor as consumer for the market, and this would eventually bring the market into the lives of the poor. The fact that the Aadhaar programme intends bringing the market into the lives of India's poor is borne out by the Aadhaar application development plans which were unveiled by the Nasscom Product Council at the Nasscom Conclave held in Bangalore on 29 October 2013 (*The Times of India* 2013a: 23).

Nasscom Product Council announced the launch of the Aadhaar Diffusion Project, which is an effort in collaboration with UIDAI to encourage start-ups to develop an application economy, and in the process, accelerate the development of applications and services that leverage the Aadhaar identity infrastructure (*Deccan Herald* 2013b: 15). The goal of the Aadhaar Diffusion Project, according to Nandan Nilekani, is to achieve widespread diffusion of the Aadhaar platform knowledge across new entrepreneurial ventures and existing companies to assist and nurture Aadhaar capabilities (*Deccan Herald* 2013b: 15). As a part of the initiative, Nasscom plans to hold a number of activities to evangelize software developers: annual developer conference, hackathons, application contests, and bootcamps (*Deccan Herald* 2013b: 15). The Aadhaar Diffusion Project also plans to run awards in varied categories as well as have certification programmes (*Deccan Herald* 2013b: 15).

According to Nandan Nilekani, Aadhaar has opened up the platform to entrepreneurs to build innovative applications. As

Nilekani points out, 'The government did the project to improve the quality of publilc services. We want to see more and more young entrepreneurs build applications for the common man using Aadhaar as an authentication mechanism' (*The Times of India* 2013b: 20). Nilekani argues that India is the only country where even the poorest and most vulnerable have got a digital identity, moving from a status of no identity (*Deccan Herald* 2013a: 8). As he told the audience at the Nasscom's Product Conclave at Bangalore, 'When 470 million people have come forward to get the Aadhaar Number, it is the real thing playing out. The life of Aadhaar is in the numbers' (*Deccan Herald* 2013a: 8). Simply put, Nilekani would have brought the market in 470 million Indian households.

Nilekani is of the view that the most fundamental transformations in the world happen in government, and for public good, before they reach the larger community (*Deccan Herald* 2013a: 8). He says:

> The Internet and GPS began in government and public work. The GPS was a military application, but has now grown to be half-a-billion dollar industry. Internet is everywhere now. So, also, Aadhaar has begun with the government, but very soon we shall see the entire private sector and civil society adopt Aadhaar...Aadhaar will have multiple applications in multiple sectors and domains. (*Deccan Herald* 2013a: 8)

Clearly, the Aadhaar programme will bring the market into the lives of the poor. The ample scope that the Aadhaar programme offers for dataveillance will make the market interested in India's poor as its potential consumers. The Aadhaar programme will facilitate the mapping of the needs and consumption patterns of India's poor by linking it to an integrated pan-India Aadhaar database, and make it possible for the market to profile the poor as consumers and understand what their needs are. It is also the Aadhaar programme which will make financial inclusion possible for the poor, bring them benefits directly in cash, and give them the wherewithal for being consumers for the market. The market, by offering a choice of goods, services, experiences, and lifestyles, will enable the poor to define who they are or want to be. It is the market that will induce in the poor the desires that they will work to satisfy. The poor will be governed into purchasing and consuming goods, products, experiences, and lifestyles through their desire. Various choices of consumption will shape the identities of the poor. That is how India's poor will now become enterprising individuals who will govern themselves and therefore, will need only limited direct governance by the state. The most tangible achievement of the Aadhaar programme will, however, be in enabling the government to propound a new political rationality in the name of giving freedom to the poor as a political project, and legitimating it through the expertize that the UIDAI embodies. Nandan Nilekani says:

> In the Indira years, the slogan was 'garibi hatao'...In the 1970s and 1980s, people's aspirations had focused on basic essentials—roti, kapada, aur makaan...Since the reforms in the 1990s, the emphasis moved to...bijli, sadak and paani. In recent years, as growth has accelerated and access to basic infrastructure has improved further, aspirations among the poor have shifted again...Today, it's all virtual things—it's about UID number, mobile phone and bank account... With that, they can access services, benefits and their rights...We are looking at a post-Aadhaar world. (Quoted in Ramakumar 2011: 4)

Nilekani's statement is significant because it tells us about how India's poor actually aspire to own an Aadhaar number, mobile phone, and bank account, so that, through them, they can access services, benefits, and their rights. The state will be there only to provide a framework so that these aspirations of the poor can fructify in an orderly manner. This is the formula of India's neo-liberal government for governing a free society in the post-Aadhaar world. The locus of the state would have changed in the discourse of this political project (Rose and Miller 1992: 199). The only thing that the state will be called upon to do now is to ensure order by providing a legal framework for social and economic life. But, within this framework, autonomous actors—market, individuals, and the poor—are to go freely about their business, making their own decisions, and controlling their own destinies (Rose and Miller 1992: 199).

Notes

1. See 'Budget 2011–12, Speech of Pranab Mukherjee, Minister of Finance', 28 February 2011, p. 5, available at http://Indiabudget.nic.in.

2. 'Budget 2011–12, Speech of Pranab Mukherjee, Minister of Finance', 28 February 2011, p. 5, available at http://Indiabudget.nic.in.

3. Ministry of Finance, 14 February 2011, available at http://pib.nic.in/newsite/PrintRelease.aspx.

4. 'Budget 2012–2013, Speech of Pranab Mukherjee, Minister for Finance', March 2012, p. 5, http://Indiabudget.nic.in.

5. 'Budget 2012–2013, Speech of Pranab Mukherjee, Minister for Finance', March 2012, p. 6, http://Indiabudget.nic.in.

Bibliography

✌১৩৯

Aggarwal, A. 2011. 'The PDS in Rural Orissa: Against the Grain?', *Economic and Political Weekly*, XLVI(36): 21–3.

Arun, T.K. 2012. 'Cleanse Politics to Make Markets Work', *The Economic Times*, Bangalore, Friday, 9 March, p. 11.

Baldwin, R. and M. Cave. 1999. *Understanding Regulation: Theory, Strategy, and Practice*. Oxford: Oxford University Press.

Basu, R. 2010. 'Reaching Out to People: Achieving Millennium Development Goals through Innovative Public Service Delivery', Paper presented at the Network of Asia-Pacific School and Institutes of Public Administration (NAPSIPAG) Annual International Conference, 2010, on 11–13 December, available at www.napispag.org/PDF/Rukmi%20 BASU.pdf, accessed 5 December 2012.

Bhatti, B., J. Dreze, and R. Khera. 2012a. 'Experiments with Aadhaar', *The Hindu*, Bangalore, Wednesday, 27 June, p. 10.

———. 2012b. 'Response to "Aadhaar and MGNREG are Made for Each Other"', *The Hindu*, Bangalore, Wednesday, 4 July, p. 11.

Bijapurkar, R. 2012. 'New Mindset to Open New Markets', *The Economic Times*, Bangalore, Friday, 2 March, p. 15.

Burchell, G., C. Gordon, and P. Miller (eds). 1991. *The Foucault Effect: Studies in Governmentality*. Chicago: University of Chicago Press.

Byatnal, A. 2010. 'Villagers Clueless in Tembhli on the Eve of Getting UID', *The Hindu*, Bangalore, Wednesday, 28 September, p. 17.

Centre for Budget and Governance Accountability. 2007. *Primer on Budget Analysis: Taking the Case of Elementary Education*. New Delhi: CBGA. Available at www.cbgaindia.org, accessed 6 September 2010.

Clarke, R. 1991. *Information Technology and Dataveillance*. Available at http://www.anu.edu.au/people/Roger.Clarke/DV/CACM88.html, accessed 5 November 2012.

———. 2006. *Introduction to Dataveillance and Information Privacy*. Available at http://www.anu.edu.au/people/Roger.Clarke/DV/Intro. html#DV. Accessed on 5 December 2012.

Council for Social Development. 2006. *Social Development Report, 2006.* New Delhi: Oxford University Press.

Cruikshank, B. 1996. 'Revolutions within: Self-government and Self-esteem', in A. Barry, T. Osborne, and N. Rose (eds), *Foucault and Political Reason: Liberalism, Neo-Liberalism, and Rationalities of Government*, pp. 215–45. Chicago: University of Chicago Press.

Das, J. and J. Leino. 2011. 'Lessons from an Experimental Information Campaign for Evaluating the RSBY', in R. Palacios, J. Das, and S. Chnagquing (eds), *India's Health Insurance Scheme for the Poor: Evidence from the Early Experience of the Rashtriya Swasthya Bima Yojana.* New Delhi: Centre for Policy Research. Available at http:/cprindia.org/publications/books/3348-indias-health-insurance-scheme-poor-evidence, accessed 13 August 2011.

Day, R.J.F. 2008. *Gramsci is Dead: Anarchist Currents in the Newest Social Movements.* Hyderabad: Orient Longman.

Deccan Herald. 2011a. 'Big Brother Watching: Inquisitive UIDAI Wants All Details about You and I', Bangalore, Saturday, 13 August, p. 1.

———. 2011b. 'Tainted by Deceit', Bangalore, Monday, 15 August, p. 10.

———. 2011c. 'UIDAI Gets its First Complaint of Misuse', Bangalore, Monday, 3 October, p. 8.

———. 2011d. 'Multi-use Smart Cards by 2013', Bangalore, Monday, 3 October, p. 8.

———. 2011e, 'Govt Changes UIDAI Task Force Norms', Bangalore, 22 September, p. 7.

———. 2012a. 'Clouds of Uncertainty over Aadhaar', Bangalore, Friday, 13 January, p. 5.

———. 2012b. 'Direct Subsidies to Poor Soon: Pranab', Bangalore, Monday, 20 February, p. 1.

———. 2012c. 'Business Correspondents for Rural Banking Proposed', Bangalore, Friday, 24 February, p. 13.

———. 2012d. '"Coriander" has Aadhaar Number', Bangalore, Friday, 13 April, p. 1.

———. 2012e. 'Direct Cash Transfer of Food Decries: It may Trigger Corruption, Says Economist Swaminathan', Bangalore, Saturday, 7 July, p. 12.

———. 2012f. 'Adopting Analytics is a Purely Biz Decision', Bangalore, Tuesday, 7 August, p. 13.

———. 2013a. 'Aadhaar will be the Basis for Almost Everything: Nilekani', Bangalore, Wednesday, 30 October, p. 8

———. 2013b. 'Aadhaar Apps Development on the Cards', Bangalore, Wednesday, 30 October, p. 15

Deshpande, R. 2012. 'UPA Hopes to Reap Dividend from Aadhaar', *The Times of India*, Bangalore, Tuesday, 16 October, p. 8.

Dey, N. 2011. 'Tool of Exclusion', *Frontline*, 28(24): 122–4.

Donzelot, J. and C. Gordon. 2008. 'Governing Liberal Societies—The Foucault Effect in the English-speaking World', *Foucault Studies*, 5(January): 48–62.

Dreze, J. 2011. 'Unique Facility, or Recipe for Trouble?', *The Hindu*, Bangalore, Thursday, 25 November, p. 11.

Duggal, R. 2009. 'Sinking Flagships and Health Budgets in India', *Economic and Political Weekly*, XLIV(33): 14–17.

Dyson, E., G. Gilder, G. Keyworth, and A. Toffler. 1996. 'Cyberspace and the American Dream', *The Information Society*, 12 (3): 295–308.

Education Commission. 1966. *Education and National Development: Report of the Education Commission (1964–66)*. New Delhi: Government of India.

Election Commission of India. 2008. 'Retention of Old EPIC Numbers for New/Duplicate EPICs and Maintenance and Upkeep of Photo-roll Image Database', Letter No. 23/ID/2008/ERS, 18 September, available at http://eci.nic.in/eci_main/eroll&epic/ins_180908.pdf, accessed 16 October 2012.

Ericson, R. and K. Haggerty. 1997. *Policing the Risk Society*. Toronto: University of Toronto Press.

Foucault, M. 1982. 'Subject and Power', in H. Dreyfus and P. Rabinow (eds), *Michel Foucault: Beyond Structuralism and Hermeneutics*, pp. 208–26. Chicago: University of Chicago Press.

———. 1991. 'Governmentality', in G. Burchell, C. Gordon, and P. Miller (eds), *The Foucault Effect*, pp. 87–104. Chicago: University of Chicago Press.

———. 1993. 'About the Beginning of the Hermeneutics of the Self' (Transcription of two lectures at Dartmouth on 17 and 24 November 1980), *Political Theory*, 21(2): 198–227.

——— (edited by P. Rabinow). 1997. *Ethics, Subjectivity and Truth: Essential Works of Michel Foucault, Vol. 1*. New York: New Press.

———. 2008. 'The Birth of Biopolitics: Lectures at the College de France 1978–1979', available at http://rauli.cbs.dk/index.php/foucault-studies/article/view/3127/3298.pdf, accessed 19 November 2011.

———. 2010. 'The Government of Self and Others: Lectures at the College de France 1982–1983', available at http://rauli.cbs.dk/index.php.foucault-studies/article/view/3127/3298.pdf, accessed 19 November 2011.

———. 2011. 'The Courage of Truth: Lectures at the College de France 1983–1984', available at http://rauli.cbs.dk/index.php.foucault-studies/article/view/3127/3298.pdf, accessed 19 November 2011.

Gandy, O. 1993. *The Panoptic Sort: A Political Economy of Personal Information*. Boulder, CO: Westview Press.

Gerth, H.H. and C. Wright Mills. 1964. *From Max Weber: Essays in Sociology*. New York: Oxford University Press.

Gooptu, N. 2009. 'Neoliberal Subjectivity, Enterprise Culture and New Workplaces: Organized Retail and Shopping Malls in India', *Economic and Political Weekly*, XLIV(22): 45–54.

Gordon, C. 1987. 'The Soul of the Citizen: Max Weber and Michel Foucault on Rationality and Government', in S. Lash and S. Whimster (eds), *Max Weber: Rationality and Modernity*, pp. 293–316. London: Allen & Unwin.

———. 1991. 'Governmental Rationality: An Introduction', in G. Burchell, C. Gordon, and P. Miller (eds), *The Foucault Effect: Studies in Governmentality*, pp. 1–51. Chicago: University of Chicago Press.

Government of India. 2000. 'Report on Long Term Grain Policy', Department of Food & Public Distribution, Ministry of Consumers Affairs, Food & Public Distribution, available at http://dfpd.nic.in/?q=node/142, accessed 17 November 2014.

———. 2010. 'Approach Paper for a Legislation on Privacy', No. 17/1/2010-IR, Department of Personnel Training, Ministry of Personnel, PG & Pensions, 18 October, available at http://persmin.gov.in/WriteReadData/RTI/approach_paper.pdf, accessed 3 October 2011.

Gupta, N.K. 2012. 'Financial Inclusion—A Way Forward', *The Times of India*, Bangalore, Wednesday, 27 June, p. 11.

India Knowledge@Wharton. 2010. 'Nandan Nilekani on What it Takes to Build the World's Biggest Social Inclusion program', available at http://knowledge,wharton.upenn.edu/india/article,cfm?articleid=4541, accessed 13 August 2011.

Jayashankar, M. and N.S. Ramnath. 2010. 'UIDAI: Inside the World's Largest Data Management Project', *Forbes India*, 29 November, available at http://business.in.com/printcontent/19632, accessed 25 September 2012.

Jore, D. 2010. 'We Have No Food, Damn the Honour', *Hindustan Times*, New Delhi, Thursday, 30 September, p. 9.

Khemka, A. 2012. 'Banking on Everyone', *The Economic Times*, Bangalore, Tuesday, 13 March, p. 12.

Khera, R. 2008. 'Access to the Targeted Public Distribution System: A Case Study in Rajasthan', *Economic and Political Weekly*, XLIII(44): 51–8.

———. 2011a. 'The UID Project and Welfare Schemes', *Economic and Political Weekly*, XLVI(9): 38–43.

————. 2011b. 'Revival of the Public Distribution System: Evidence and Explanations', *Economic and Political Weekly*, XLVI(44–45): 36–50.

Krishnan, D. 2011. 'The Phone as a Bank', *The Economic Times*, Bangalore, Friday, 28 October, p. 14.

Kurup, D. 2012a. 'What the Aadhaar Payment Pipe Offers,' *The Hindu*, Bangalore, Sunday, 26 February, p. 7.

————. 2012b. 'Big Data that's Worth Big Bucks', *The Hindu*, Bangalore, Sunday, 29 July, p. 8.

Lemke, T. 2000. 'Foucault, Governmentality and Critique', Paper presented at the Rethinking Marxism Conference, University of Amherst, 21–4 September.

————. 2001. 'The Birth of Bio-politics: Michel Foucault's Lectures at the College de France on Neoliberal Governmentality', *Economy and Society*, 30(2): 1–17, available at http://www.thomaslemkeweb.de/engl.%20texte/The%20Birth%20of%20Biopolitics%203.pdf, accessed 28 October 2011.

Mann, N., V. Pande, and J. Ramesh. 2012. 'Aadhaar and MGNREGA are Made for Each Other', *The Hindu*, Bangalore, Wednesday, 4 July, p. 11.

Mehmood, T. 2011. 'Registration and the Poor: Why UIDAI Wants to Register the Poor in India', 17 September, pp. 1–10, available at http://aadhaararticles.blogspot.com/2011/09/1603-registration-and-poor-why-uidai.html, accessed 28 October 2011.

Michman, R.D. 1991. *Lifestyle Market Segmentation*. New York: Praeger.

Ministry of Education. 1985. *Challenge of Education: A Policy Perspective*. New Delhi: Government of India.

Ministry of Finance. 2011a. *Report of the Technical Advisory Group for Unique Projects (TAGUP)*. New Delhi: Ministry of Finance, Government of India. Available at http://finmin.nic.in/reports/TAGUP_Report.pdf, accessed 13 August 2011.

————. 2011b. *Interim Report of the Task Force on Direct Transfer of Subsidies on Kerosene, LPG and Fertilizer*. New Delhi: Ministry of Finance, Government of India, available at http://finmin.nic.in/reports/Interim report Task Force DTS.pdf, accessed 16 October 2011.

————. 2011c. *Report of the Task Force on an IT Strategy for PDS and an Implementable Solution for the Direct Transfer of Subsidy for Food and Kerosene*. New Delhi: Ministry of Finance, Government of India. Available at http://finmin.nic.in/reports/it_strategy_pds.pdf, accessed 15 February 2012.

Ministry of Human Resource Development. 2009. 'Model Rules under the Right of Children to Free and Compulsory Education Act, 2009',

Government of India, available at education.nic.in/Elementary/RTI_ Model_Rules.pdf, accessed 16 November 2010.

Ministry of Law and Justice. 2005. *The National Rural Employment Guarantee Act, No. 42 of 2005*, Legislative Department. New Delhi: Government of India.

Ministry of Law and Justice. 2009. *The Right of Children to Free and Compulsory Education Act, 2009*. New Delhi: Government of India.

Ministry of Rural Development. 2008. *The National Rural Employment Guarantee Act 2005, Operational Guidelines 2008*. New Delhi: Government of India.

Narayana, D. 2010. 'Review of the Rashtriya Swasthya Bima Yojana', *Economic and Political Weekly*, XLV(29): 13–18.

National Council of Applied Economic Research (NCAER). 1994. *Non-enrolment, Drop-out and Private Expenditure on Elementary Education: A Comparison across States and Population Groups*. New Delhi: NCAER.

National Council of Educational Research and Training (NCERT). 2005. *Seventh All-India Educational Survey: Provisional Statistics*. New Delhi: NCERT.

Nayar, L. 2012. 'The Budget Sets Foot in Kitchens: An Experiment in Cash Transfers in a Delhi Slum Gets Mixed Reception', *Outlook*, 15 October, pp. 40–1.

Nilekani, N. 2008. *Imagining India: Ideas for the New Century*. New Delhi: Penguin/Allen Lane.

Noorani, A.G. 2011. 'A Case for Privacy,' *Frontline*, 28(24): 14–15.

Palacios, R. 2011. 'A New Approach to Providing Health Insurance to the Poor in India: The Early Experience of Rashtriya Swasthya Bima Yojana', in *India's Health Insurance for the Poor: Evidence from the Early Experience of the Rashtriya Swasthya Bima Yojana*, pp. 1–37. New Delhi: Centre for Policy Research. Available at http://cprindia.org/publications/books/3348-indias-healthinsurance-scheme-poor-evidence, accessed 16 October 2012.

Panagariya, A. 2012. 'Empowering the Poor', *The Times of India*, Bangalore, Saturday, 25 August, p. 20.

Paranjpe, N. 2012. 'The Practitioner', *The Economic Times*, Bangalore, Friday, 2 March, p. 15.

Paul, S., S. Balakrishnan, G. Thampi, S. Sekhar, and M. Vivekananda. 2006. *Who Benefits from India's Public Services? A People's Audit of Five Basic Services*. New Delhi: Academic Foundation.

Planning Commission. 2008a. *Eleventh Five Year Plan, 2007–12, Vol. I: Inclusive Growth*. New Delhi: Oxford University Press.

———. 2008b. *Eleventh Five Year Plan, 2007–12, Vol. II: Social Sector*. New Delhi: Oxford University Press.

PRS Legislative Research. 2010a. *The National Identification Authority of India Bill:*
Bill Summary. New Delhi: Centre for Policy Research. Available at www.prsindia.org, accessed 2 March 2012.

———. 2010b. *The National Identification Authority of India Bill: Legislative Brief.* New Delhi: Centre for Policy Research. Available at www.prsindia.org, accessed 2 March 2012.

———. 2010c. *The National Identification Authority of India Bill, 2010.* Available at www.prsindia.org/.../The%20National%20Identification%20Authority%20of%20India%2, accessed 22 November 2012.

———. 2011. *The National Food Security Bill, 2011.* Available at http://www.prsindia.org/uploads/media/Food%20Security/National%20Food%20Security%20Bill%202011.pdf, accessed 15 November 2012.

Rabinow, P. (ed.). 1984. *The Foucault Reader.* New York: Pantheon Books.

Raghunandan, P.M. 2012. 'State Sheds Bogus Card Burden,' *Deccan Herald*, Bangalore, Wednesday, 18 January, p. 5.

Rajshekhar, M. 2012a. 'Bank Accounts Opened: 80 Million, Working: 15 Million', *The Economic Times*, Bangalore, Tuesday, 28 February, p. 13.

———. 2012b. 'Many Blueprints for a Transaction', *The Economic Times*, Bangalore, Tuesday, 17 April, p. 13.

Ramachandran, R. 2011. 'How Reliable is UID?', *Frontline*, 28(24): 25–8.

Ramakrishnan, V. 2011. 'In Two Minds?', *Frontline*, 28(24): 11–12.

Ramakumar, R. 2009. 'High-cost, High-risk', *Frontline*, 26(16), 10 August, available at http://www.hindu.com/fline/fl2616/stories/20090814261604900.html, accessed 25 July 2010.

———. 2010. 'What the UID Conceals', *The Hindu*, Bangalore, Thursday, 21 October, p. 12.

———. 2011a. 'Identity Concerns', *Frontline*, 28(24): 4–10.

———. 2011b. 'PDS in Peril', *Frontline*, 28(24): 16–18.

———. 2012. 'UID Road to Exclusion', *The New Indian Express*, Bangalore, Thursday, 16 February, p. 8.

Ramanathan, U. 2010. 'A Unique Identity Bill', *Economic and Political Weekly*, XLV(30): 10–14.

Rao, M. 2011. 'False Promises', *Frontline*, 28(24): 19–21.

Rao, U. 2013. 'Biometric Marginality: UID and the Shaping of Homeless Identities in the City', *Economic and Political Weekly*, XLVIII(13): 71–7.

Ravishankar, G.V. 2012. 'The Quality Mantra', *The Economic Times*, Bangalore, Friday, 3 February, p. 15.

Ray, A. 2012. 'Govt. to Include More Villages into Financial Inclusion Drive', *The Economic Times*, Bangalore, Wednesday, 6 June, p. 10.

Reserve Bank of India (RBI). 2006a. 'Financial Inclusion by Extension of Banking Services—Use of Business Facilitators and Correspondents', DBOD No. BL.BC.58/22.01.001/2005–06, 25 January, available at http:/rbidocs.rbi.org.in/rdocs/notification/PDFs/68417.pdf, accessed 19 November 2011.

———. 2006b. 'Guidelines on Managing Risks and Code of Conduct in Outsourcing of Financial Services by Banks', DBOD No. BP.40/21.04.158/2006-7, 3 November, available at http://rbidocs.rbi.org.in/rdocs/notification/PDFs/73713.pdf, accessed 19 November 2011.

———. 2008. 'Mobile Payments in India—Operative Guidelines for Banks', 12 June, available at http://rbidocs.rbi.org.in/rdocs/PressReleas/PDFs/84979.pdf, accessed 19 November 2011.

———. 2009. 'Financial Inclusion by Extension of Banking Services—Use of Business Correspondents (BCs)', DBOD No. BL.BC.63/22.01.2009/2009–10, 30 November, available at http://rbidocs.rbi.org.in.rdocs/notification/PDFs/IBC301109FV.pdf, accessed 19 November 2011.

———. 2010a. 'Discussion Paper on Engagement of "For-profit" Companies as Business Correspondents', 2 August, available at http://rbi.org.in/scripts/bs_viewcontent.aspx?Id=2234, accessed 19 November 2011.

———. 2010b. 'Financial Inclusion by Extension of Banking Services—Use of Business Correspondents', DBOD No. BL.BC.43/22.01.009/2010–11, 28 September, available at http://www.rbi.org.in/scripts/NotificationUser.aspx?Id=6017&Mode=0, accessed 19 November 2011.

———. 2012. 'Financial Inclusion by Extension of Banking Services—Use of Business Correspondents (BCs)', DBOD No. BL.BC.82/22.01.009/2011–12, 2 March, available at http://www.rbi.org.in/scrpts/NotificationUser.aspx?Id=7038&Mode=0, accessed 3 May 2012.

Rose, N. 1992. 'Towards a Critical Sociology of Freedom', Inaugural Lecture, Goldsmith College, London, 5 May.

———. 1996. *Inventing Our Selves*. Cambridge: Cambridge University Press.

———. 1999. *Powers of Freedom: Reframing Political Thought*. Cambridge: Cambridge University Press.

Rose, N. and P. Miller. 1992. 'Political Power beyond the State: Problematics of Government', *The British Journal of Sociology*, 43(2): 173–205.

Rose, N., P. O'Malley, and M. Valverde. 2006. 'Governmentality', *Annual Review of Law and Social Science*, 2: 83–104.

Saini, S. 2012. 'Banks Told to Give Big Push to E-Fund Transfer', *The New Indian Express*, Bangalore, Saturday, 7 July, p. 13.

Sastry, A.K. 2012. 'Biometric System will Help Remove Bogus Ration Cards', *The Hindu*, Bangalore, Saturday, 13 October, p. 5.

Scaria, J.A. 2012. 'No Reason Why Our PDS can't be on Cloud', *The Economic Times*, Bangalore, Wednesday, 25 July, p. 14.

Selvaraj, S. and A.K. Karan. 2009. 'Deepening Health Insecurity in India: Evidence from National Sample Surveys since 1980s', *Economic and Political Weekly*, XLIV(40): 55–60.

Shariff, A. and P.K. Ghosh. 2000. 'Indian Education Scene and the Public Gap', *Economic and Political Weekly*, 35(15): 1396–406.

Shariff, A., P. Ghosh, and S. Mondal. 2002. 'Indian Public Expenditures on Social Sector and Poverty Alleviation Programmes during the 1990s', Working Paper 169, Human Development Division, NCAER, New Delhi.

Sheila, R. 2010. 'Reimagining Citizenship: Debating India's Unique Identification Scheme', *Economic and Political Weekly*, XLV(2): 31–6.

Singh, M.K. 2012. 'Unique Identification Scheme to Stay', *The Times of India*, Bangalore, Thursday, 19 January, p. 11.

Singh, S. 2012a. 'When 93.5% isn't Good Enough', *The Economic Times*, Bangalore, Tuesday, 17 April, p. 13.

———. 2012b. 'Banking on Biometrics to Give You a Unique Identity', *The Economic Times*, Bangalore, Thursday, 26 April, p. 13.

Srinivasan, G. 2011. 'The Aim is Inclusion', *Frontline*, 28(24): 8.

Surveillance Studies Network. 2006. *A Report on the Surveillance Society for the Information Commissioner*. Available at http://www.ico.gov.ul/upload/documents/library/data_protection/practical_application/surveillance_society_full_report_2006.pdf, accessed on 3 November 2011.

Swamy, R.K. 2011. 'Cards to Nowhere—Inclusion', pp. 1–9, available at http:/aadhaararticles.blogspot.com, accessed 16 October 2012.

Swamy's Manual of Office Procedure. 2004. Chennai: Swamy Publishers (P) Ltd.

Swarup, A. 2012. 'A Winning Model of Health Insurance for the Poor', *The Economic Times*, Bangalore, Friday, 3 February, p. 15.

Szreter, S. 2011. 'The Right of Registration: Development, Identity Registration and Social Security', available at http://www.historyandpolicy.org/papers.policy-paper-53.html, accessed 13 August 2011.

Tehelka. 2010. 'We Raised the Issue of Privacy Long before Anyone Else', Saturday, 6 November, 7(44): 26–9.

The Dayafter. 2010. 'Ambitious UID Project Endangers Privacy', Mumbai, 16–30 September, pp. 32–3.

The Economic Times. 2011a. 'Bank A/cs Must for MGNREGA Beneficiaries', Bangalore, Saturday, 6 August, p. 9.

————. 2011b. 'The Wannabe Village Bankers'. Bangalore, Tuesday, 20 September, p. 13.

————. 2011c. 'The Rupees 3,00,000 cr Muddle', Bangalore, Tuesday, 20 September, p. 13.

————. 2011d. 'Welfare Muddle: The Shift to Cash Transfers won't Happen in a Day, but We Need to Do It', Bangalore, Wednesday, 21 September, p. 12.

————. 2011e. 'Is Nilekani's Dream Run Over?', Bangalore, Tuesday, 27 September, p. 13.

————. 2011f. 'Plan Panel Wants UIDAI Finances to be Tracked', Bangalore, Wednesday, 28 September, p. 1.

————. 2011g. 'Nilekani Defends Aadhaar, to Propose 10,000-cr Demand', Bangalore, Friday, 30 September, p. 5.

————. 2011h. 'The Slum Economy Rises', Bangalore, Tuesday, 11 October, p. 15.

————. 2011i. 'UIDAI Finance Advisor's Role, Powers Clipped', Bangalore, Friday, 21 October, p. 13.

————. 2011j. 'Reach and Reliability: A Safe Passage for Wages', Bangalore, Tuesday, 6 December, p. 15.

————. 2011k. 'Reach and Reliability: All Banks in All Panchayats', Bangalore, Tuesday, 6 December, p. 15.

————. 2011l. 'Government Introduces National Food Security Bill in Lok Sabha', 23 December, available at http://articles.economictimes.com/2011-12-23/news/30550903_1_food-subsidy, accessed 25 December 2011.

————. 2012a. 'India's Health: Reality Check', Bangalore, Friday, 3 February, p. 15.

————. 2012b. 'Doing Well by Doing Good', Bangalore, Friday, 2 March, p. 15.

————. 2012c. 'Who's Responsible for Protecting Data in Cloud?', Bangalore, Thursday, 5 April, p. 4.

————. 2012d. 'Identity to Transactions', Bangalore, Tuesday, 17 April, p. 13.

————. 2012e. 'Basics of Biometrics', Bangalore, Thursday, 26 April, p. 13.

————. 2012f. 'Aadhaar: Much More than Just a Number', Bangalore, Saturday, 21 July, p. 10.

————. 2012g. 'Rural India—An Emerging Powerhouse', Bangalore, Tuesday, 24 July, p. 7.

————. 2012h. 'A Revolution', Bangalore, Monday, 22 October, p. 12.

————. 2012i. 'Day After, UPA Declares Elections with Cash Transfers', Bangalore, Saturday, 24 November, p. 1.

The Economic Times on Sunday. 2010. 'UID for Faster Delivery of Services: Nilekani', Bangalore, Sunday, 29 August, p. 4.

The Electronic Delivery Services Bill, 2011, 16 November, available at http://www.mit.gov.in/sites/upload_files/dit/files/Electronic_Delivery_of_Services_Bill_2011_16thNov_Legal_17112011.pdf, accessed 23 September 2011.

The Hindu. 2010a. 'Implications of Registering, Tracking, Profiling', Bangalore, 5 April, p. 1.

————. 2010b. 'Unique Facility, or Recipe for Trouble', Bangalore, Thursday, 25 November, p. 11.

————. 2010c. 'Tembhli becomes First Aadhaar Village in India', pp. 1–2, available at www.thehindu.com/news/national/tembhli-becomes-first-aadhar-village-in-india/article802538.ece?ref=relaedNews, accessed 28 August 2011.

————. 2010d. 'Keep UID out of MGNREGA', Bangalore, 1 December 2010, available at http://www.thehindu.com/opinion/op-ed/keep-uid-out-of-mgnrega/article924219.ece, accessed 17 November 2014.

————. 2011a. 'Aadhaar: On a Platform of Myths', Bangalore, Monday, 18 July, p. 8.

————. 2011b. 'UIDAI Clarifies on Aadhaar', Bangalore, Thursday, 15 September, p. 15.

————. 2012a. 'Group Looking at Merging Registries, Says Nilekani', Bangalore, Saturday, 21 January 2012, p. 1.

————. 2012b. 'LPG Cap Part of Larger Aadhaar-linked Plans', Bangalore, Tuesday, 18 September, p. 4.

————. 2012c. 'Aadhaar-enabled Service Delivery System Launched', Bangalore, Sunday, 21 October, p. 14.

————. 2012d. 'PM Sets up National Committee on Direct Cash Transfers', Bangalore, Friday, 26 October, p. 12.

————. 2012e. '49 Lakh Ration Cards Cancelled: State', Bangalore, Friday, 16 November, p. 7.

The New Indian Express. 2011. 'Govt to Launch E-payment Gateway for Direct Subsidy Payment', Bangalore, Saturday, 29 October, p. 15.

————. 2012A. 'UIDAI Invades Privacy, Endangers Security', Bangalore, Saturday, 21 January, p. 8.

————. 2012b. '10 L Micro ATMs Mooted: Task Force on Aadhaar-enabled E-payment System Submits Report', Bangalore, Friday, 24 February, p. 15.

————. 2012C. 'UIDAI Probing Cases of Data Misuse', Bangalore, Monday, 30 April, p. 10.

The New Sunday Express. 2011. 'Mera Gaon, Mera Desh', Bangalore, Sunday, 9 October, p. 11.

The Times of India. 2011a. 'Cracking the UID Code: Japan, France Send Teams to Study Tech behind Aadhaar's Mind-boggling Scale', Bangalore, Monday, 19 September, p. 3.

————. 2011b. 'Aadhaar Not Enough to Open Bank Accounts: RBI', Bangalore, Thursday, 29 September, p. 23.

————. 2012a. 'No-frills a/cs aren't a Nuisance: Subbarao Pulls up Banks for Ignoring Bottom of Pyramid', Bangalore, Saturday, 7 July, p. 21.

————. 2012b. 'Reboot Subsides', Bangalore, Tuesday, 25 September, p. 10.

————. 2012c. 'Assured Delivery: UID-linked Cash Transfer can Revolutionalise Our Welfare System', Bangalore, Wednesday, 17 October, p. 14.

————. 2013a. 'UIDAI, Nasscom to Push Aadhaar App Development', Bangalore, Tuesday, 29 October, p. 23.

————. 2013b. 'Aadhaar Apps can Enable Day-to-day Payments', Bangalore, Wednesday, 30 October, p. 20.

Thyagarajan, S. and J. Venkatesan. 2008. 'Cost–Benefit and Usage Behaviour Analysis of No Frills Accounts: A Study Report of Cuddalore District', Mimeo, December.

Tilak, J.B.G. 2002. 'Education Poverty in India', *Review of Development and Change*, 7(1): 1–44.

————. 2006. 'Education: A Saga of Spectacular Achievements and Conspicuous Failures', in Council for Social Development, *Social Development Report*, pp. 39–49. New Delhi: Oxford University Press.

Unique Identification Authority of India (UIDAI). 2009. 'Office Memorandum No. 33/DG_UIDAI/2009', 9 October, Planning Commission, Government of India.

————. 2010a. 'UIDAI Strategy Overview: Creating a Unique Identity Number for Every Resident in India', Planning Commission, Government of India, April, available at http://uidai.gov.in/UID_PDF/ Front_Page_Articles/Documents/Strategy_Overview-001.pdf, accessed 30 April 2012.

————. 2010b. 'A UID Numbering Scheme', Planning Commission, Government of India, May, available at http://uidai.gov.in/UID_PDF_ Working_Papers/A_UID_Numbering_Scheme.pdf, accessed 30 April 2012.

————. 2010c. 'Envisioning a Role for Aadhaar in the Public Distribution System', Working Paper Version 1, Planning Commission, Government of India, 24 June, available at http://uidai-gov.in/UID_PDF/Working_ Papers/Circulated_Aadhaar_PDS_Note.pdf, accessed 30 April 2012.

———. 2010d. 'From Exclusion to Inclusion with Micropayments', Planning Commission, Government of India, April, available at http:// www.uidai.gov.in/UID_PDF/Front Page Articles/Strategy/Exclusion to Inclusion with Micropayments.pdf, accessed 30 April 2012.

———. 2010e. 'Training Module on Aadhaar Enrolment Process', available at http://uidai.gov.in/UID_PDF/Front_Page_Articles/Training/Module2-Aadhaar_Enrolment_Process-Ver1.0.pdf, accessed 30 April 2012.

———. 2010f. 'Training Module on Enrolment Centre Setup & Management', available at http://uidai.gov.in/UID_PDF/Front_Page_ Articles/Training/Module3-Setting_up&Managing_an_Enrolment_ Centre-Ver1.0.pdf, accessed 30 April 2012.

———. 2010g. 'Aadhaar Technology', available at http://uidai.gov.in/ aadhaar-technology.html, accessed on 30 April 2012.

———. 2010h. 'Training Module on UIDAI and Aadhaar', available at http://uidai.gov.in/UID_PDF/Front_Page_Articles/Training/Module1-UIDandAADHAAR-VER1.0.PDF, accessed 30 April 2012.

———. 2010i. 'Aadhaar Enrolment Client Installation—Read Me', available at http://uidai.gov.in, accessed 30 April 2012.

———. 2010j. 'Rules and Procedures for Testing and Certification of Biometric Devices for UID Application (BDCS-03-01)', available at http://uidai.gov.in/images/FrontPageUpdates/stqc_docs/Rules%20%20 procedure.pdf, accessed on 30 April 2012.

———. 2010k. 'Operator Manual for the Enrolment Process, Version 1.1', available at http://uidai.gov.in/UID_PDF/Front_Page_Articles/Training/ Enrolmentclient_OperatorManual.pdf, accessed 30 April 2012.

———. 2011a. 'Guidelines for Recruitment of Volunteers', available at http://uidai.gov.in/images/FrontPageUpdates/volunteer_guidelines_ 2011.pdf, accessed 4 July 2012.

———. 2011b. 'Guidelines for Recruitment of Personnel on Sabbatical/ Secondment', Available at http://uidai.gov.in/images/FrontPgeUpdates/ sabbatical_guidelines_2011.pdf, accessed 4 July 2012.

———. 2012a. 'About UIDAI', Planning Commission, Government of India, available at http://www.uidai.gov.in/about-uidai.html, accessed 25 July 2012.

———. 2012b. 'Internship Guidelines, 2012', available at http://www.uidai. gov.in/images/internship_guidelines_2012.pdf, accessed 25 July 2012.

UK Cabinet Office, Performance and Innovation Unit (PIU). 2002. *Privacy and Data-sharing: The Way Forward for Public Services*. London: Cabinet Office.

Venkatsubramanian, A.K. 2006. 'The Political Economy of the Public Distribution System in Tamil Nadu', in Vikram K. Chand (ed.), *Reinventing Public Service Delivery in India: Selected Case Studies*, pp. 266–294. New Delhi: Sage.

Weiser, M. 1991. 'The Computer for the 21st Century', *Scientific American*, 265(September): 94–104.

Whitley, E. 2011. 'Why it Failed in U. K.', *Frontline*, 28(24): 29–32.

Yadav, Y. 2012. 'Fake Names are the Fruits of Aadhaar', *The New Indian Express*, Bangalore, Monday, 9 July, p. 1.

Index

❧

About the Author

❧❧

S.K. Das is a former civil servant. He retired as Member (Finance), Space Commission and Atomic Energy Commission, and Ex-officio Secretary to Government of India. He has published *Civil Service Reform and Structural Adjustment* (1998), *Public Office, Private Interest: Bureaucracy and Corruption in India* (2001), *Rethinking Public Accounting: Policy and Practice of Accrual Accounting in Government* (2006), *Building a World-Class Civil Service for Twenty-First Century India* (2010), *The Civil Services in India* (2013), and *India's Rights Revolution: Has it Worked for the Poor?* (2013), with Oxford University Press. His book, *Touching Lives: The Little Known Triumphs of the Indian Space Programme* (Penguin, 2007), won the Luigi Napolitano Book Award of the International Academy of Astronautics, and has been translated into many regional languages.